SpringerBriefs in Business

SpringerBriefs present concise summaries of cutting-edge research and practical applications across a wide spectrum of fields. Featuring compact volumes of 50 to 125 pages, the series covers a range of content from professional to academic. Typical topics might include:

- A timely report of state-of-the art analytical techniques
- A bridge between new research results, as published in journal articles, and a contextual literature review
- A snapshot of a hot or emerging topic
- An in-depth case study or clinical example
- A presentation of core concepts that students must understand in order to make independent contributions

SpringerBriefs in Business showcase emerging theory, empirical research, and practical application in management, finance, entrepreneurship, marketing, operations research, and related fields, from a global author community.

Briefs are characterized by fast, global electronic dissemination, standard publishing contracts, standardized manuscript preparation and formatting guidelines, and expedited production schedules.

More information about this series at http://www.springer.com/series/8860

Yong Shi • Lingling Zhang • Yingjie Tian
Xingsen Li

Intelligent Knowledge

A Study Beyond Data Mining

Yong Shi
Research Center on Fictitious Economy
and Data Science
Chinese Academy of Sciences
Beijing
China

Yingjie Tian
Research Center on Fictitious Economy
and Data Science
Chinese Academy of Sciences
Beijing
China

Lingling Zhang
School of Management
University of Chinese Academy of Sciences
Beijing
China

Xingsen Li
School of Management,
Ningbo Institute of Technology, Zhejiang
University
Ningbo
Zhejiang
China

ISSN 2191-5482
ISSN 2191-5490 (electronic)
SpringerBriefs in Business
ISBN 978-3-662-46192-1
ISBN 978-3-662-46193-8 (eBook)
DOI 10.1007/978-3-662-46193-8

Library of Congress Control Number: 2014960237

Springer Berlin Heidelberg New York Dordrecht London

Printed on acid-free paper

Springer Berlin Heidelberg is part of Springer Science+Business Media (www.springer.com)

To all of Our Colleagues and Students at Chinese Academy of Sciences

Preface

This book provides a fundamental method of bridging data mining and knowledge management, which are two important fields recognized respectively by the information technology (IT) community and business analytics (BA) community. For a quit long time, IT community agrees that the results of data mining are "hidden patterns", not "knowledge" yet for the decision makers. In contrast, BA community needs the explicit knowledge from large database, now called Big Data in addition to implicit knowledge from the decision makers. How to human experts can incorporate their experience with the knowledge from data mining for effective decision support is a challenge. There some previous research on post data mining and domain-driven data mining to address this problem. However, the findings of such researches are preliminary; either based on heuristic learning, or experimental studies. They have no solid theoretical foundations. This book tries to answer the problem by a term, called "Intelligent Knowledge."

The motivation of the research on Intelligent Knowledge was started with a business project carried out by the authors in 2006 (Shi and Li, 2007). NetEase, Inc., a leading China-based Internet technology company, wanted to reduce its serious churn rate from the VIP customers. The customers can be classified as "current users, freezing users and lost users". Using a well-known tool of decision tree classification algorithm, the authors found 245 rules from thousands of rules, which could not tell the knowledge of predicting user types. When the results were presented to a marketing manager of the company, she, with her working experience (domain knowledge), immediately selected a few rules (decision support) from 245 results. She said, without data mining, it is impossible to identify the rules to be used as decision support. It is data mining to help her find 245 hidden patterns, and then it is her experience to further recognize the right rules. This lesson trigged us that the human knowledge must be applied on the hidden patterns from data mining. The research is to explore how human knowledge can be systematically used to scan the hidden patterns so that the latter can be upgraded as the "knowledge" for decision making. Such "knowledge" in this book is defined as Intelligent Knowledge.

When we proposed this idea to the National Science Foundation of China (NSFC) in the same year, it generously provided us its most prestigious fund, called "the Innovative Grant" for 6 years (2007–2012). The research findings presented in this book is part of the project from NSFC's grant as well as other funds.

Chapter 1–6 of this book is related to concepts and foundations of Intelligent Knowledge. Chapter 1 reviews the trend of research on data mining and knowledge management, which are the basis for us to develop intelligent knowledge. Chapter 2 is the key component of this book. It establishes a foundation of intelligent knowledge management over large databases or Big Data. Intelligent Knowledge is generated from hidden patterns (it then called "rough knowledge" in the book) incorporated with specific, empirical, common sense and situational knowledge, by using a "second-order" analytic process. It not only goes beyond the traditional data mining, but also becomes a critical step to build an innovative process of intelligent knowledge management—a new proposition from original data, rough knowledge, intelligent knowledge, and actionable knowledge, which brings a revolution of knowledge management based on Big Data. Chapter 3 enhances the understanding about why the results of data mining should be further analyzed by the second-order data mining. Through a known theory of Habitual Domain analysis, it examines the effect of human cognition on the creation of intelligent knowledge during the second-order data mining process. The chapter shows that people's judgments on different data mining classifiers diverge or converge can inform the design of the guidance for selecting appropriate people to evaluate/select data mining models for a particular problem. Chapter 4 proposes a framework of domain driven intelligent knowledge discovery and demonstrate this with an entire discovery process which is incorporated with domain knowledge in every step. Although the domain driven approaches have been studied before, this chapter adapts it into the context of intelligent knowledge management to using various measurements of interestingness to judge the possible intelligent knowledge. Chapter 5 discusses how to combine prior knowledge, which can be formulated as mathematical constraints, with well-known approaches of Multiple Criteria Linear Programming (MCLP) to increase possibility of finding intelligent knowledge for decision makers. The proposed is particular important if the results of a standard data mining algorithm cannot be accepted by the decision maker and his or her prior (domain) knowledge can be represented as mathematical forms. Following the similar idea of Chapter 5, when the human judgment can expressed by certain rules, then Chapter 6 provides a new method to extract knowledge, with a thought inspired by the decision tree algorithm, and give a formula to find the optimal attributes for rule extraction. This chapter demonstrates how to combine different data mining algorithms (Support vector Machine and decision tree) with the representation of human knowledge in terms of rules.

Chapter 7–8 of this book is about the basic applications of Intelligent Knowledge. Chapter 7 elaborates a real-life intelligent knowledge management project to deal with customer churn in NetEase, Inc.. Almost all of the entrepreneurs desire to have brain trust generated decision to support strategy which is regarded as the most critical factor since ancient times. With the coming of economic globalization era, followed by increasing competition, rapid technological change as well as gradually accrued scope of the strategy. The complexity of the explosive increase made only by the human brain generates policy decision-making appeared to be inadequate.

Chapter 8 applies a semantics-based improvement of Apriori algorithm, which integrates domain knowledge to mining and its application in traditional Chinese Medicines. The algorithm can recognize the changes of domain knowledge and re-mining. That is to say, the engineers need not to take part in the course, which can realize intellective acquirement.

This book is dedicated to all of our colleagues and students at the Chinese Academy of Sciences. Particularly, we are grateful to these colleagues who have working with us for this meaningful project: Dr. Yinhua Li (China Merchants Bank, China), Dr. Zhengxiang Zhu (the PLA National Defense University, China), Le Yang (the State University of New York at Buffalo, USA), Ye Wang (National Institute of Education Sciences, China), Dr. Guangli Nie (Agricultural Bank of China, China), Dr. Yuejin Zhang (Central University of Finance and Economics, China), Dr. Jun Li (ACE Tempest Reinsurance Limited, China), Dr. Bo Wang (Chinese Academy of Sciences), Mr. Anqiang Huang (BeiHang University, China), Zhongbiao Xiang(Zhejiang University, China)and Dr. Quan Chen (Industrial and Commercial Bank of China, China). We also thank our current graduate students at Research Center on Fictitious Economy and Data Science, Chinese Academy of Sciences: Zhensong Chen, Xi Zhao, Yibing Chen, Xuchan Ju, Meng Fan and Qin Zhang for their various assistances in the research project.

Finally, we would like acknowledge a number of funding agencies who supported our research activities on this book. They are the National Natural Science Foundation of China for the key project “Optimization and Data Mining,” (#70531040, 2006–2009), the innovative group grant “Data Mining and Intelligent Knowledge Management,” (#70621001, #70921061, 2007–2012); Nebraska EPScOR, the National Science Foundation of USA for industrial partnership fund “Creating Knowledge for Business Intelligence” (2009–2010); Nebraska Furniture Market—a unit of Berkshire Hathaway Investment Co., Omaha, USA for the research fund “Revolving Charge Accounts Receivable Retrospective Analysis,” (2008–2009); the CAS/SAFEA International Partnership Program for Creative Research Teams “Data Science-based Fictitious Economy and Environmental Policy Research” (2010–2012); Sojern, Inc., USA for a Big Data research on “Data Mining and Business Intelligence in Internet Advertisements” (2012–2013); the National Natural Science Foundation of China for the project “Research on Domain Driven Second Order Knowledge Discovering” (#71071151, 2011–2013); National Science Foundation of China for the international collaboration grant “Business Intelligence Methods Based on Optimization Data Mining with Applications of Financial and Banking Management” (#71110107026, 2012–2016); the National Science Foundation of China, Key Project “Innovative Research on Management Decision Making under Big Data Environment” (#71331005, 2014–2018); the National Science Foundation of China, “Research on mechanism of the intelligent knowledge emergence of innovation based on Extenics” (#71271191, 2013–2016) the National Natural Science Foundation of China for the project “Knowledge Driven Support Vector Machines Theory, Algorithms and Applications” (#11271361, 2013–2016) and the National Science Foundation of China. “The Research of Personalized Recommend System Based on Domain Knowledge and Link Prediction” (#71471169,2015-2018).

Contents

About the Authors

Yong Shi serves as the Executive Deputy Director, Chinese Academy of Sciences Research Center on Fictitious Economy & Data Science. He is the Union Pacific Chair of Information Science and Technology, College of Information Science and Technology, Peter Kiewit Institute, University of Nebraska, USA. Dr. Shi's research interests include business intelligence, data mining, and multiple criteria decision making. He has published more than 20 books, over 200 papers in various journals and numerous conferences/proceedings papers. He is the Editor-in-Chief of International Journal of Information Technology and Decision Making (SCI), Editor-in-Chief of Annals of Data Science (Springer), and a member of Editorial Board for a number of academic journals. Dr. Shi has received many distinguished awards including the Georg Cantor Award of the International Society on Multiple Criteria Decision Making (MCDM), 2009; Fudan Prize of Distinguished Contribution in Management, Fudan Premium Fund of Management, China, 2009; Outstanding Young Scientist Award, National Natural Science Foundation of China, 2001; and Speaker of Distinguished Visitors Program (DVP) for 1997-2000, IEEE Computer Society. He has consulted or worked on business projects for a number of international companies in data mining and knowledge management.

Lingling Zhang received her PhD from Bei Hang University in 2002. She is an Associate Professor at University of Chinese Academy of Sciences since 2005. She also works as a Researcher Professor at Research Center on Fictitious Economy and Data Science and teaches in Management School of University of Chinese Academy of Sciences. She has been a visiting scholar of Stanford University. Currently her research interest covers intelligent knowledge management, data mining, and management information system. She has received two grant supported by the Natural Science Foundation of China (NSFC), published 4 books, more than 50 papers in various journals and some of them received good comments from the academic community and industries.

Yingjie Tian received the M.Sc. degree from Beijing Institute of Technology, in 1999, and the Ph.D. degree from China Agricultural University, Beijing, China, in 2005. He is currently a Professor with the Research Center on Fictitious Economy and Data Science, Chinese Academy of Sciences, Beijing, China. He has authored four books about support vector machines, one of which has been cited over 1000 times. His current research interests include support vector machines, optimization theory and applications, data mining, intelligent knowledge management, and risk management.

Xingsen Li received the M.Sc degree from China University of Mining and Technology Beijing in 2000, and the Ph.D. degree in management science and engineering from Graduate University of Chinese Academy of Sciences in 2008. He is currently a Professor in NIT, Zhejiang University and a director of Chinese Association for Artificial Intelligence (CAAI) and the Secretary-General of Extension engineering committee, CAAI. He has authored two books about intelligent knowledge management and Exteincs based data mining. His current research interests include intelligent knowledge management, big data, Extenics-based data mining and Extenics-based innovation.

Chapter 1
Data Mining and Knowledge Management

Data mining (DM) is a powerful information technology (IT) tool in today's competitive business world, especially as our human society entered the Big Data era. From academic point of view, it is an area of the intersection of human intervention, machine learning, mathematical modeling and databases. In recent years, data mining applications have become an important business strategy for most companies that want to attract new customers and retain existing ones. Using mathematical techniques, such as, neural networks, decision trees, mathematical programming, fuzzy logic and statistics, data mining software can help the company discover previously unknown, valid, and actionable information from various and large sources (either databases or open data sources like internet) for crucial business decisions. The algorithms of the mathematical models are implemented through some sort of computer languages, such as C++, JAVA, structured query language (SQL), on-line analysis processing (OLAP) and R. The process of data mining can be categorized as selecting, transforming, mining, and interpreting data. The ultimate goal of doing data mining is to find knowledge from data to support user's decision. Therefore, data mining is strongly related with knowledge and knowledge management.

According to the definition of Wikipedia, knowledge is a familiarity with someone or something. Knowledge contains "specific" facts, information, descriptions, or skills acquired through experience or education. Generally, knowledge can be divided as "implicit" (hard to be transformed) or "explicit" (easy to be transformed). Knowledge Management (KM) refers to strategies and practices for individual or an organization to find, transmit, and expand knowledge. How to use human knowledge into the data mining process has drawn challenging research problems over the last 30 years when data mining became important knowledge discovery mechanism.

This chapter reviews the trend of research on data mining and knowledge management as the preliminary findings for intelligent knowledge, the key contribution of this book. In Sect. 1.1, the fundamental concepts of data mining is briefly outlined, while Sect. 1.2 provides a high-level description of knowledge management mainly from personal point of view. Section 1.3 summarizes three popular existing research directions about how to use human knowledge in the process of data mining: (1) knowledge used for data preprocessing, knowledge for post data mining and domain-driven data mining.

Y. Shi et al., *Intelligent Knowledge*, SpringerBriefs in Business,
DOI 10.1007/978-3-662-46193-8_1

1.1 Data Mining

The history of data mining can be traced back to more than 200 years ago when people used statistics to solve real-life problems. In the area of statistics, Bayes' Theorem has been playing a key role in develop probability theory and statistical applications. However, it was Richard Price (1723–1791), the famous statistician, edited Bayes' Theorem after Thomas Bayes' death (Bayes and Price 1763). Richard Price is one of scientists who initiated the use of statistics in analyzing social and economic datasets. In 1783, Price published "Northampton table", which collected observations for calculating of the probability of the duration of human life in England. In this work, Price showed the observations via tables with rows for records and columns for attributes as the basis of statistical analysis. Such tables now are commonly used in data mining as multi-dimensional tables. Therefore, from historical point of view, the multi-dimensional table should be called as "Richard Price Table" while Price can be honored as a father of data analysis, late called data mining. Since 1950s, as computing technology has gradually used in commercial applications, many corporations have developed databases to store and analyze collected datasets. Mathematical tools employed to handle datasets evolutes from statistics to methods of artificial intelligence, including neural networks and decision trees. In 1990s, the database community started using the term "data mining", which is interchangeable with the term "Knowledge Discovery in Databases" (KDD) (Fayyad et al. 1996). Now data mining becomes the common technology of data analysis over the intersection of human intervention, machine learning, mathematical modeling and databases.

There are different versions of data mining definitions varying from deferent disciplines. For data analysts, data mining discovers the hidden patterns of data from a large-scale data warehouse by precise mathematical means. For practitioners, data mining refers to knowledge discovery from the large quantities of data that stored in computers. Generally speaking, data mining is a computing and analytical process of finding knowledge from data by using statistics, artificial intelligence, and/or various mathematics methods.

In 1990s, mining useful information or discovering knowledge from large databases has been a key research topic for years (Agrawal et al. 1993; Chen et al. 1996; Pass 1997). Given a database containing various records, there are a number of challenging technical and research problems regarding data mining. These problems can be discussed as data mining process and methodology, respectively.

From the aspect of the process, data mining consists of four stages: (1) selecting, (2) transforming, (3) mining, and (4) interpreting. A database contains various data, but not all of which relates to the data mining goal (business objective). Therefore, the related data has to first be selected as identification. The data selection identifies the available data in the database and then extracts a subset of the available data as interested data for the further analysis. Note that the selected variables may contain both quantitative and qualitative data. The quantitative data can be readily represented by some sort of probability distributions, while the qualitative data can be first numericalized and then be described by frequency distributions. The selection criteria are changed with the business objective in data mining. Data transformation converts the selected data into the mined data through certain mathematical (analytical data) models. This type of model building is not only technical, but also a state-of-art (see the following discussion). In general, the consideration of model building could be the timing of data processing, the simple and standard format, the aggregating capability, and so on. Short data processing time reduces a large amount of total computation time in data miming. The simple and standard format creates the environment of information sharing across different computer systems. The aggregating capability empowers the model to combine many variables into a few key variables without losing useful information. In data mining stage, the transformed data is mined using data mining algorithms. These algorithms developed according to analytical models are usually performed by computer languages, such as C++, JAVA, SQL, OLAP and/or R. Finally, the data interpretation provides the analysis of the mined data with respect to the data mining tasks and goals. This stage is very critical. It assimilates knowledge from different mined data. The situation is similar to playing "puzzles". The mined data just like "puzzles". How to put them together for a business purpose depends on the business analysts and decision makers (such as managers or CEOs). A poor interpretation analysis may lead to missing useful information, while a good analysis can provide a comprehensive picture for effective decision making.

From the aspect of methodology, data mining can be achieved by Association, Classification, Clustering, Predictions, Sequential Patterns, and Similar Time Sequences (Cabena et al. 1998). In Association, the influence of some item in a data transaction on other items in the same transaction is detected and used to recognize the patterns of the selected data. For example, if a customer purchases a laptop PC (X), then he or she also buys a Mouse (Y) in 60 % cases. This pattern occurs in 5.6 % of laptop PC purchases. An association rule in this situation can be "X implies Y, where 60 % is the confidence factor and 5.6 % is the support factor". When the confidence factor and support factor are represented by linguistic variables "high" and "low", respectively (Jang et al. 1997), the association rule can be written as a fuzzy logic form: "X implies Y is high, where the support factor is low". In the case of many qualitative variables, the fuzzy association is a necessary and promising technique in data mining.

In Classification, the methods intend to learn different functions that map each item of the selected data into one of predefined classes. Given a set of predefined classes, a number of attributes, and a "learning (or training) set", the classification methods can automatically predict the class of other unclassified data of the learning set. Two key research problems related to classification results are the evaluation of misclassification and the prediction power. Mathematical techniques that are often used to construct classification methods are binary decision trees, neural networks, linear programming, and statistics. By using binary decision trees, a tree induction model with "Yes-No" format can be built to split data into different classes according to the attributes. The misclassification rate can be measured by either statistical estimation (Breiman et al. 1984) or information entropy (Quinlan 1986). However, the classification of tree induction may not produce an optimal solution in which the prediction power is limited. By using neural networks, a neural induction model can be built on a structure of nodes and weighted edges. In this approach, the attributes become input layers while the classes associated with data are output layers. Between input layers and output layers, there are a larger number of hidden layers processing the accuracy of the classification. Although the neural induction model has a better result in many cases of data mining, the computation complexity of hidden layers (since the connection is nonlinear) can create the difficulty in implementing this method for data mining with a large set of attributes. In linear programming approaches, the classification problem is viewed as a linear program with multiple objectives (Freed and Glover 1981; Shi and Yu 1989). Given a set of classes and a set of attribute variables, one can define a related boundary value (or variables) separating the classes. Then each class is represented by a group of constraints with respect to a boundary in the linear program. The objective function can be minimizing the overlapping rate of the classes and maximizing the distance between the classes (Shi 1998). The linear programming approach results in an optimal classification. It is also very feasible to be constructed and effective to separate multi-class problems. However, the computation time may exceed that of statistical approaches. Various statistical methods, such as linear discriminant regression, the quadratic discriminant regression, and the logistic discriminant regression are very popular and commonly used in real business classifications. Even though statistical software has been well developed to handle a large amount of data, the statistical approaches have disadvantage in efficiently separating multi-class problems, in which a pair-wise comparison (i.e., one class vs. the rest of classes) has to be adopted.

Clustering analysis uses a procedure to group the initially ungrouped data according to the criteria of similarity in the selected data. Although Clustering does not require a learning set, it shares a common methodological ground with Classification. In other words, most of mathematical models mentioned above for Classification can be applied to Clustering analysis. Predictions are related to regression techniques. The key idea of Prediction analysis is to discover the relationship between the dependent and independent variables, the relationship between the independent variables (one vs. another; one vs, the rest; and so on). For example, if the sales are an independent variable, then the profit may be a dependent variable. By using historical data of both sales and profit, either linear or nonlinear regression techniques can produce a fitted regression curve which can be used for profit prediction in the future. Sequential Patterns want to find the same pattern of data transaction over a business period. These patterns can be used by business analysts to study the impact of the pattern in the period. The mathematical models behind Sequential Patterns are logic rules, fuzzy logic, etc. As an extension of Sequential Patterns, Similar Time Sequences are applied to discover sequences similar to a known sequence over the past and current business periods. Through the data mining stage, several similar sequences can be studied for the future trend of transaction development. This approach is useful to deal with the databases which have time-series characteristics.

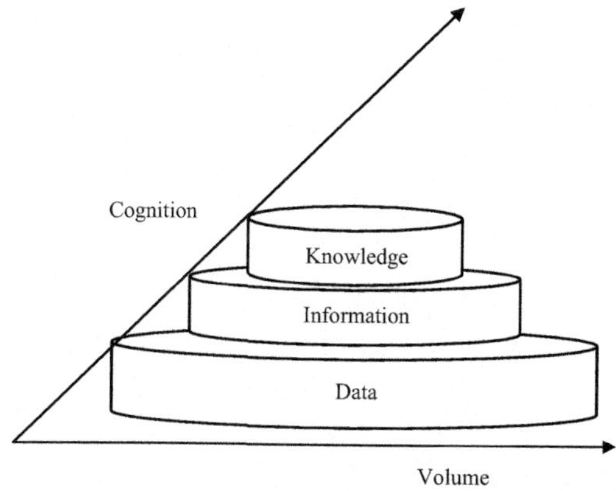

Fig. 1.1 Relationship of Data, Information and Knowledge

1.2 Knowledge Management

Even before data mining, knowledge management is another field which brings numerous impacts on human society. Collecting and disseminating knowledge has been human beings' important social activity for thousands of years. In Western culture, Library of Alexandria in Egypt (200 B.C.) collected more than 500,000 works and hard written copies. The Bible also contains knowledge and wisdom in addition to the religious contents. In Chinese culture, the Lun Yu, Analects of Confucius, the Tao Te Ching of Lao Tsu, and The Art of War of Sun Tzu have been affecting human beings for generations. All of them have served as knowledge sharing functions.

The concepts of the modern knowledge management started from twentieth century and the theory of knowledge management gradually formulated in the last 30 years. Knowledge Management can be regarded as an interdisciplinary business methodology within the framework of an organization as its focus (Awad and Ghaziri 2004). In the category of management, the representations of the knowledge can be (1) state of mind; (2) object; (3) process; (4) access to information; and (5) capacity. Furthermore, knowledge can be classified as tacit (or implicit) and explicit (Alavi 2000; Alavi and Leidner 2001). For a corporation, the tasks of knowledge management inside organization consist of knowledge innovation, knowledge sharing, knowledge transformation and knowledge dissemination. Since explicit knowledge may be converted into different digital forms via a systematical and automatics means, such as information technology, development of knowledge management naturally relates with applications of information technology, including data mining techniques. Basic arguments between knowledge management and data mining can be shown as in Fig. 1.1. Data can be a fact of an event or record of transaction. Information is data that has been processed in some way. Knowledge can be useful information. It changes with individual, time and situation (see Chap. 2 for definitions).

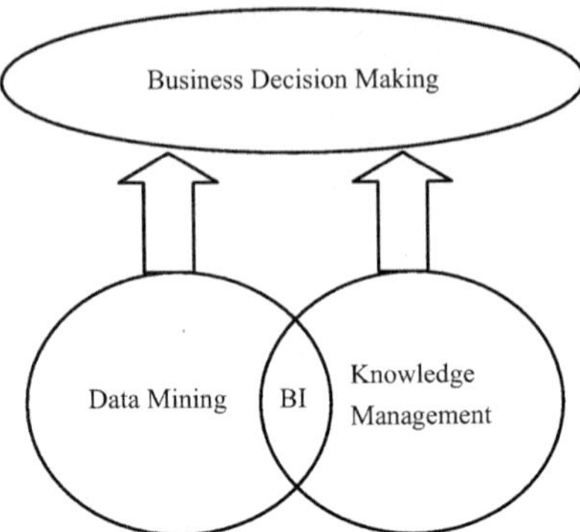

Fig. 1.2 Data Mining and Knowledge Management

Although data mining and knowledge management have been developed independently as two distinct fields in academic community, data mining techniques have playing a key role in the development of corporative knowledge management systems. In terms of support business decision making, their general relationship can be demonstrated by Fig. 1.2. Figure 1.3, however, is used to shown how they can act each other with business intelligence in a corporative decision support system (Awad and Ghaziri 2004).

1.3 Knowledge Management Versus Data Mining

Data mining is a target-oriented knowledge discovering process. Given a business objective, the analysts have to first transfer it into certain digital representation which can be hopefully discovered from the hidden patterns resulted from data

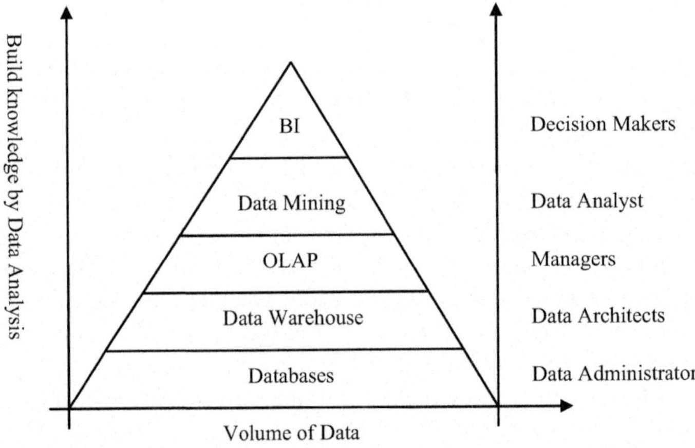

Fig. 1.3 Data Mining, Business Intelligence and Knowledge Management

mining. This knowledge can be considered as the target knowledge. The purpose of data mining is to discover such knowledge. We note that in order to find it in the process of using and analyzing available data, the analysts have to use other related knowledge to achieve target knowledge the different working stages. Researchers have been extensively studied how to incorporate knowledge in the data mining process for the target knowledge. This section will briefly review the following approaches that differ from the proposed intelligent knowledge.

1.3.1 Knowledge Used for Data Preprocessing

In terms of data mining process, the four stages mentioned in Sect. 1.1 can be reviewed as three categories: (1) data preprocessing that encloses selecting and transforming stages; (2) mining, and (3) post mining analysis which is interpreting. Data preprocessing is not only important, but also tedious due to the variety of tasks have to carry out, such as data selections, data cleaning, data fusion on different data sources (especially in the case of Big Data where semi-structural and non-structural data come with traditionally structural data), data normalization, etc. The purpose of data preprocessing is to transfer dataset into a multi-dimensional table or pseudo multi-dimensional table which can be calculated by available data mining algorithms. There are a number of technologies to deal with the components of data preprocessing. However, the existing research problem is how to choose or employ an appropriate technique or method for a given data set so as to reach the better trade-off between the processing time and quality.

From the current literature, either direct human knowledge (e.g., the experience of data analysts) or knowledge agent (e.g., computer software) may be used to both save the data preprocessing time and maintain the quality. The automated intelligent agent of Eliza (Weizenbaum 1966) is one of the earlier knowledge agent versions, which performs natural language processing to ask users questions and used those answers to create subsequent questions. This agent can be applied to guide the analysts who may lack the understanding of data to complete the processing tasks. Recently, some researcher implement well-known methods to design particular knowledge based agent for data preprocessing. For example, Othman et al. (2009) applied the Rough Sets to construct knowledge based agent method for creating the data preprocessing agent's knowledge. This method first to create the preprocessing agent's Profile Data and then use rough set modeling to build agent's knowledge for evaluating of known data processing techniques over different data sets. Some particular Profile Data are the number of records, number of attributes, number of nominal attributes, number of ordinal attribute, number of continuous attributes, number of discrete attributes, number of classes and type of class attribute. These meta data formed a structure of a multi-dimensional table as a guided map for effective data preprocessing.

1.3.2 Knowledge for Post Data Mining

Derive knowledge from the results of data mining (it is called Interpreting stage in this chapter) has been crucial for the whole process of data mining. All experts of data mining agree that data mining provides "hidden patterns", which may not be regarded as "knowledge" although it is later called "rough knowledge" in this book. The basic reason is that knowledge is changed with not only individuals, but also situations. To one person, it is knowledge while it not knowledge for another person. Knowledge is for someone today, but not tomorrow. Therefore, conducting post data mining analysis for users to identify knowledge from the results of data mining has drawn a great deal of research interests. The existing research findings, however, related how to develop automatic algorithms to find knowledge in the domain of computing areas, which differs from our main topics of intelligent knowledge in the book. There are a number of particular methods by designing the algorithms for knowledge from post data mining.

A general approach in post data mining is to define the measurements of "interestingness" on the results of data mining that can provide a strong interests, such as "high ranked rules", "high degree of correlations" and so on for the end users as their knowledge (for instance, see Shekar and Natarajan 2004). Based on interestingness, model evaluation of data mining is supposed to identify the real interesting knowledge model, while knowledge representation is to use visualization and other techniques to provide users knowledge after mining (Guillet and Hamilton 2007). Interestingness can be divided into objective measure and subjective measure. Objective measure is mainly based on the statistical strength or attributes of models found, while subjective measure derives from the users' belief or expectation (Mcgarry 2005).

There is no unified view about how the interestingness should be used. Smyth and Goodman (1992) proposed a J-Measure function that can be quantified information contained in the rules. Toivonen et al. (1995) used cover rules that is a division of mining association rule sets based on consequent rules as interestingness. Piatetsky-Shapiro et al. (1997) studied rules measurement by the independence of events. Aggarwal and Yu (1998) explored a collection of intensity by using the idea of "greater than expected" to find meaningful association rules. Tan et al. (2002) investigated correlation coefficient for interestingness. Geng and Hamilton (2007) provided nine standards of most researchers' concerns and 38 common objective measurement methods. Although these methods are different in forms, they all concern about one or several standards of measuring interestingness. In addition, many researchers think a good interestingness measure should include generality and reliability considerations (Klosgen 1996; Piatetsky et al. 1997; Gray and Orlowska 1998; Lavrac et al. 1999; Yao 1999; Tan et al. 2002). Note that objective measurement method is based on original data, without any additional knowledge about these data. Most of the measurement methods are based on probability, statistics or information theory, expressing the correlation and the distribution in strict formula and rules. Mathematical nature is easy to analyze and be compared with, but these methods do not consider the detailed context of application, such as decision-making objectives, the users' background knowledge and preferences into account (Geng and Hamilton 2007).

In the aspect of subjective interestingness, Klemettinen et al. (1994) studied rule templates so that users can use them to define one certain type of rules that is valuable to solve the value discriminant problem of rules. Silberschatz and Tuzhilin (1996) used belief system to measure non-anticipatory. Kamber and Shinghal (1996) provided necessity and sufficiency to evaluate the interest degree of characteristic rules and discriminant rules. Liu et al. (1997) proposed the rules which could identify users' interest through the method of users' expectations. Yao et al. (2004) proposed a utility mining model to find the rules of greatest utility for users. Note that subjective measure takes into account users as well as data. In the definition of a subjective measure, the field and background knowledge of users are expressed as beliefs or expectations. However, the expression of users' knowledge by the subjective measure is not an easy task. Since the effectiveness of using the subjective measure depends on users' background knowledge, users who have more experiences in a data mining process could be efficient than others.

Because these two measurement methods have their own advantages and disadvantages, a combination of objective and subjective measure were merged (Geng and Hamilton 2007). Freitas (1999) even considered the objective measure can be used as the first-level filter to select the mode of potential interest and then use subjective measure for second-level screening. In this way, knowledge that users feel genuinely interested in can be formed.

While there are a number of research papers contributing to the interestingness of associations, few can be found for the interestingness of classification except for using the accuracy rate to measure the results of classification algorithms. This approach lacks the interaction with users. Arias et al. (2005) constructed a framework for evaluation of classification results of audio indexing. Rachkovskij (2001) constructed DataGen to generate datasets used to evaluate classification results.

The clustering results are commonly evaluated from two criteria. One is to maximize the intra-class similarity and another is to minimize inter-class similarity. Dunn (1974) proposed an indicator for discovering the separate and close clustering based on the basic criteria. The existing data mining research on model evaluation of data mining and knowledge representation indicates that in order to find knowledge for specific users from the results of data mining, more advanced measurements that combine the preferences of users should be developed, in conjunction with some concepts of knowledge management. A variety of methods have been proposed along with this approaches. For example, Zhang et al. (2003) studied a post data mining method by transferring infrequent itemsets to frequent itemsets, which implicitly used the concept of "interestingness" measure to describe the knowledge from the results of data mining. Gibert et al. (2013) demonstrated a tool to bridge logistic regression and the visual profile's assessment grid methods for indentifying decision support (knowledge) in medical diagnosis problems. Yang et al. (2007) considered how to convert the decision tree results into the users' knowledge, which may not only keep the favorable results like desired results, but also change unfavorable ones into favorable ones in post data mining analysis. These findings are close to the concept of intelligent knowledge proposed in this book. They, however, did not get into the systematic views of how to address the scientific issues in using human knowledge to distinguish the hidden patterns for decision support.

1.3.3 Domain Driven Data Mining

There has been a conceptual research approach called "domain driven data mining", which considers multiple aspects by incorporating human knowledge into the process of data mining (see Cao et al. 2006, 2010; Cao and Zhang 2007). This approach argues that knowledge discovered from algorithm-dominated data mining process is generally not interesting to business needs. In order to identify knowledge for taking effective actions on real-world applications, data mining, conceptually speaking, should involve domain intelligence in the process. The modified data mining process has six characteristics: (i) problem understanding has to demonstrate domain specification and domain intelligence, (ii) data mining is subject to constraint-based context, (iii) in-depth patterns can result in knowledge, (iv) data mining is a loop-closed iterative refinement process, (v) discovered knowledge should be actionable in business, and (vi) a human-machine-cooperated infrastructure should embedded in the mining process (Cao and Zhang 2007).

Although this line of research provided a macro view of the framework to address how important human (here called domain) knowledge can play in the process of data mining to assist in identifying actionable decision support to the interested users, it did not show the theoretical foundation how to combine domain knowledge with data mining in abstract format, which can give a guidance to analysts to construct an automatic way (the algorithm associated with any know data mining algorithm that can be embedded in the data mining process) if the domain knowledge is quantitatively presented. One of goals of this book is to fill this open research problem.

1.3.4 Data Mining and Knowledge Management

There are some cross-field study between data mining and knowledge management in the literature. For example, Anand et al. (1996) proposed that the prior knowledge of the users and previously discovered knowledge should be jointly considered to discover new knowledge. Piatesky-Shapiro and Matheus (1992) explored how domain knowledge can be used in initial discovery and restrictive searching. Yoon and Kerschberg (1993) discussed the coordination of new and old knowledge in a concurrent evolution thinking of knowledge and database. However, there is no a systematic study and concrete theoretical foundation for the cross-field study between data mining and knowledge management.

Management issues, such as expert systems and decision support systems, have been discussed by some data mining scholars. Fayyad et al. (1996) described knowledge discovery project based on the knowledge through data mining. Cauvin et al. (1996) studied knowledge expression based on data mining. Lee and Stolfo (2000) constructed an intrusion detection system based on data mining. Polese et al. (2002) established a system based on data mining to support tactical decision-making. Nemati et al. (2002) constructed a knowledge warehouse integrating knowledge management, decision support, artificial intelligence and data mining technology. Hou et al. (2005) studied an intelligent knowledge management model, which is different from what we discuss in the book.

We observe that the above research of knowledge (we late call rough knowledge) generated from data mining has attracted academic and users' attention, and in particular, the research of model evaluation has been investigated, but is not fully adaptable for the proposed study in the paper based on the following reasons. First, the current research concentrates on model evaluation, and pays more attention to the mining of association rules, especially the objective measure. As we discussed before, objective measurement method is based on original data, without any additional knowledge about these data. Most of the measurement methods are based on probability, statistics or information theory, expressing the correlation and the distribution in strict formula and rules. They are hardly to be combined with expertise. Second, the application of domain knowledge is supposed to relate with research of actionable knowledge that we will discuss late, but should not be concentrated in the data processing stage as the current study did. The current study favored more on technical factors than on the non-technical factors, such as scenario, expertise, user preferences, etc. Third, the current study shows that there is no framework of knowledge management technology to well support analytical original knowledge generated from data mining, which to some extent means that the way of incorporating knowledge derived from data mining into knowledge management areas remains unexplored. Finally, there is lack of systematic theoretical study in the current work from the perspective of knowledge discovery generated from data based on the organizational level. The following chapter will address the above problems.

Chapter 2
Foundations of Intelligent Knowledge Management

Knowledge or hidden patterns discovered by data mining from large databases has great novelty, which is often unavailable from experts' experience. Its unique irreplaceability and complementarity has brought new opportunities for decision-making and it has become important means of expanding knowledge bases to derive business intelligence in the Big Data era. Instead of considering how domain knowledge can play a role in each stage of data mining process, this chapter concentrates on a core problem: whether the results of data mining can be really regarded as "knowledge". The reason is that if the domain knowledge is quantitatively presented, then the theoretical foundation can be explored for finding automatic mechanisms (algorithms) to use domain knowledge to evaluate the hidden patterns of data mining. The results will be useful or actionable knowledge for decision makers. To address this issue, the theory of knowledge management should be applied. Unfortunately, there appears little work in the cross-field between data mining and knowledge management. In data mining, researchers focus on how to explore algorithms to extract patterns that are non-trivial, implicit, previously unknown and potentially useful, but overlook the knowledge components of these patterns. In knowledge management, most scholars investigate methodologies or frameworks of using existing knowledge (either implicit or explicit ones) support business decisions while the detailed technical process of uncovering knowledge from databases is ignored.

This chapter aims to bridge the gap between these two fields by establishing a foundation of intelligent knowledge management over large databases or Big Data. Section 2.1 addresses the challenging problems to data mining. Section 2.2 enables to generate "special" knowledge, called intelligent knowledge base on the hidden patterns created by data mining. Section 2.3 systematically analyzes the process of intelligent knowledge management—a new proposition from original data, *rough* knowledge, *intelligent* knowledge, and *actionable* knowledge as well as the four transformations (4 T) of these items. This study not only promotes more significant research beyond data mining, but also enhances the quantitative analysis of knowledge management on hidden patterns from data mining. Section 2.4 will outline some interesting research directions that will be elaborated in the rest of chapters.

Y. Shi et al., *Intelligent Knowledge,* SpringerBriefs in Business,
DOI 10.1007/978-3-662-46193-8_2

2.1 Challenges to Data Mining

Since 1970s, researchers began systematically exploring various problems in knowledge management (Rickson 1976). However, people have been interested in how to collect, expand and disseminate knowledge for a long time. For example, thousands of years ago, Western philosophers studied the awareness and understanding of the motivation of knowledge (Wiig 1997). The ancient Greek simply believed that personal experience forms all the knowledge. Researchers at present time pay more attention to management of tacit knowledge and emphasize on management of people as focusing on people's skills, behaviors and thinking patterns (Wang 2004; Zhang et al. 2005).

Thanks to the rapid development of information technology, many western companies began to widely apply technology-based tools to organize the internal knowledge innovation activities. Thus it drove a group of researchers belonging to technical schools to explore how to derive knowledge from data or information. For instance, Beckman (1997) believes that knowledge is a kind of humans' logical reasoning on data and information, which can enhance their working, decision-making, problem-solving and learning performance. Knowledge and information are different since knowledge can be formed after processing, interpretation, selection and transformation of information (Feigenbaum 1977).

In deriving knowledge by technical means, data mining becomes popular for the process of extracting knowledge, which is previously unknown to humans, but potentially useful from a large amount of incomplete, noisy, fuzzy and random data (Han and Kamber 2006). Knowledge discovered from algorithms of data mining from large-scale databases has great novelty, which is often beyond the experience of experts. Its unique irreplaceability and complementarity has brought new opportunities for decision-making. Access to knowledge through data mining has been of great concern for business applications, such as business intelligence (Olson and Shi 2007).

However, from the perspective of knowledge management, knowledge discovery by data mining from large-scale databases face the following challenging problems.

First, the main purpose of data mining is to find hidden patterns as decision-making support. Most scholars in the field focus on how to obtain accurate models. They halt immediately after obtaining rules through data mining from data and rarely go further to evaluate or formalize the result of mining to support business decisions (Mcgarry 2005). Specially speaking, a large quantity of patterns or rules may be resulted from data mining. For a given user, these results may not be of interest and lack of novelty of knowledge. For example, a data mining project that classifies users as "current users, freezing users and lost users" through the use of decision tree classification algorithm produced 245 rules (Shi and Li 2007). Except for their big surprise, business personnel cannot get right knowledge from these rules (Shi and Li 2007). The expression of knowledge should not be limited to numbers or symbols, but also in a more understandable manner, such as graphics, natural languages and visualization techniques. Knowledge expressions and qualities from different data mining algorithms differ greatly, and there are inconsistencies, even conflicts, between the knowledge so that the expression can be difficult. The current data mining research in expressing knowledge is not advanced. Furthermore due to the diversification of data storages in any organizations, a perfect data warehouse may not exist. It is difficult for data mining results based on databases or data warehouses to reflect the integration of all aspects of data sources. These issues lead to the situation that the data mining results may not be genuinely interesting to users and can not be used in the real world. Therefore, a "second-order" digging based on data mining results is needed to meet actual decision-making needs.

Second, many known data mining techniques ignore domain knowledge, expertise, users' intentions and situational factors (Peng 2007). Note that there are several differences between knowledge and information. Knowledge is closely related to belief and commitment and it reflects a specific position, perspective or intention. Knowledge is a concept about operations and it always exists for "certain purposes". Although both knowledge and information are related to meaning, knowledge is in accordance with the specific situation and acquires associated attributes (Nonaka et al. 2000; Zeleny 2007). From the culture backgrounds of knowledge, Westerners tend to emphasize on formal knowledge, while Easterners prefer obscure knowledge. It is also believed that these different kinds of knowledge are not totally separated but complementary to each other. In particular, they are closely linked in terms of how human and computer are interacted in obtaining knowledge. Because of the complexity of knowledge structure and the incrementality of cognitive process, a realistic knowledge discovery needs to explore interactively different abstraction levels through human-computer interaction and then repeat many times. Keeping the necessary intermediate results in data mining process, guiding role of human-computer interaction, dynamic adjusting mining target, and users' background knowledge, domain knowledge can speed up the process of knowledge excavation and ensure the effectiveness of acquired knowledge. Current data mining tools are unable to allow users to participate in excavation processes actually, especially for second-order excavation. In addition, both information and knowledge depend on specific scenarios, and they are relevant with the dynamic creation in humans' social interaction. Berger and Luckman (1966) argued that interacting people in certain historical and social scenario share information derived from social knowledge. Patterns or rules generated from data mining must be combined with specific business context in order to use in the enterprise. The context here includes relevant physics, business and other externally environmental and contextual factors, which also covers cognition, experience, psychology and other internal factors of the subject. It is the key element to a complete understanding of knowledge, affecting people's evaluation about knowledge. A rule may be useful to enterprises in a certain context, for a decision maker, at a certain time, but in another context it might be of no value. Therefore, context is critical for data mining and the process of the data mining results. In the literature, the importance of context to knowledge and knowledge management has been recognized by a number of researchers (Dieng 1999; Brezillion 1999; Despres 2000; Goldkuhl 2001; Cap 2002). Though people rely on precise mathematical expressions for scientific findings, many scientific issues cannot be interpreted by mathematical forms. In fact in the real world, the results of data mining should be interacted effectively with the company reality and some non-quantitative factors before they are implemented as actionable knowledge and business decision support. These factors include the bound of specific context, expertise (tacit knowledge), users' specific intentions, domain knowledge and business scenarios (Zhang et al. 2008).

Third, common data mining process stops at the beginning of knowledge acquisition. The organizations' knowledge creation process derived from data should use different strategies to accelerate the transformation of knowledge in different stages of the knowledge creation, under the guidance of organizational objectives. Then a spiral of knowledge creation is formed, which creates conditions for the use of organizational knowledge and the accumulation of knowledge assets. At present, data mining process only covers knowledge creation part in this spiral, but does not involve how to conduct a second-order treatment to apply the knowledge to practical business, so as to create value and make it as a new starting point for a new knowledge creation spiral. Therefore, it cannot really explain the complete knowledge creation process derived from data. There is currently very little work in this area. In the ontology of data mining process, the discovered patterns are viewed as the end of the work. Little or no work involving the explanation of knowledge creation process at organizational level is studied in terms of implementation, authentication, internal process of knowledge, organizational knowledge assets and knowledge recreation. From the epistemological dimension, it lacks a deep study about the process of data - information - knowledge –wisdom, and the cycle of knowledge accumulation and creation is not revealed. A combination of organizational guides and strategies needs to decide how to proceed with the knowledge guide at the organizational level so that a knowledge creation process derived from data (beyond data mining process) and organizational strategies and demands can be closely integrated.

Based on the above analysis, in the rest of this book, the knowledge or hidden patterns discovered from data mining will be called "rough knowledge." Such knowledge has to be examined at a "second-order" in order to derive the knowledge accepted by users or organizations. In this book, the new knowledge shall be called "intelligent knowledge" and the management process of intelligent knowledge is called intelligent knowledge management. Therefore, the focus of the study has the following dimensions:

- The object of concern is "rough knowledge".
- The stage of concern is the process from generation to decision support of rough knowledge as well as the "second-order" analysis of organizational knowledge assets or deep-level mining process so as to get better decision support.
- Not only technical factors but also non-technical factors such as expertise, user preferences and domain knowledge are considered. Both qualitative and quantitative integration have to be considered.
- Systematic discussion and application structure are derived for the perspective of knowledge creation.

The purposes of proposing intelligent knowledge management are:

- Re-define rough knowledge generated from data mining for the field of knowledge management explicitly as a special kind of knowledge. This will enrich the connotation of knowledge management research, promote integration of data mining and knowledge management disciplines, and further improve the system of knowledge management theory in the information age.
- The introduction of expertise, domain knowledge, user intentions and situational factors and the others into "second-order" treatment of rough knowledge may help deal with the drawbacks of data mining that usually pays too much emphasis on technical factors while ignoring non-technical factors. This will develop new methods and ideas of knowledge discovery derived from massive data.
- From the organizational aspect, systematic discussion and application framework derived from knowledge creation based on massive data in this paper will further strengthen and complement organizational knowledge creation theory.

2.2 Definitions and Theoretical Framework of Intelligent Knowledge

In order to better understand intelligent knowledge management, basic concepts and definitions are introduced in this subsection.

The research of intelligent knowledge management relates to many basic concepts such as original data, information, knowledge, intelligent knowledge and intelligent knowledge management. It is also associated with several relevant concepts such as congenital knowledge, experience, common sense, situational knowledge etc. In order to make the proposed research fairly standard and rigorous from the beginning, it is necessary to give the definition of these basic concepts. Moreover, the interpretation of these concepts may provide a better understanding of intrinsic meanings of data, information, knowledge, and intelligent knowledge.

Definition 2.1 Data is a certain form of the representation of facts.

The above definition that is used in this paper has a general meaning of "data." There are numerous definitions of data from different disciplines. For example, in computing, data is referred to distinct pieces of information which can be translated into a different form to move or process; in computer component or network environment, data can be digital bits and bytes stored in electronic memory; and in telecommunications, data is digital-encoded information (Webopedia 2003; Whatis.com 2005). In information theory, data is abstractly defined as an object (thing) that has the self-knowledge representation of its state and the state's changing mode over time (Zhong 2007). When it is a discrete, data can be expressed mathematically a vector of n-dimensional possible attributes with random occurrences. Without any physical or analytic processing to be done, given data will be treated as "original" in this paper. Therefore, original data is the source of processing other forms (such as information, rough knowledge, intelligent knowledge and others).

From the perspective of forms, the data here includes: text, multimedia, network, space, time-series etc.

From the perspective of structure, the data includes: structured, unstructured and semi-structured data; as well as more structured data which current data mining or knowledge discovery can deal with.

From the perspective of quantity, the data includes: huge amounts of data, general data and small amounts of data etc.

Data, judging from its nature, is only the direct or indirect statements of facts. It is raw materials for people to understand the world.

Therefore, the characteristics of the original data here include: roughness (original, roughness, specific, localized, isolated, superficial, scattered, or even chaotic), extensive (covering a wide range), authenticity and manipulability (process through data technology). After access to original data, appropriate processing is needed to convert it into abstract and universal applicable information. Thus, the definition of information is given as:

Definition 2.2 Information is any data that has been pre-processed to all aspects of human's interests.

Traditionally, information is the data that has been interpreted by human using certain means. Both scientific notation and common sense share the similar concepts of information. If the information has a numerical form, it may be measured through the uncertainty of an experimental outcome (The American Heritage Dictionary of the English Language 2003), while if it cannot be represented by numerical form, it is assigned for an interpretation through human (Dictionary of Military and Associated Terms 2005). Information can be studied in terms of information overload. Shi (2000) classified information overload by exploring the relationships between relevant, important and useful information. However, definition 2 used in this paper is directly for describing how to get knowledge from data where information is an intermediate step between these two. It is assumed that the pre-processed data by either quantitative or qualitative means can be regarded as information. Based on the concepts of data and information, the definition of rough knowledge is presented as follows:

Definition 2.3 Rough Knowledge is the hidden pattern or "knowledge" discovered from information that has been analyzed by the known data mining algorithms or tools.

This definition is specifically made for the results of data mining. The data mining algorithms in the definition means any analytic process of using artificial intelligence, statistics, optimization and other mathematics algorithms to carry out more advanced data analysis than data pre-processing. The data mining tools are any commercial or non-commercial software packages performing data mining methods. Note that data pre-processing normally cannot bring a qualitative change of the nature of data and results in information by definition 2, while data mining is advanced data analysis that discovers the qualitative changes of data and turns information into knowledge that has been hidden from human due to the massive data. The representation of rough knowledge changes with a data mining method.

For example, rough knowledge from association method is rules, while it is a confusion matrix for the accuracy rates by using a classification method.

The purpose of defining data, information and rough knowledge is to view a general expression of the data mining process. This paper will call the process and other processes of knowledge evolution as "transformations."

The transformation from data (or original data) to rough knowledge via information is called the first transformation, denoted as T_1. Let K_R stand for the rough knowledge and D denote as data. Then the first type of transformation can be expressed as:

$$T_1 : D \rightarrow K_R \quad or \quad K_R = T_1(D)$$

As it stands, T_1 contains any data mining process that consists of both data preprocessing (from data to information) and data mining analysis (from information to rough knowledge). Here the main tasks of T_1 can include: characterization, distinction, relevance, classification, clustering, outlier analysis (abnormal data), evolution analysis, deviation analysis, similarity, timing pattern and so on. Technologies of T_1 include extensively: statistical analysis, optimization, machine learning, visualization theory, data warehousing, etc. Types of rough knowledge are potential rules, classification tags, outlier labels, clustering tags and so on.

Characteristics of rough knowledge can be viewed as:

(i) Determined source: from results of data mining analysis;
(ii) Part usability: the possibility of direct support for business may exist, but much may not be used directly.
(iii) Rough: without further refinement, rough knowledge contains much redundant, one-sided or even wrong knowledge. For example, the knowledge generated from over-training has high prediction accuracy rate about the test set, but the effect is very poor;
(iv) Diversity: knowledge needs to be shown by a certain model for decision-making reference. There are many forms of rough knowledge, for instance, summary description, association rules, classification rules (including decision trees, network weights, discriminant equations, probability map, etc.), clusters, formulas and cases and so on. Some representations are easy to understand, such as decision trees, while some manifestations have poor interpretability, such as neural networks.
(v) Timeliness: compared with humans' experience, rough knowledge is derived from data mining process in a certain time period, resulting in short cycle. It may degrade in the short term with environmental changes. In addition, there are conflicts sometimes between the knowledge generated from different periods. As a result, as the environment changes the dynamic adaptability can be poor.

While rough knowledge is a specific knowledge derived from the analytic data mining process, the human knowledge has extensively been studied in the field of knowledge management. The item knowledge has been defined in many different ways. It is generally regarded as individual's expertise or skills acquired through learning or experience (Wikipedia 2008). In the following, knowledge is divided as five categories in terms of its contents. Then, these can be incorporated into rough knowledge from data mining results for our further discussion on intelligent knowledge.

Definition 2.4 Knowledge is called Specific Knowledge, denoted by K_S if it contains the certain state and rules of an object expressed by human.

Specific knowledge is a cognitive understanding of certain objects and can be presented by its form, content and value (Zhong 2007). Specific knowledge has a strict boundary in defining its meanings. Within the boundary, it is knowledge; otherwise, it is not (Zeleny 2002).

Definition 2.5 Knowledge is called Empirical Knowledge, denoted by K_E if it directly comes from human's experience gained from empirical testing.

Note that the empirical testing in definition 5 is referred to specifically non-technical, but practical learning process from which human can gain experience. If it is derived from statistical learning or mathematical learning, knowledge is already defined as rough knowledge of definition 2.2. Empirical testing here can be also referred to as intermediate learning, such as reading from facts, reports or learning from others' experiences. When these experiences are verified through a scientific learning, they will become "knowledge". Otherwise, they are still "experiences" (Zhong 2007).

Definition 2.6 Knowledge is called Common Sense Knowledge, denoted as K_C if it is well known and does not need to be proved.

Common sense is the facts and rules widely accepted by most of humans. Some knowledge, such as specific knowledge or empirical knowledge can become common sense as they are gradually popularized. Therefore, it is also called "post-knowledge" (Zhong 2007).

Definition 2.7 Knowledge is called Instinct Knowledge, denoted by K_H if it is innate as given functions of humans.

Instinct knowledge is heritage of humans through the biological evolution and genetic process. It does not need to be studied and proved. If instinct knowledge is viewed as a "root" of the knowledge mentioned above, then a "knowledge ecosystem" can be formed. In the system, instinct knowledge first can be changed into empirical knowledge after training and studying. Then, if empirical knowledge is scientifically tested and confirmed, it becomes specific knowledge. As the popularity of specific knowledge develops, it is common sense knowledge. However, the system is premature since the creation of human knowledge is quite complex and could not be interpreted as one system (Zhong 2007).

Definition 2.8 Knowledge is called Situational Knowledge, denoted as K_U if it is context.

The term *context* used in this paper, associated with knowledge and knowledge activities, is relevant to conditions, background and environment. It includes not only physical, social, business factors, but also the humans' cognitive knowledge, experience, psychological factors (Pan 2005).

Situational knowledge or context has the following characteristics:

(i) It is an objective phenomenon which exists widely;
(ii) It is independent of knowledge and knowledge process, but keeps a close interaction with knowledge and knowledge process;
(iii) It describes situational characteristics of knowledge and knowledge activities. Its function is to recognize and distinguish different knowledge and knowledge activities. To humans, their contexts depict personal characteristics of one engaging in intellectual activities (Pan 2005).

Based on the above definitions of different categories of knowledge, a key definition of this paper is given as:

Definition 2.9 Knowledge is called Intelligent Knowledge, denoted as K_I if it is generated from rough knowledge and/or specific, empirical, common sense and situational knowledge, by using a "second-order" analytic process.

If data mining is said as the "first-order" analytic process, then the "second-order" analytic process here means quantitative or qualitative studies are applied to the collection of knowledge for the pre-determined objectives. It can create knowledge, now intelligent knowledge, as decision support for problem-solving. The "second-order" analytic process is a deep study beyond the usual data mining process. While data mining process is mainly driven by a series of procedures and algorithms, the "second-order" analytic process emphasizes the combinations of technical methods, human and machine interaction and knowledge management.

Some researchers in the field of data mining have realized its importance of handling the massive rules or hidden patterns from data mining (Ramamohanarao 2008; Wong 2008; Webb 2008). However, they did not connect the necessary concepts from the filed of knowledge management in order to solve such a problem for practical usage. Conversely, researchers in knowledge management often ignore rough knowledge created outside humans as a valuable knowledge base. Therefore, to bridge the gap between data mining and knowledge management, the proposed study on intelligent knowledge in the paper is new.

As discussed above, the transformation from information to rough knowledge T_1 is essentially trying to find some existing phenomenological associations among specific data. T_1 is some distance away from the knowledge which can support decision-making in practice. The "second-order" analytic process to create intelligent knowledge from available knowledge, including rough knowledge, can be realized in general by transformation T_2, defined as follows:

$$T_2 : K_R \cup K \rightarrow K_I \quad or \quad K_I = T_2(K_R \cup K),$$
$$where\ K = \rho(K_S, K_E, K_C, K_H, K_U)\ is\ a\ power\ set.$$

K_S Specific Knowledge;
K_E Empirical Knowledge;

K_C Common Sense Knowledge;
K_H Instinct Knowledge;
K_U Situational Knowledge.

The above transformation is an abstract form. If the results of the transformation are written in terms of the components of intelligent knowledge, then the following mathematical notations can be used:

(i) Replacement transformation: $K_I = K_R$

(ii) Scalability transformation: $K_I = \alpha K_R,\ where -\infty < \alpha < +\infty$

(iii) Addition transformation: $K_I = K_R + K_I$

(iv) Deletion transformation: $K_I = K_R - K_I$

(v) Decomposition transformation:

$$K_I = \alpha_1 K_{R1} + \alpha_2 K_{R2} + \alpha_2 K_{R3} + \ldots,\ where -\infty < \alpha_i < +\infty$$

In the above, replacement transformation is a special case of scalability transformation, and they, together with addition and deletion transformations are parts of decomposition transformation.

The coefficients of $\{\alpha_1, \alpha_2, \alpha_2 \ldots\}$ in the decomposition represent the components of $K = \rho(K_S, K_E, K_C, K_H, K_U)$ distributed in the knowledge creation process.

The intelligent knowledge has the following characteristics:

(i) The process of intelligent knowledge creation fully integrates specific context, expertise, domain knowledge, user preferences and other specification knowledge, and makes use of relevant quantitative algorithms, embodying human-machine integration principle;
(ii) Since intelligent knowledge is generated from the "second-order" analytic process, it is more valuable than rough knowledge;
(iii) It provides knowledge to people who need them at the right time, under appropriate conditions.
(iv) The objective of intelligent knowledge is to provide significant inputs for problem-solving and support strategic action more accurately.

To explore more advanced issues in the meaning of knowledge management, intelligent knowledge can be further employed to construct a strategy of problem-solving by considering goal setting, specific problem and problem environment.

Restricted by the given problem and its environmental constraints, aiming at the specific objectives, a strategy of solving the problem can be formed based on related intelligent knowledge. To distinguish the strategy that has been used in different fields, the strategy associated with intelligent knowledge is called intelligent strategy.

If P is defined as the specific problems, E is for problem solving environment and G is goal setting, then the information about issues and environment can be expressed as $I(P,E)$. Given intelligent knowledge K_I, an intelligent strategy S is another transformation, denoted as:

$$T_3 : K_I \times I(P,E) \times G \to S, or$$
$$S = T_3(K_I \times I(P,E) \times G)$$

Transformation T_3 differs from T_2 and T_1 since it relates to forming an intelligent strategy for intelligent action, rather than finding knowledge. Achieving the transformation from intelligent knowledge to a strategy is the mapping from a product space of $K_I \times I(P,E) \times G$ to strategy space S.

Action usually refers to the action and action series of humans. Intelligent action (a high level transformation) is to convert an intelligent strategy into actionable knowledge, denoted as T_4:

$$T_4 : S \to K_A, or$$
$$K_A = T_4(S)$$

Term K_A is denoted as actionable knowledge. Some K_A can ultimately become intangible assets, which is regarded as "wisdom" (Zeleny 2006). For example, much actionable knowledge produced by great military strategists in history gradually formed as wisdom of war. A smart strategist should be good at using not only his/her actionable knowledge, but also the wisdom from history (Nonaka 2009). When processing qualitative analysis in traditional knowledge management, people often pay more attention to how intelligent strategy and actionable knowledge generated from tacit knowledge and ignore their source of quantitative analysis, where intelligent knowledge can be generated from combinations of data mining and human knowledge. Intelligent strategy is its inherent performance, while actionable knowledge is its external performance. Transformation T_4 is a key step to produce actionable knowledge that is directly useful for decision support. Figure 2.1 is the process of transformations from data to rough knowledge, to intelligent knowledge and to actionable knowledge.

The management problem of how to prepare and process all of four transformations leads to the concept of intelligent knowledge management:

Definition 2.10 Intelligent Knowledge Management is the management of how rough knowledge and human knowledge can be combined and upgraded into intelligent knowledge as well as management issues regarding extraction, storage, sharing, transformation and use of rough knowledge so as to generate effective decision support.

Intelligent knowledge management proposed in this paper is the interdisciplinary research field of data mining and knowledge management. One of frameworks can be shown as Fig. 2.2.

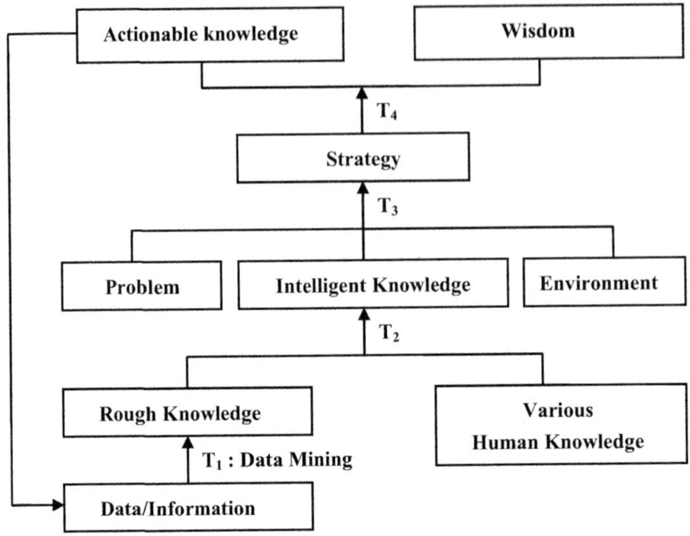

Fig. 2.1 Data → Rough Knowledge → Intelligent Knowledge → Actionable Knowledge

The features of intelligent knowledge management are as follows:

(i) The main source of intelligent knowledge management is rough knowledge generated from data mining. The purpose of doing this is to find deep-seated knowledge and specifically to further discover relationships on the basis of existing relationships.
(ii) Intelligent knowledge managementrealizes decision support better, so as to promote the practicality of knowledge generated from data mining, reduce information overload and enhance the knowledge management level.
(iii) Intelligent knowledge management can be used tobuildorganization-based and data-derived knowledge discovery projects, realizing the accumulation and sublimation of organizational knowledge assets.
(iv) It is a complex multi-method and multi-channel process. The technical and non-technical factors, as well as specification knowledge (expertise, domain knowledge, user preferences, context and other factors) are combined in the process of intelligent knowledge management. As a result, the knowledge found should be effective, useful, actionable, understandable to users and intelligent.
(v) Essentially, intelligent knowledge management is the process of combining machine learning (or data mining) and traditional knowledge management, of which the key purpose is to acquire problem-solving knowledge. The study source is knowledge base and the study means is a combination of inductive and deductive approaches. Ultimately not only the *fact* knowledge but also the *relationship* knowledge can be discovered. It is closely related to the organization of knowledge base and ultimate knowledge types that users seek. Adopted reasoning means may involve many different logical fields.

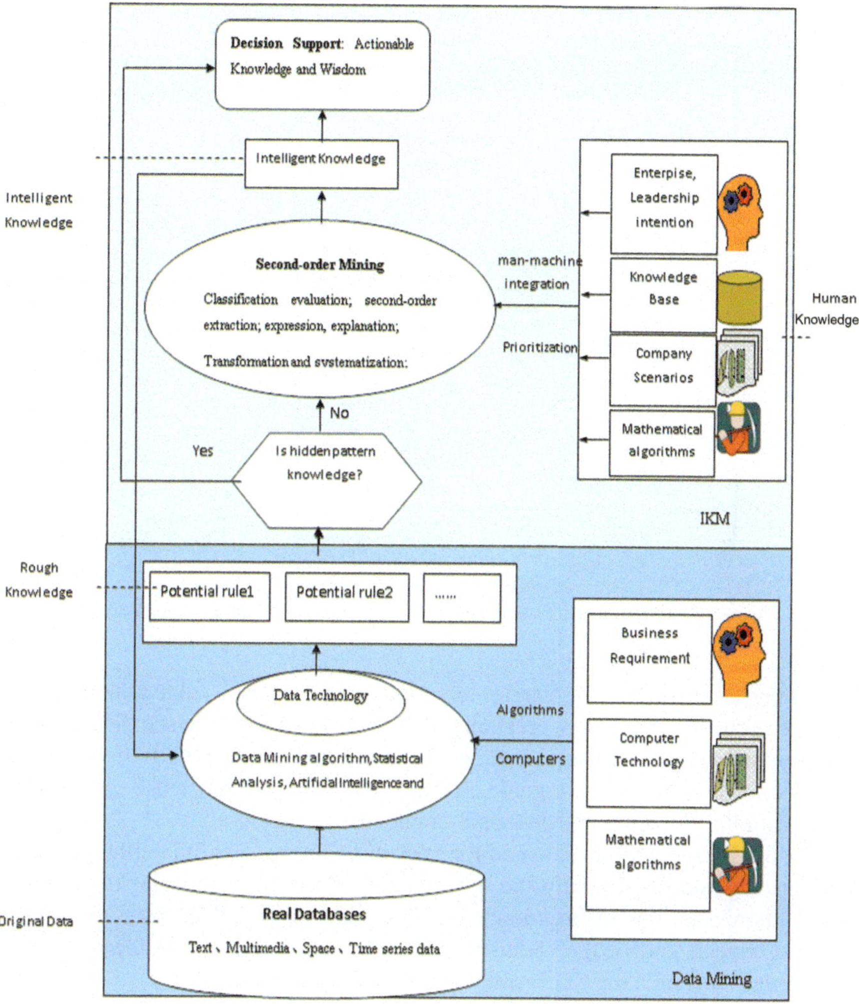

Fig. 2.2 A Framework of Intelligent Knowledge Management (IKM)

2.3 T Process and Major Steps of Intelligent Knowledge Management

As the leading representative of knowledge creation process derived from experience, Nonaka et al. (2000) proposed SECI model of knowledge creation, the value of the model is given as in Fig. 2.3:

This model reveals that through externalization, combination and internalization, highly personal tacit knowledge ultimately becomes organizational knowledge assets and turns into tacit knowledge of all the organizational members. It accurately shows the cycle of knowledge accumulation and creation. The concept of "Ba"

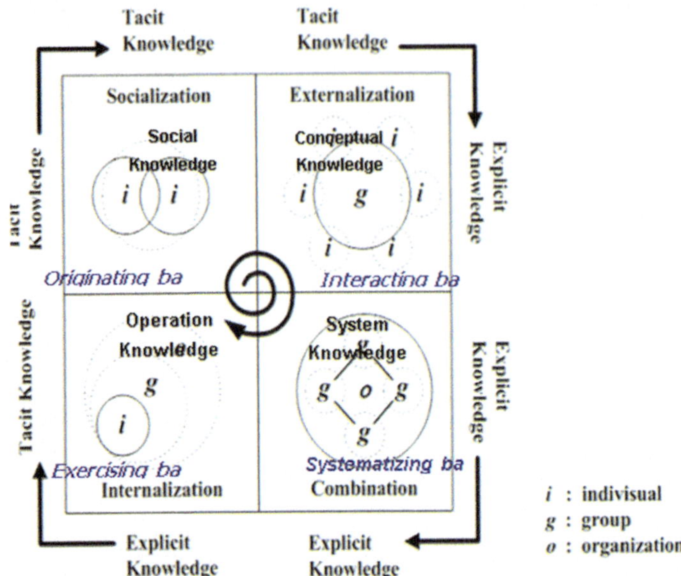

Fig. 2.3 Knowledge Creation as the Self-Transcending Process. (Source: Nonaka et al. (2000))

means that using different strategies in various stages of knowledge transformation can accelerate the knowledge creation process. It can greatly enhance the efficiency and operating performance of enterprises' knowledge innovation. It also provides an organizational knowledge guide so that the process of knowledge creation and organizational strategies and demands can be integrated closely.

The SECI model can be adopted for explaining the process of intelligent knowledge management, especially the 4 T process of transformation including data–rough knowledge-intelligent knowledge- actionable knowledge. From the organizational aspect, knowledge creation derived from data should be the process of knowledge accumulation like a spiral, which is shown in Fig. 2.4:

The transformation process includes:

T_1 (from data to rough knowledge): after the necessary process of processing and analyzing original data, the preliminary result (hidden Pattern, rules, weights, etc.) is rough knowledge, as a result from a kind of primary transformation.

T_2 (from rough knowledge to intelligent knowledge): on the basis of rough knowledge, given user preferences, scenarios, domain knowledge and others, the process carries out a "second-order" mining for knowledge used to support intelligent decision-making and intelligent action. The process carries out deep processing of the original knowledge, which is the core step in intelligent knowledge management.

T_3 (from intelligent knowledge to intelligent strategy): in order to apply intelligent knowledge in practice, one must first convert intelligent knowledge into intelligent strategy through consideration of problem statement and solving environment. It is the process of knowledge application.

T_4 (from intelligent strategy to actionable knowledge): once actionable knowledge is obtained, it can be re-coded as "new data", which are either intangible assets

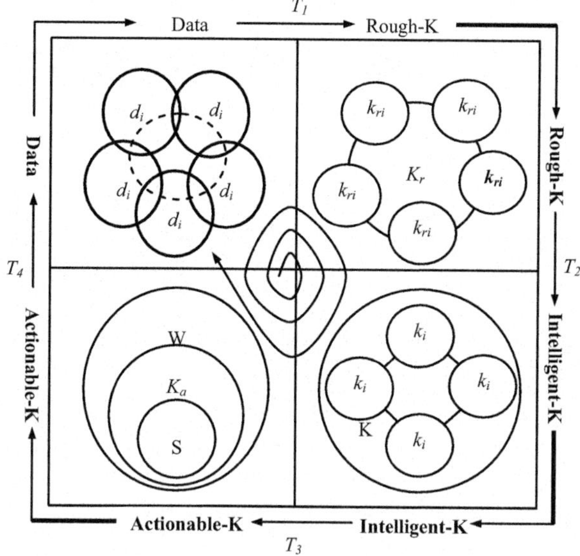

Fig. 2.4 Transformation Process of Data–Rough knowledge-Intelligent Knowledge- Actionable Knowledge

or wisdom can be used as data source for decision support. The new process of rough knowledge-intelligent knowledge-actionable knowledge begins. However, the new round of knowledge discovery is a higher level of knowledge discovery on the basis of existing knowledge.

Therefore, it is a cycle, spiraling process for the organizational knowledge creation, and from the research review, the current data mining and KDD would often be halted when it is up to stage T_3 or T_4, leading to the fracture of spiral, which is not conducive to the accumulation of knowledge.

It also needs to be noted that in this process, different stages require different disciplines and technologies for support. Stage T_1 generally focuses on technical factors such as computer and algorithms, while stage T_2 needs expertise, domain knowledge, user preferences, scenarios, artificial intelligence for constraint and support. Stage T_3 needs a higher level of expertise to make it into actionable knowledge or even the intelligence. Stage T_4 generates new data primarily by computers, networks, sensors, records, etc. However, technical factors and non-technical factors are not totally separate, but the focus should be different at different stages.

2.4 Related Research Directions

Intelligent knowledge management can potentially be a promising research area that involves interdisciplinary fields of data technology, knowledge management, system science, behavioral science and computer science. The feature of intelligent knowledge management research is shown in Fig. 2.5. There are a number of research directions remaining to be explored. Some of them can be described below.

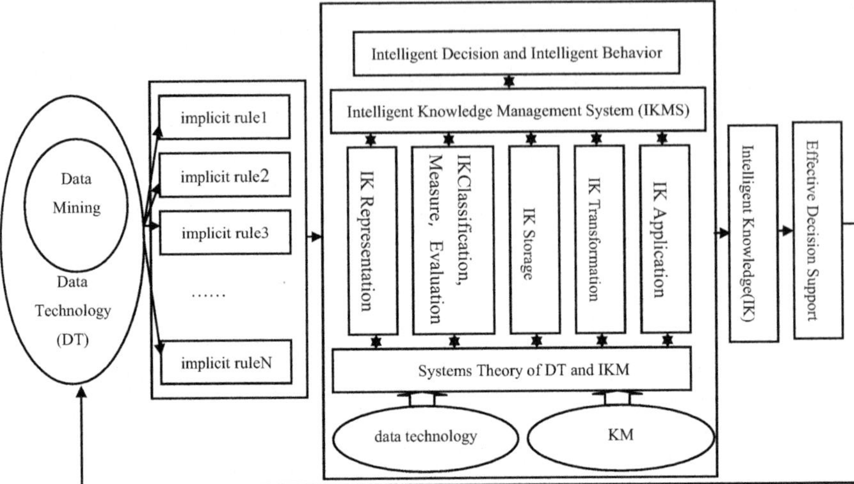

Fig. 2.5 Interdisciplinary Feature of Intelligent Knowledge

2.4.1 The Systematic Theoretical Framework of Data Technology and Intelligent Knowledge Management

Related to the above issues discussed in this paper, a general term, data technology, is used to capture a set of concepts, principles and theories of quantitative methodologies to analyze and transform data to information and knowledge. In accordance with the principles of system science, the following issues need to be raised and studied in the future:

a. How to classify, describe and organize known data technologies, including data mining, artificial intelligence, statistics and others based on the treatment capacity and characteristics. How to effectively use the results of data mining as rough knowledge to discuss the logical relationship between intelligent knowledge and traditional knowledge structure? How to establish the mathematical model about intrinsic links between data technology and intelligent knowledge? These can be used to explain the characteristics of intelligent knowledge generated from the results of data analysis.
b. From the perspective of knowledge creation derived from data, how to study the process of knowledge creation, establish knowledge creation theory derived from data and build a systematic framework of data mining and intelligent knowledge management.

As a class of "special" knowledge, the process management theory including extraction, transformation, application, innovation of intelligent knowledge in specific circumstances should be studied. In the study, not only knowledge itself, but also the tacit knowledge of decision-makers and users and other non-technical factors, such as domain knowledge, user preferences, scenarios, etc. should be considered. In addition, artificial intelligence, psychology, complex systems, integrated integration as well as some empirical research methods should be employed to understand the systematic framework.

2.4.2 *Measurements of Intelligent Knowledge*

Finding appropriate "relationship measurement" to measure the interdependence between data, information and intelligent knowledge is a challenging task. This research on appropriate classification and expression of intelligent knowledge may contribute to the establishment of the general theory of data mining, which has been a long-term unresolved problem.

The classification and evaluation of intelligent knowledge include analyzing features of intelligent knowledge generated from data mining, classifying intelligent knowledge, selecting appropriate indicators for different types of intelligent knowledge to do the effectiveness evaluation, and building a classification and evaluation system of intelligent knowledge.

In measure of intelligent knowledge, the theory and methods of subjective and objective measure of intelligent knowledge should be studied. The mathematical method of the measurement for intelligent knowledge value should be more carefully studied. Measure is a "relationship". The establishment of intelligent knowledge measures can be very challenging.

Given applied goals and information sources, what data mining system must do is to evaluate the validity of intelligent knowledge structure. Results of the evaluation should not only quantify the usefulness of the existing intelligent knowledge, but also decide whether there is a need for other intelligent knowledge. The exploring of this area needs three aspects to conduct an in-depth study: (1) analysis of intelligent knowledge complexity; (2) analysis of the correlation between intelligent knowledge complexity and model effectiveness; (3) analysis of across heterogeneous intelligent knowledge effectiveness. In short, how to identify the results from data mining, and how to accurately measure the valuable intelligent knowledge and evaluate the quality of intelligent knowledge management are key issues of the application of knowledge management. The research in this area (Benchmark of Data Mining and Intelligent Knowledge) still remains unexplored, in need of much further work.

Furthermore, intelligent knowledge is viewed as a class of "special" knowledge, and the meaning and structure in mathematics and management of its preservation, transformation and application should be further studied.

The link between intelligent knowledge and intelligent action, intelligent decision-making and action, and how to apply intelligent knowledge to improve decision-making intelligence and decision-making efficiency are also interesting research issues.

2.4.3 Intelligent Knowledge Management System Research

Based on the framework of the relevance and features of the intelligent knowledge management system, management information system and knowledge management system in this paper, both data mining and intelligent knowledge management are used to support enterprise management decision-making. For different industries, such as finance, energy policy, health care, communications, auditing with large-scale data infrastructures, an intelligent knowledge management system can be established, through the integration of data mining and intelligent knowledge management, to improve their knowledge management capability and overall competitiveness.

With the development of information technology, knowledge management and data mining have become popular research fields. However, the cross-over study of knowledge management and data mining is very limited. Particularly in the field of data mining, most scholars focus on how to obtain accurate rules, but rarely classify, evaluate or formalize the result of knowledge excavation to support business decisions better(Mcgarry 2005). In addition, human knowledge, such as expertise and user preferences, is often not incorporated into the process of identifying knowledge from the hidden patterns using data mining algorithms.

There have been a lack of management and applications of its properties as well as a systematic theory and applied research from the perspective of the creation of knowledge from data. These problems led to the interdisciplinary development behind the practical demands of business applications. For a class of "special" knowledge created by data mining, this paper systematically analyzes the background of intelligent knowledge management—a new scientific proposition, defines original data, rough knowledge, rule knowledge, intelligent knowledge, intelligent action, actionable knowledge, intelligent decision-making, intelligent knowledge management and other related concepts and explains their relationship. A 4 T transformation model involving data, rough knowledge, intelligent knowledge, and actionable knowledge, as well as the research direction, content and framework of future intelligent knowledge management has been proposed. This study greatly enriches the content of data mining and knowledge management and opens new avenues for exciting interdisciplinary research in the area.

Chapter 3
Intelligent Knowledge and Habitual Domain

This paper is to enhance our understanding about the second-order data mining. In particularly, we examine the effect of human cognition on the creation of intelligent knowledge during the second-order data mining process. Prior studies have suggested that human cognition plays an important role in the second-order data mining process during which intelligent knowledge was discovered (Baker et al. 2009). Given the knowledge that no single data mining model outperforms others for all problems, a common practice in data mining projects is to run multiple data mining models at first and then invite a group of people to collaboratively make judgments on these data mining models' performance. These judgments often diverge. Little research exists to explain why these variations of human judgments occur.

The theory of habitual domains (Yu 1990, 1991, 2002; Yu and Chen 2010) provides a useful theoretical base for explaining the behavioral mechanism that guides human minds' operations. Drawing on the theory of habitual domains, in this article, we develop a theoretical model to explain the influence of habitual domains' characteristics on human judgments made on data mining models' performance. Specifically, among the many data mining models, this study chose to use the classifiers. A field survey was administrated at a multidisciplinary research. A social network data analysis technique was used to test the proposed relationships in the model. The specific research question of this study is:

What are the relationships between human habitual domain characteristics and the convergence of human judgments on data mining performance in the second-order data mining process?

Intelligent knowledge was created during second-order data mining through human judgments. A clear understanding about why people's judgments about classifiers diverge or converge will inform the design of the guidance for selecting appropriate people to evaluate/select data mining models for a particular problem. Thus, costly mistakes can be avoided when appropriate people are selected.

The rest of the chapter is organized as follows. Section 3.1 introduces the theory of habitual domains and related hypotheses. Then the overall research design and experimental results are presented in Sect. 3.2. Section 3.3 discusses the limitations of the study. In Sect. 3.4 and 3.5, we present the discussion and conclusion of our study.

Y. Shi et al., *Intelligent Knowledge*, SpringerBriefs in Business,
DOI 10.1007/978-3-662-46193-8_3

3.1 Theory of Habitual Domain

3.1.1 Basic Concepts of Habitual Domains

The analysis of intelligent knowledge, rough knowledge, and human knowledge leads us to wonder how various types of human knowledge along with the results from data mining classifiers contribute to the creation of intelligent knowledge. The theory of habitual domains provides us a theoretical foundation. The theory of habitual domains (Shi and Yu 1987; Yu 1990, 1991, 2002; Yu and Chen 2010) attempts to describe and explain the human's behavior mechanism that guides people in making decisions and judgments. The central proposition of habitual domain theory is that an individual thinks and acts in a habitual way, which is influenced by one's habitual domains. The theory of habitual domains builds on three necessary conditions: (1) our perceptions of the environment can be reached at steady states in our brain, (2) most of daily problems we counter happen regularly, and (3) human tends to take the most convenience way of dealing with daily problems (Yu 1990). In this chapter, we suggest that the theory of habitual domains is useful in explaining the elusive process involved in our minds in the process of intelligent knowledge creation.

Yu and Chen (2010, p. 11) defined the habitual domains as "the set of ideas and concepts which we encode and store in our brain can over a period of time gradually stabilize in certain domain". According to the theory of habitual domains, human attain knowledge or make decisions based on external stimulus and self suggestion. Unless there is an occurrence of extraordinary events, an individual tends to make decisions by following a stable mental model established in his/her mind. As a result, we can observe that each of us has his/her own set of habitual ways of doing cognitive related tasks, such as problem solving, decision making, and learning.

The theoretical building blocks of the habitual domains are ideas and operators. Ideas refer to specific thoughts resides in our minds. Operators are the actions, specifically the "thinking processes or judging methods" (Yu 1990, p. 118). The theory of habitual domains developed eight hypotheses to capture the basics to how our minds work. In particular, the analogy/association hypothesis is most relevant to this study. The analogy/association hypothesis is stated as follows:

"The perception of new events, subjects or ideas can be learned primarily by analogy and/or association with what is already known. When faced with a new event, subject or idea, the brain first investigates its features and attributes in order to establish a relationship with what is already known by analogy and/or association. Once the right relationship has been established, the whole of the past knowledge (preexisting memory structure) is automatically brought to bear on the interpretation and understanding of the new event, subject or idea (Yu and Chen 2010, p. 8)."

According to this hypothesis, analogy/association enables the brain to comprehend and interpret the new arriving information from the external environment. People with different habitual domain characteristics will perceive rough knowledge differently and thus make different judgments on the classifiers' performance.

Though there are a variety of variables constitute people's habitual domain characteristics, we choose these specific characteristics—level of education, areas of specialty, and prior experience with data mining—which are most relevant to the context of second-order data mining. The linkages between these three characteristics and the theory of habitual domains are explained in the next subsection. Hypotheses are developed.

3.1.2 Hypotheses of Habitual Domains for Intelligent Knowledge

The theory of habitual domains (Yu 1990) identifies four basic components of habitual domains. These four components are: potential domain, actual domain, activation probabilities, and reachable domain.

Potential domain is a collection of ideas and operators that can be potentially activated. Actual domain is the activated ideas and operators. The overall potentially reachable collection of ideas and operators based on the potential domain and the actual domain is called reachable domain. The activation probabilities define the degree to which subsets of potential domain can be actually activated at a particular time. Subsets of potential domain vary in the degree of their likelihood to be activated for given problems.

In most cases, a large size of potential domain is preferable. That is because holding all other things equal, the larger the potential domain, the more likely that a larger set of ideas, concepts or thoughts will be activated. Moreover, if the ideas, thoughts, and knowledge are stored in a systematical way and are integrated seamlessly, individuals are more likely to make judgments and cope with problems better.

The size of a potential domain is greatly contingent on an individual's habitual domain formation. The theory of habitual domains proposed eight approaches by which individuals form their habitual domains. The eight approaches are: active learning, projecting from a higher position, self awareness, active association, changing the relevant parameters, retreating, changing the environment, and brainstorming. Based on these eight approaches of habitual domains formation, this paper proposed that an individual's habitual domain's characteristics can be described by examining an individual's background in these eight areas. The assumption we made here is that for each of the eight approaches, if people follow different paths within the approach, then people's habitual domains will be formed differently. In other words, peoples' habitual domains' characteristics can be described by assessing peoples' background in each of the approaches by which s/he form the habitual domains.

Considering the purpose of this study along with the consideration of empirical assessment, this paper focused on the active learning dimension. The habitual domain is a multi-dimensional and complex concept. The theory of habitual domain has identified three dimensions of one's domain, namely behavior function, events, and external interaction. Each dimension has several specific components. Given the multidimensional nature of habitual domains, checking one's habitual domain thoroughly is challenging. Yu (1990) suggest that a study could only focus on one component based on the study's purpose. Given the purpose of the study is to understand why people make different judgments on classifiers' performance on data sets and plus people's such decision making is to a large extent influenced by ones' learning experience, therefore, it is adequate to only check the active learning experience of people at this point. More approaches should be considered when different goals of the study are taken.

Active learning emphasizes on the various external sources (such as experts, media, and school education) around us. Active learning will not only give us a higher chance of getting new and innovative ideas but will also enable us to be able to more efficiently integrate ideas we have before and make those ideas more accessible.

We specifically identified three areas related to active learning. Those three areas are: level of education, areas of specialty, and prior experience with data mining. We posit that these three areas make up a significant high proportion of one's active learning experience. People who have similar background in each of the three areas of active learning will possess similar habitual domains and thus make similar judgments on data mining classifiers' performance. In the following paragraphs of this section, we will describe each of these three areas in details and develop hypotheses.

First, level of education is concerned with how many years of formal school education one has taken. From many years of education in school, each of us has been exposed to many new ideas and new knowledge from reading books, listening to lectures, and interacting with our classmates. Attending classes not only provides us new ideas and knowledge but also facilitates the absorption of these new ideas and knowledge in our minds by repetitions. In an experimental study, Macpherson (1996) found that educational background, specifically the number of years of education, has a significant positive effect on individuals' capabilities of generating insights. Another study reveals that education can decrease the anxiety toward the use of computer (Igbaria et al. 1989). Bower and Hilgard's study (1981) suggest that higher level of education would enhance individual's cognitive capabilities and thus accelerate the individual's learning process especially in novel situations. Considering the situations people face to the hidden patterns—which usually reveals unknown rules or hidden patterns, we construct the following hypothesis.

H1: The closer the levels of education between individuals, the higher the degree to which people agree on judging performance of classifiers for a particular database.

Second, areas of specialty refer to the: (1) research areas and majors that individuals peruse in college (2) individuals' domain knowledge. Working or studying in a special area will provide one with relatively in-depth knowledge in that particular area. Further, working in a specific specialized area enables one communicate with a group of peers and can help one gain new knowledge and insights (Astin 1993). A study conducted by Paulsen and Wells (1998) found that students who studied in similar majors (according to hard-soft, pure-applied dimensions of Biglan's (1973) classification of academic fields) held similar epistemological beliefs, which are beliefs about the nature of knowledge and learning. Their study found that students majored in soft and pure fields were less likely than others to hold naïve beliefs in certain knowledge.

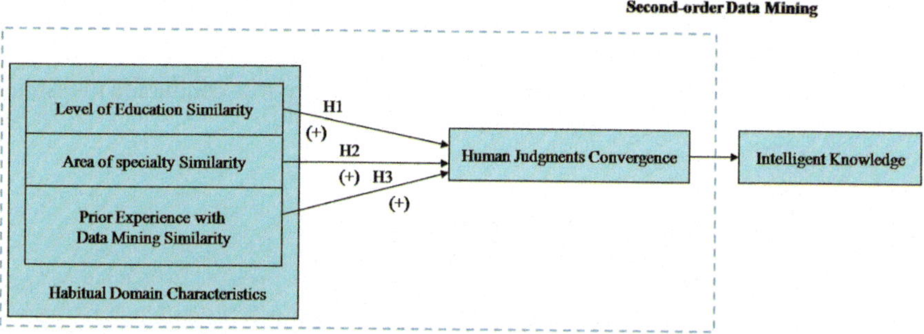

Fig. 3.1 Influence of Habitual Domains on Human Judgments Convergence

The importance of areas of specialty on the successful application of data mining has also been recognized in the field of data mining. For example, Ambrosino and Buchanan (1999) found that models that incorporated domain knowledge performed significantly better than models without considering domain knowledge in predicting the risk of mortality in patients with a specific disease. In a study of applying data mining to bank loans problem, Sinha and Zhao (2008) examined and compared performances of seven well-known classifiers. They found that models that incorporated the pre-derived expert rules outperformed models without those expert rules.

Thus, we have the following hypothesis.

H2: The closer the areas of specialty between individuals, the higher the degree to which people agree on judging performance of classifiers for a particular database.

Third, prior experience with data mining is about individuals' past experience related to data mining. Such experience can be gained by attending data mining related classes, leading or participating in data mining projects, using data mining software, developing data mining algorithms, and reading books or literatures related data mining. We suggest that an individual's experience with data mining greatly influences one's attitude toward various data mining classifiers. Empirical studies have found that previous experience with certain technologies can either hinder or foster one's adoption of a new technology (Harrison et al. 1992). For example, one study found that users resisted using an unfamiliar technology because of switching costs (Scholtz et al. 1990). Thus, we build the following hypothesis.

H3: The closer the experience with data mining between individuals, the higher the degree to which people agree on judging performance of classifiers for a particular database.

The research model is shown in Fig. 3.1. Building on the theory of habitual domains, the conceptual model describes the convergence of human judgments on data mining is positively influenced by the similarity of people's level of education, by the similarity of people's areas of specialty, and by the similarity of people's prior experience with data mining. The model is constructed and examined at the team level. The creation of intelligent knowledge from rough knowledge during second-order data mining is a complex process, this article focuses on studying the influence of habitual domain characteristics on the convergence of human judgments on classifiers' performance.

3.2 Research Method

The overall research design is a field survey. A pilot study was conducted to test the reliability and validity of the survey and the field procedure.

3.2.1 *Participants and Data Collection*

Considering the purpose of the study is to test if habitual domain characteristics affect people's judgments on data mining, it is necessary to have subjects with diverse background. Thus, the study collected data from members employed in a multi-disciplinary research institute in China. The research institute has conducted several large data mining projects in the past. This research institute consists of a total of five research labs concentrating on various areas, ranging from e-commerce, green energy, to data mining. Researchers in the institute have backgrounds as varied as management information systems, computer science, economics, and biology. Of the 38 respondents, 42 percent of the respondents were male and 58 percent of the respondents were female. The distribution of respondents' age is shown in Table 3.1.

In the study, we first run eight classifiers[1] on two data sets and recorded the performance of each classifier given a set of measures. Then we administrated the survey questionnaire. The session lasted for a total of 4 h. An author of the paper gave an introduction to the background of the survey. The questionnaire collected participants' demographic information and also asked the participants to rate the performances of eight classifiers on the two large-scale data sets. The participants rated the performance of the classifiers on each of the two data sets according to the seven standard evaluation criteria (as is shown in Appendix A).

The Nursery Database is a public data set from the Machine Learning Repository of the University of California, at Irvine (UCI). It was derived from a hierarchical decision model originally developed to rank applications for nursery schools. It was used during several years in 1980's when there was excessive enrollment to these schools in Ljubljana, Slovenia, and the rejected applications frequently needed an objective explanation[2]. PBC Dataset is a data set related to credit scoring from

Table 3.1 Frequency on Subjects' Age

Age	Frequency	Percentage (%)
20–30	28	73.68
30–40	6	15.79
40–50	3	7.89
Above 50	1	2.63

[1] The eight methods are J48, Nbtree, Baysnet, Naivebays, Logistic, Support Vector Machine (SVM), Multiple Criteria Linear Programming (MCLP), and Multiple Criteria Quadratic Programming (MCQP).

[2] Http://archive.ics.uci.edu/ml/datasets/Nursery

China. After preprocess, we got a data set with 1600 samples. 800 of them were classified as good customers and 800 of them were classified as bad customers. 80 variables were designed to reflect the behaviors of the customers.

3.2.2 Measures

3.2.2.1 Habitual Domains Characteristics

Measures for habitual domain characteristics—level of educational, prior experience with data mining, and areas of specialty—were enabled by asking participants to check the items that best describe their current status. Specifically, to assess subjects' educational background, we asked each participant to answer one multiple choice question that asks their highest degree (IV1). Second, area of specialty was measured by asking subjects' current major and research area (IV2). Third, to assess subjects' prior experience with data mining (IV3), we used multiple measures, including: their level of acquaintance with data mining, if ever participated in data mining related projects, if ever studied data mining related courses, level of acquaintance with data mining methods, and level of familiarity with data mining software.

3.2.2.2 Dependent Variables

Dependent variables in this study were participants' judgments on data mining classifiers' performance. Specifically, dependent variables consist of participant's ratings on performance of each of the eight classifiers on the data sets. We ran eight data mining classification algorithms on two large-set data sets. The second section of the questionnaire presented the results of performance of data mining algorithms on two datasets according to the selected standard measures. We asked subjects to evaluate the performance of the data mining algorithm on each of the seven measures, using a 10-point response scale (1 = very bad performance and 10 = outstanding performance).

3.2.3 Data Analysis and Results

3.2.3.1 Descriptive Analysis

We first analyze the psychometric properties of the acquaintance with data mining (IV3) by running a reliability analysis in SPSS. Results showed the subscales of IV3 have good internal consistency, $\alpha = 0.93$. Table 3.2 shows the frequency of individuals' educational background.

The descriptive statistic of the areas of specialty of individuals is shown in Table 3.3.

Table 3.2 Frequency on Subjects' Educational Background—Level of Study

Degree	Frequency	Percentage (%)
Master Graduate Student	14	36.8
Doctoral Graduate Student	14	36.8
Doctor	10	26.3
Total	38	100

Table 3.3 Frequency on Subjects' Educational Background—Major

Major	Frequency	Percentage (%)
Social Science	0	0
Management Science	28	73.7
Information Technology	10	26.3
Total	38	100

Table 3.4 Ratings on Classifiers' Performance on the Nursery Database

Classifier	Mean	SD
J48	8.11	1.29
Nbtree	7.78	1.61
Baysnet	6.11	1.90
Naivebays	6.22	1.61
Logistic	7.22	1.79
SVM	8.81	1.29
MCLP	8.46	1.69
MCQP	7.84	1.59

Table 3.5 Ratings on Classifiers' Performance on the PBC Database

Classifier	Mean	SD
J48	8.03	1.62
Nbtree	7.30	1.75
Baysnet	5.65	1.79
Naivebays	5.22	1.70
Logistic	7.11	1.52
SVM	5.41	1.84
MCLP	7.16	1.35
MCQP	7.65	1.46

Results showed that participants were generally somewhat familiar with data mining (M=2, SD=0.81).

The descriptive analysis of subjects' judgments on the eight classifiers' performance on Nursery Database indicated that SVM got the highest average score (M=8.81, SD=1.29) and Baysnet got the lowest average score (M=6.11, SD=1.9). Table 3.4 showed the descriptive statistics.

For classifiers' performance on the PBC database, results showed that J48 received the highest average score (M=8.03, SD=1.62). Naivebays received the lowest average score (M=5.22, SD=1.70). Table 3.5 presented the descriptive statistics for all classifiers' scores on the PBC database.

3.2.3.2 Geary's C Analysis

We identify Geary's C (1954) statistic as a perfect fit for testing the type of hypotheses in the present study. Geary's C is adapted for social network analysis from their origins in geography, where they were developed to measure the extent to which the similarity of the geographical features of any two places was related to the spatial distance between them (Geary 1954). Geary's C has been widely used in social network analysis for testing the homophily hypothesis which asks a question of: Is there a tendency for actors who have more similar attributes to be located closer to one another in network? Since the hypotheses of present study concerned about if the closeness of experts' habitual domain characteristics would affect their judgments on data mining algorithms' performance, thus it is obvious for us to use Geary's C for testing the hypotheses of this study. This social network data analysis method, Geary's C statistic has two advantages. First, it avoids merely focusing on subjects' answers to individual question, rather it provides a global view of the subject's responses to all of the questions. Second, it simplifies the dependent variables and makes it easy to conduct the correlation analysis.

It should be noted that although MANOVA method allows the analysis of the effects of more than one independent variable on two or more dependent variables, MANOVA method has strict assumptions on the data, such as normality of dependent variables, linearity of all pairs of dependent variables, and homogeneity of variances. The robustness of MANOVA results will be significantly affected when these important assumptions are violated. Unfortunately, we explored the two data sets on all the three assumptions of MANOVA. Two of the assumptions (normality and linearity of dependent variables) were violated, and only the homogeneity of variances assumption was met.

Therefore, we consider Geary's C statistic to test the effects of independent variables on dependent variables. To apply Geary's C statistic in our study, for each of the two datasets, we used the affiliation network method[3] in UCINET (Borgatti et al. 2002) to get an adjacency matrix[4] of all participants based on their judgments on data mining algorithm performance. This adjacency matrix thus described the "closeness" of each pair of participants on their overall perceptions on the data mining algorithm performance. Then, we create another attribute table that contains all information of participants' habitual domain characteristics. UCINET was used to calculate the Geary's C measure. Table 3.6 and 3.7 present the Geary's C statistic results.

Correlation results indicated that educational level is highly positively correlated with the closeness between individual's judgments on classifier's performance. To

[3] Affiliation network is a one mode network, which has been first applied to study the southern women and the social events in which they attended. The affiliation network describes how many same events each two of women have attended. Then affiliation network has been applied in many cases to establish the pairwise ties between actors Wasserman, S., and Faust, K. Social Network Analysis, 1995.

[4] The computational process to get the Geary's C and the adjacency was shown in Appendix C.

Table 3.6 Geary's C Correlation Analysis on the Nursery Database

IV	DV	Geary's C
LES	Closeness between individual's judgments on classifier's performance	0.99[a]
ASS	Closeness between individual's judgments on classifier's performance	1.004
PEDMS	Closeness between individual's judgments on classifier's performance	0.98[b]

IV independent vriable, *DV* dependent variable, *LES* level of education similarity, *ASS* area of specialty similarity, *PEDMS* prior experience with data mining similarity

[a] Indicates a correlation is significant at 0.1

[b] Indicates a correlation is significant at 0.01

Table 3.7 Geary's C Correlation Analysis on the PBC Database

IV	DV	Geary's C
LES	Closeness between individual's judgments on classifier's performance	0.99[a]
ASS	Closeness between individual's judgments on classifier's performance	1.005
PEDMS	Closeness between individual's judgments on classifier's performance	0.98[a]

IV independent vriable, *DV* dependent variable, *LES* level of education similarity, *ASS* area of specialty similarity, *PEDMS* prior experience with data mining similarity

[a] Indicates a correlation is significant at 0.1

[b] Indicates a correlation is significant at 0.01

put it another way, the degree to which individuals agree on classifier's performance is positively influenced by the similarity between individual's educational levels. Prior experience with data mining also indicated a significant influence on individual's agreements on data mining algorithms performance. However, on both two data sets, areas of specialty didn't show a significant relationship with people's judgments on classifier's performance. Overall, Hypothesis 1 and Hypothesis 3 were supported. Hypothesis 2 was rejected.

3.3 Limitation

Prior to discussing the findings of the study, limitations of the study must be acknowledged. First, the sample itself offers some important limitations. The setting for the study was a research institution and respondents were mostly students and a few faculties who worked in this institution. Thus, the generalizability of the respondents' behaviors to a more general population may be somewhat limited. One mostly mentioned drawback of using students as subjects is that the significant differences between students and the targeting groups. In this study, the targeting groups will be the data mining customers who propose, sponsor, evaluate, and eventually implement a data mining project. The targeting groups may possess very different background in terms of educational background, areas of specialty, and previous experience compared to students of this study.

Additionally, this study only asks participants' opinions on classifiers' performance on two data sets. Moreover, a data set is from UCI rather than a real-world data set. One major criticism with UCI data set is that the data set in UCI is often biased because pre-processing of the data. Future study should provide classifiers' performance on more data sets so that the bias resulting from the data sets can be reduced.

Another limitation of the study comes from the type of data analysis we conducted. Geary's C analysis doesn't allow an interaction analysis of data. This autocorrelation method can only detect the association between subjects' attributes and subjects' responses on a set of questions. The impact of interactions among subjects' attributes, such as level of education, areas of specialty, and prior experience with data mining, cannot be obtained. Future research can acquire larger sample of data and conduct a MANOVA analysis to see if there are interaction effects of individuals' habitual domain characteristics on their judgments on data mining classifiers.

Finally, this study is a first attempt in applying habitual domain theory in understanding peoples' judgments made on data mining classifiers' performance. Therefore, the three constructs, level of education, areas of specialty, and experiences in data mining, need further refinement. For example, while we gave a formal description of areas of specialty in this study, the study did not specify which several areas of specialty should be considered in the assessment of individuals' habitual domains.

3.4 Discussion

People intend to take full advantage of data mining through discovering intelligent knowledge from the data mining results. Accordingly, data mining researchers have begun to explore deriving intelligent knowledge from data mining in this stage (Bendoly 2003; Zhang et al. 2009). Research activities that are interested in transforming data mining results into actionable intelligent knowledge are called "second-order" data mining. This paper proposed that the theory of habitual domain provides a useful theoretical lens to study "second-order" data mining. Habitual domain theory is proposed to account for the mechanism through which human make decisions and judgments. The theory of habitual domain operationalized habitual domain in four specific domains: potential domain, actual domain, activation probabilities, and reachable domain. Further, the theory proposed that such human habitual domains are expanded through active learning, specifically formal school education and important personal experience.

This paper derived empirically testable hypotheses based on the habitual domain theory. In our experiments, we found support for our hypotheses that people's judgments on data mining classifiers' performance are influenced by people's education and prior experience with data mining. Education was found to be an important factor on peoples' perceptions on classifiers' performance. People's prior experience with data mining was also revealed as a predictor to peoples' evaluation on classifiers' performance with statistic significance.

The analysis, however, didn't confirm the hypothesized positive effect of areas of specialty similarity on people's convergence on classifiers' performance. To put it another way, this results indicated that individuals' judgments on classifier's performance will not be significantly influenced by individuals' majors. One possible explanation is that the majors of participants in the study were not diverse enough. This study only had individuals from these three majors: Computer Science, Financial Engineering, and Management Science. It is possible that students from these three majors show similar attitudes on data mining classifiers' performance on various data sets. A study conducted by Tikka (2000) found that students of majors related to technology and economics showed similar attitude toward the environment adopted a more negative attitude toward the environment and, on average, had fewer nature-related hobbies than students in general.

One key advantage of understanding what habitual domains characteristics influence people's judgments making on data mining methods is the opportunity it presents for training interventions to manipulate people's perceptions about a classifier. Since education and previous experience with data mining have significant effect on people's perceptions on classifiers, designing better training will increase the likelihood that novice data mining developers make quality judgments as data mining experts do.

Having a group of people with similar habitual domains characteristics can benefit data mining project teams in terms of reducing conflicts in data mining algorithms. Since 1980s, numerous data mining algorithms have been developed. But no single one data mining algorithm has been proved to be able to outperform all the other algorithms in all tasks. Therefore, in the real world data mining projects, data mining teams have to carefully compare among more than one data mining methods and choose one that has the best functioning performance. Depending upon ones' past educational background and experience with data mining, people will possess different views toward the data mining methods' performance. Having people with similar habitual domains characteristics will help the team establish a shared understanding about the data mining methods' advantages and disadvantages, and thus help the data mining project team to reach a convergent opinion on which data mining method to be used. But having people with similar habitual domains may also place a potential risk of entering a decision trap to the data mining project team. For instance, it is possible that all people converge on a wrong decision when the team faces an unusual problem of data mining. With the coming of the big data era (i.e. large scale of data and integration of both structured and unstructured data) (Chen et al. 2012), the chance of dealing with unfamiliar data mining task or using unfamiliar data mining tools increases significantly. Therefore, given unusual data mining tasks or unfamiliar data mining algorithms, it is important for the data mining project teams to choose team members with diverse educational background and data mining experience, so that the team can make an optimal decision on choosing a data mining method.

3.5 Remarks and Future Research

The broad goal of the chapter is to enhance our understanding about the second-order data mining, particularly the creation of intelligent knowledge by human from data mining results. This study drew on the theory of habitual domains to develop a conceptual model that explains why human judgments on data mining performance are different. The study further conducted a field survey to empirically test the model. The study adopted a social network analysis method, Geary's C, for analyzing the data to get a global view of the correlation between participants' attributes and their responses. The study findings support two of the three hypotheses proposed in the model. First, the hypothesis of education's influence on human judgments is supported. Second, the empirical study identifies a significant correlation between human's previous experience with data mining and human's judgments on data mining performance.

This chapter took the first step in empirically testing the effect of human cognitive psychology characteristics on the creation of intelligent knowledge at second-order data mining. The findings of this paper provide evidence for the variations of human judgments on classifiers' performance when human possess varied cognitive psychology characteristics. These findings are valuable in understanding the important role of human in the stage of second-order data mining. Most of present studies of data mining either ignore the role of human or symbolize human as agents in the post-stage of data mining. While it could be argued from this study that human's complex cognitive psychology characteristics play a significant role in the creation of intelligent knowledge from data mining results. It should be noted that intelligent knowledge is created based on human judgments made on rough knowledge. Such human judgments are a function of various human prior knowledge, rough knowledge, and human's habitual domain characteristics.

This research presents interesting directions for future research. Since there is no one data mining method outperform all the other data mining methods in all kinds of tasks, choosing a most appropriate data mining method for a given task is one important step influencing the overall data mining project success. Experts of data mining possess implicit knowledge that guides them in selecting the best data mining method. The findings of this research lead us to wonder that implicit knowledge of data mining experts can have linkages with experts' past experience and educational background. Understanding what type of experience and educational background are mostly founded in data mining experts is crucial in training data mining analysts. Future research could focus on understanding this issue thoroughly.

It is unknown from this study that what interaction effects there are between the habitual domain characteristics and the data mining methods' performance evaluation. Future research can conduct a survey with a larger sample size to test if the interaction effects exist.

Another future research direction is to apply the habitual domains theory in understanding the overall data mining project success. Just as the case with all types of project, a data mining project that is accepted and actually used by the end users is a true successful project. As is said thousands of times in the data mining literature, customers of data mining want to discover innovative ideas from the hidden patterns of data mining. But, without domain knowledge or being lacking in the domain knowledge, it is challenging for data mining analysts to understand what ideas count for innovative ideas from the customers' perspective. Understanding the preferences of customers and being able to have a shared understanding with customers about what ideas are innovative ideas is of critical importance to the overall success of data mining project. The habitual domains theory not only conceptually describes how human obtain, store, process and apply information from the world in terms of concepts and propositions, but also prescribes ways of expanding humans' habitual domains and discussed the characteristics of information that would catch people's eyes. The theory of habitual domains possesses great potential in developing useful constructs to predict the acceptance and continuing usage of data mining.

Appendix A: Summary Of Data Sets, Classifiers and Measures (Table A)

Table A Data Sets, Classifiers, and Measures

Data sets	The Nursery Database
	The PBC Database
DMC	Decision Tree
	NbTree
	Baysnet
	Naivebays
	Logistic Regression
	SVM
	MCLP
	MCQP
Measures	Correctly Classified Instances
	Kappa Statistic
	Mean Absolute Error
	Negative—TP Rate
	Negative—FP Rate
	Positive—TP Rate
	Positive—FP Rate

DMC Data Mining Classifiers

Appendix B: Questionnaires for Measuring Dependent Variables (Table B-1 and B-2)

Table B-1 Questionnaire Used For the Nursery Database

Score of Algorithm									
Measure		J48	Nbtree	Baysnet	Naivebays	Logistic	SVM	MCLP	MCQP
Correctly Classified Instances		0.97	0.97	0.9	0.9	0.93	0.99	0.99	0.97
Kappa Statistic		0.96	0.96	0.86	0.86	0.89	0.98	0.98	0.94
Mean Absolute Error		0.02	0.02	0.08	0.08	0.04	0.01	0.01	0.03
Not_Recom	TP Rate	1	1	1	1	1	1	0.98	0.99
	FP Rate	0	0	0	0	0	0	0	0.04
	F-Measure	1	1	1	1	1	1	0.98	0.96
Recommend	TP Rate	0	0	0	0	0	0	1	0.96
	FP Rate	0	0	0	0	0	0	0.02	0.01
	F-Measure	0	0	0	0	0	0	0.99	0.98
Priority	TP Rate	0.95	0.96	0.9	0.9	0.89	0.98		
	FP Rate	0.02	0.02	0.1	0.1	0.06	0.01		
	F-Measure	0.96	0.96	0.86	0.86	0.89	0.98		
Very_Recom	TP Rate	0.73	0.7	0.06	0.06	0.74	0.9		
	FP Rate	0.01	0	0	0	0.01	0		
	F-Measure	0.76	0.79	0.11	0.11	0.77	0.94		
Spec_Prior	TP Rate	0.98	0.99	0.87	0.87	0.9	0.99		
	FP Rate	0.02	0.02	0.05	0.05	0.05	0.01		
	F-Measure	0.97	0.98	0.88	0.88	0.9	0.98		

Table B-2 Questionnaire Used For the PBC Database

Score of Algorithm									
Measure		J48	Nbtree	Baysnet	Naivebays	Logistic	SVM	MCLP	MCQP
Correctly Classified Instances		0.87	0.86	0.75	0.70	0.84	0.71	0.84	0.86
Kappa statistic		0.74	0.72	0.50	0.39	0.69	0.43	0.68	0.84
Mean absolute error		0.18	0.16	0.25	0.30	0.21	0.29	0.16	0.16
Negative	TN rate	0.94	0.89	0.83	0.93	0.85	0.53	0.88	0.86
	FN rate	0.20	0.17	0.33	0.54	0.16	0.10	0.20	0.18
	F-measure	0.88	0.86	0.77	0.75	0.84	0.65	0.85	0.85
Positive	TP rate	0.80	0.83	0.67	0.46	0.84	0.90	0.80	0.82
	FP rate	0.06	0.11	0.17	0.07	0.15	0.47	0.12	0.14
	F-measure	0.86	0.85	0.73	0.60	0.84	0.76	0.83	0.83

APPENDIX C: Geary'S C Statistics

We illustrate how to manually compute the Geary's c measure using the following example.

Suppose we have three subjects x, y, z. For each of them, we measured three attributes A, B, C. Table C-1 shows the three subjects' attributes' values. We also computed an adjacency matrix W in Table 3.2 that describes the closeness for each pair of the three subjects.

Table C-1 Attributes' Values of Three Subjects

Subjects	Attribute A	Attribute B	Attribute C
x	3	4	5
y	5	3	6
z	4	7	8

Step 1: Construct the adjacency matrix, that is, the W, using the minimum method from affiliation network method.

The minimum method examines two subjects' values on each of the attributes, selects the lowest scores and then sums. For example, for subjects x and y, it yields 3+3+5=11, it might means the extent to which subject x and y jointly agree on the three attributes A, B and C. Using this method, we filled out the adjacency matrix. (Table C-2)

Table C-2 Adjacency Matrix for Three Subjects

	x	y	z
x	12	11	12
y	11	14	13
z	12	13	19

Step 2: Calculate the Geary's c for each pair of subjects on each of the three attributes. First, let us calculate the Geary's c attribute A.

$$C = \frac{(N-1)\sum_i \sum_j \omega_{ij} \left(X_i - X_j\right)^2}{2W \sum_i \left(X_i - \bar{X}\right)^2}$$

$$N = 3, X_1 = 3, X_2 = 3, w_{12} = 11, w_{13} = 12, w_{23} = 13$$

$$C_A = \frac{(3-1)*2*[11(3-5)^2 + 12(3-4)^2 + 13(5-4)^2]}{2*107*[(3-4)^2 + (5-4)^2 + (4-4)^2]} = 0.65$$

Chapter 4
Domain Driven Intelligent Knowledge Discovery

Data mining algorithms, making use of powerful computation ability of computers, can make up the weakness of logical computation of human and extract novel, interesting, potentially useful and finally understandable knowledge (Fayyad et al. 1996). As a main way to acquire knowledge from data and information, data mining algorithms can generate knowledge that cannot be obtained from experts, thus become a new way to assist decision makings. As the critical technology of knowledge acquisition and the key element of business intelligence, data mining has been a hot research area over the last several decades and made a great progress (Han and Kamber 2001). Scholars in this area proposed many popular benchmark algorithms and extensions, and applied them in many applications ranging from banking, insurance industries to retail industry (Frawley et al. 1992).

However, the problem is that there exists a big gap between "hidden patterns" from data mining algorithms and their practical applications. Thus, data mining cannot directly provide effective support for decision makings. This motivates us to find new methods to find real intelligent knowledge that are different from "hidden patterns" (or "rough knowledge") to efficiently and intelligently support decision makings in certain domain applications. In this chapter, we propose our framework of domain driven intelligent knowledge discovery and demonstrate this with an entire discovery process which is incorporated with domain knowledge in every step.

This chapter is organized as following: Sect. 4.1 points out the importance of domain driven intelligent knowledge discovery and some relevant definitions are given. Section 4.2 is the framework of domain driven intelligent knowledge discovery (DDIKD). Some relevant literatures are reviewed, and our conceptual model of DDIKM is presented with every step described in details. Section 4.3 proposes the method of domain driven association rules mining based on unexpectedness. This method corporate domain knowledge with the whole intelligent knowledge discovery process (including preprocessing, data mining, and post analysis period) and we validated this method in supermarket data analysis. Section 4.4 concludes this chapter.

Y. Shi et al., *Intelligent Knowledge,* SpringerBriefs in Business,
DOI 10.1007/978-3-662-46193-8_4

4.1 Importance of Domain Driven Intelligent Knowledge Discovery (DDIKD) and Some Definitions

4.1.1 Existing Shortcomings of Traditional Data Mining

Some important problems generate a gap between the data mining results and the practical applications, thus cannot directly assist decision makings. We classify the problems into three categories: rule-overload, separation from context, ignorance of the existing experience and knowledge.

First, rule-overload denies the applied significance of data mining.

Traditional data mining is a trial and error procedure, extracts rules from historic data according to the fixed pattern, aims at creating new rules, but lack the deep analysis of the rules (Cao and Zhang 2007). Two kinds of rule-overload come from traditional data mining, one is Rule-Overload in Depth (ROID), for example, data mining generate so long as a relation-rule that people must judge 20 times if they use the rule. And the other is Rule-Overload in Quantity (IORQ), which means algorithms produce so many rules that people are too confused to choose the suitable ones, for example, a data mining project used decision tree algorithm to generate as many as 200 rules. The workers were very exciting, but soon they were confused by the problem that they could not decide which rule they should select. Both kinds of rule-overload make data mining results unable to be effectively used in the factual decision.

Second, separation from context makes data mining results do not agree with the fact.

Context is the related condition, background, and environment of knowledge and its activities (Brezillon and Pomerol 1999). The difference between knowledge and information lies in the fact that knowledge represents a special standpoint, aspect or intention and has the characters which depend on special context (Nonaka et al. 2000). Knowledge created in a particular context will not easily be understood if separated from its context. All the knowledge has its conditions, beyond which it will be not correct any longer.

An increasing number of experts are pay attention to the significance of context. Dieng et al. (1999) said context and uniqueness of knowledge management were very important. Despres and Chauval (2000) hold the idea that context is the perception of the things around you, and all knowledge will be nothing if separated from their contexts. Brezillon and Pomerol (1999) argued that context is a critical part that help people to understand knowledge completely.

Traditional knowledge discovery does not be integrated with real context, So the results often deviate heavily from the real world (Goldkuhl and Braf 2001).

Thirdly, ignorance of existing knowledge and expert experience enhances the difficulty of knowledge discovery and wastes the chance of debating the two formers' effects.

4.1.2 Domain Driven Intelligent Knowledge Discovery: Some Definitions and Characteristics

Based on analysis of weakness of traditional data mining above, we propose domain knowledge driven intelligent knowledge discovery (DKIKD) and gave out three declarations:

(1) Domain knowledge: those knowledge added to guide or constrain the activity of searching interesting knowledge domain knowledge or background knowledge (Zhang et al. 2009). In this chapter, domain knowledge specially denotes expert experience, context, interest, and user preference.
(2) DDIKD is a kind of deep knowledge discovery, which has three meanings: the first is knowledge from data mining is crude knowledge, we can mine this data to get more refined results, and we call this mining based on the crude knowledge derived from data mining "secondary data mining". The second is DDIKD, compared with traditional data mining, attaches more importance to applying domain knowledge in the mining process to make mining results more actionable. The third is DDIKD considers knowledge discovery as a complete circulation from data to knowledge, instead of just focusing on the fore part of knowledge discovery.
(3) In manner of constraints, codes, formulas or templates, DDIKD adds domain knowledge to every stage of knowledge discovery, especially to "secondary mining" stage, so as to transfer traditional trial-and-error data mining to more accurate data mining and display the results in a interesting manner.

To sum up, DDIKD, integrated with knowledge management and data mining theories, has the following characters:

(1) Knowledge based data mining: in the real world, both knowledge discovery and decision making depend on some specific constraints, such as context, domain, user preference, environment, etc. Constraints are the basic condition of efficient and effective data mining.
(2) A deep mining process: instead of stopping when the crude patterns come out, DDIKD continues to mine the crude derived knowledge, which is one of the most distinctive characters.
(3) A human-machine interactive process: in DDIKD process, domain experts play an very important role. Many jobs, such as understanding business and data, selecting attributes, picking algorithms, extracting domain knowledge and so on, need experts help, Meanwhile, using computers' powerful calculation ability, people can solve very complex computation that can not imagined before. Human-machine interactivity is the main work pattern of DDIKD
(4) A circular and spiral mining process: different from traditional data mining considering new patterns as the end of mining, DDIKD splits the complete discovery process into three steps, including data selection—pattern discovery—second order mining—knowledge practice—data selection. Every step can be carried out several times and every circulation will make data

mining better. By this spiral process, DDIKD accumulates knowledge derived from data mining and this knowledge can guide next data mining process to work better.

(5) A process of definite quantity and definite quality combination: domain knowledge, such as expert experience, context and so on, is qualitative knowledge, and algorithms solve quantitative computation, so DDIKD is a knowledge discovery process which combines qualitative analysis with quantitative analysis.

4.2 Domain Driven Intelligent Knowledge Discovery (DDIKD) Process

4.2.1 Literature Review

There are few researches that combine data mining and knowledge management: we just sporadically find some researches about this issue and list them as follows. In 1996, Anand et al. (1996) said that prior knowledge and existing knowledge can be added to the data mining process. Piatesky-Shapiro and Matheus (1992) advanced the idea that using domain knowledge to help with initial data mining focus and constrained search in the process of developing his knowledge discovery platform called KDW. In recent years, researchers generated some domain driven data mining methods to make up traditional data mining weakness, but few systematically researched this issue.

Graco et al. (2007) brought forth knowledge oriented data mining. They argued that data mining is not just the business of algorithms, it involved four kinds of issues: (1) using expert knowledge to generate smart data mining algorithms. (2) Obtaining smart data. (3) Combining business knowledge and technique knowledge.

Cao and Zhang (2007) pointed out that data mining might generate a large number of rules, but traditional knowledge evaluation was unable to tell actionable knowledge from the sea of derived rules, consequently it is necessary to add domain knowledge to judge really significant actionable knowledge. In order to judge actionable knowledge, knowledge evaluation should involve two dimensions which include four aspects, which means that people should pay attention to subjective factors (domain knowledge), objective factors, technical factors and business factors. Knowledge which meets all the above constraints is real actionable knowledge. According to this idea they put forward a new kind data mining method called DDID-PD (Domain-Driven In-depth Pattern Discovery). When they used DDID-PD to analyze the transaction association in Australia stock market, they got some actionable rules that could really support decision making.

Kuo et al. (2007) used domain driven data mining to search the cause of chronic kidney disease from the victim data. They utilized a medical ontology to preserve domain knowledge, and then, helped by domain knowledge they categorized

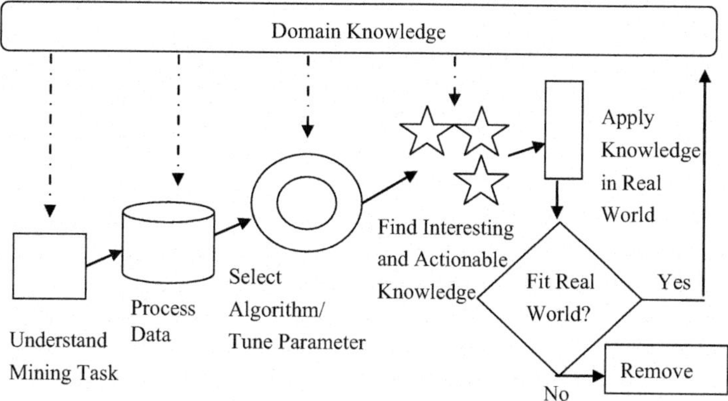

Fig. 4.1 Conceptual Model of DDIKD

variables and eliminated reduplicate data. They also categorized variables into several groups according to semantic relations and mined at different semantic levels and got better results than that of traditional data mining.

There are some researches combining data mining with expert system and decision support system. Fayyad et al. (1996) gave the conception of knowledge discovery engineer which obtains knowledge from data mining; Nemati et al. (2002)composed knowledge warehouse which fuse several technologies, such as knowledge management, decision support, AI and data mining, into the comprehensive one.

To sum up, although there are already some domain driven data mining researches starting pay attention to the significance of domain knowledge, these researches mostly use domain knowledge in the data preprocessing and data mining, two issues are overlooked, including the secondary mining on crude derived knowledge and accumulating and using derived knowledge to guide the future mining. Most researches just focus on a part of knowledge discovery. Considering this fact, this chapter will systematically introduce Domain Driven Intelligent Knowledge Discovery (DDIKD) (Fig. 4.1).

4.2.2 Domain Driven Intelligent Knowledge Discovery Conceptual Model

In this conceptual model, we can finish DKDIKD through 5 steps (Huang et al. 2009).

Step 1 understanding data mining task

Before data mining, experts and user must think the answers of the following questions: who use, why use, what to use, where to use and how to use (W4H) (Zhu et al. 2008). They also have to understand the constraints they face and existing domain knowledge.

Step 2 preprocessing data

According to expert experience, domain knowledge, and real world constraints, this step figures out data characters, removes non-interesting data, create new derived attributes, etc. If data is not enough to generate useful regularities, domain experts can create "artificial data" and this "artificial data" can be added to training data (Zhu et al. 2008). An efficient mechanism for constructing "artificial data" is one of the new approaches for data preprocess, which strongly depend on domain expert knowledge and experience (Silberschatz and Tuzhilin 1996).

Step 3 selecting algorithm and tuning parameter

On the basis of understanding task and data characters, some method must be employed to select proper algorithm and tune parameter values, which may impose much influence on the final results. Considering the complexity of this work, it may involve human-machine cooperation and multi-agent system which can automatically choose algorithm automatically, and what expert need to do is to decide repeatedly whether to accept the parameter value according to feedback or not till he is satisfied.

Step 4 finding interesting and actionable knowledge

Algorithm may generate so much knowledge that users are just not able to judge which are really useful and profitable. In order to fulfill the final aim of data mining which is to discover interesting and actionable knowledge to support decision, it is necessary to evaluate result produced by data mining. What should be emphasized is evaluation should not be limited to subjective and technical methods, and objective and business ones should also be included.

Step 5 applying and enriching domain knowledge

All the final knowledge got from data mining must be applied to and validated in the real world. Those which survive the real-world tests are added to existing domain knowledge and can be used in next mining process. When algorithm does not generate satisfying results, this five-step procedure can be looped till ideal results come out.

The key point of the concept is to make use of the domain knowledge in every level of knowledge discovering.

4.2.3 Whole Process of Domain Driven Intelligent Knowledge Discovery

We will demonstrate the whole process of domain driven intelligent knowledge discovery by a case. Figure 4.2 represents technologies and their functions in every step in this case.

(1) Data Mining Recommending Service

This step is for customers who are not familiar with data mining system to recommend a data mining technology based on specific problems of the customers. To achieve this, knowing the customer data type and their expected results are needed. Meanwhile all the related functions of all the data algorithms then match the users'

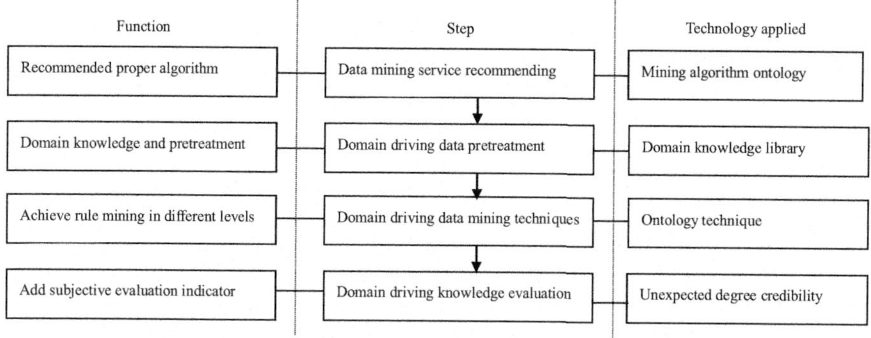

Fig. 4.2 Technologies applied in every step

information to algorithm's information and select a most matched algorithm as a recommend one. We build up ontology of data mining algorithm to describe the functions of all the algorithms.

The important information about a data mining algorithms contains; 1) name of the algorithm (N), for example: tree C5.0;2)function of algorithm (F), for example: classification, cluster, prediction, association rules etc.; 3) condition of algorithm (C), for example, some algorithm's need continuous data; 4) structure of algorithm (S), includes time complexity of algorithm, output formats, intelligibility, etc. So we could use a 4 tuple to make algorithm ontology: MO:=(N, F, C, S).

Our customers' need could also be described as a four tuple DM Requirement:=(ID, aim, data, resultrequirement). ID is the number of customers' need. Aim is the goal customers want to achieve, for example, classification or cluster or prediction. Data type is the description for the data that users process. For example, discrete or continuous time series data or cross-sectional data etc. Result requirement is the specific description of algorithm results, includes result output format requirements, users' tolerance of algorithm's runtime, mining results and intelligibility.

Elements that users needed correspond to the elements in algorithm ontology, as Figure 4.3 shows.

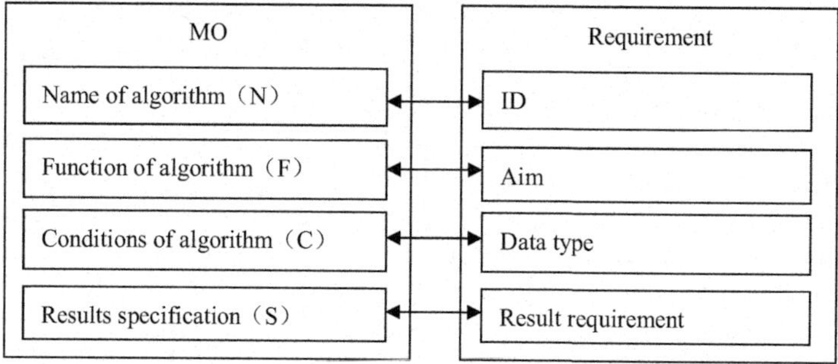

Fig. 4.3 Correspondence of technique ontology and service elements

When we get a user's need, and represent it in the form of four tuple, according to the corresponding relation in Fig. 4.3, figure out the similarity between the ontology and users' need; finally find the most matched algorithm as a recommended one.

We could take Surdeanu M and Turmo T's method to calculate the similarity based on semantics (Surdeanu and Turmo 2005)

$$\mathrm{Sim}(\mathrm{S}_1,\mathrm{S}_2)=\frac{\alpha(1_1+1_2)}{(\mathrm{dis}(\mathrm{S}_1,\mathrm{S}_2)+\alpha)\max(|1_1-1_2|,1)}$$

In the chart above, Sim< (s1, s2) shows the similarity between s1 and s2. Dis (s, s2) shows their distance; l1 and l2 stand for the level of ontology semantic tree where s1 and s2 locate. α is a distance between s1 and s2 when similarity is 0.5, an adjustable parameter. Similarity between users' required DMR and technical entities should be integrated semantic similarity of all terms.

$$Sim(DMR,MO)=\frac{\sum_{i=1}^{n} Sim(DMR_i,MO_i)}{n},DMR_i\in DMR,MO_i\in MO$$

Take above as a basement, data mining algorithm based on ontology specific steps are:

1) Firstly identify user's need, and break it into a simple atomic requirement ordered set which can be achieved by algorithm. $\{FR_i\},(i=1,\ldots,n)$. Every atomic requirement specification language expressed as user purpose, data type, results requirement. Denoted as $FR_i := (i,\ aim,\ datatype,\ \mathrm{resultrequirement})$
2) According to the customer's demand, identify relevant domain A_i, find A_i's data mining ontology technology from ontology set $\left\{MO_K^{A_i}\right\},(K=1,\ldots,m)$.
3) Calculate algorithm ontology similarity between FR_i and $\left\{MO_K^{A_i}\right\}$, if $MO_l^{A_i}$ exists ,then $Sim(FR_i,MO_l^{A_i})=\max\limits_{K\in 1,\ldots,m}(sim(FR_i,MO_K^{A_i})),l\in 1,\ldots,m$, so $MO_l^{A_i}$ stands for algorithm Fuc_i is the recommend algorithm for FR_i.
4) All the need will be implemented to step 2 and step 3. At last, a corresponding ordered set of algorithm $\{Fuc_i\},(i=1,\ldots,n)$, which is the whole set algorithm recommended to the customers.

(2) Domain Knowledge Driven Data Preprocessing

Data preprocessing is an important step of knowledge discovery and a necessity of data mining preparation. Domain driven data preprocessing is to use domain knowledge for the introduction of data preprocessing. Domain knowledge in data preprocessing level should pay attention to the relationship between data attributes, records and its range limit of each attribute instead of reasoning.

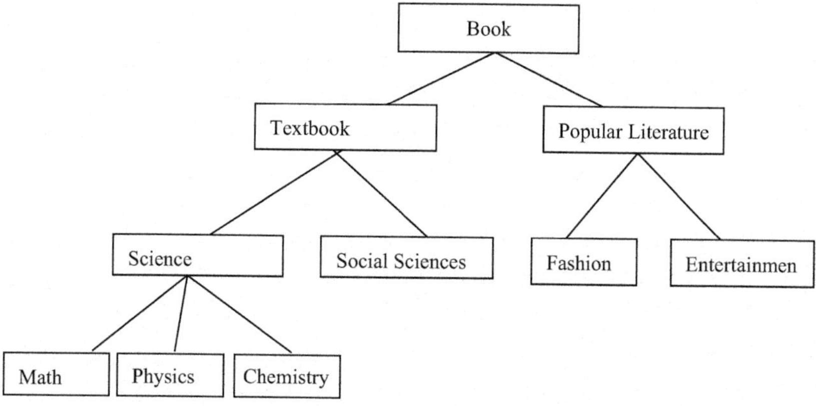

Fig. 4.4 Conceptual hierarchy tree

We believe that in the process of data mining data constantly change. Therefore, the previous mathematic statistical knowledge is not suitable for the later dataset. Only range knowledge, hierarchy knowledge, and rule knowledge are really useful domain knowledge in data mining. Range knowledge stands for a certain property's range, which mainly comes from expertise. It reduces data only selecting data in the range, in this way the amount of data is significantly reduced.

Range knowledge is expressed as: AtrName=<min,max>

Hierarchy knowledge stands for the relationship between different data granularity of a certain attribute, similar with Fig. 4.4 conceptual hierarchy tree denotation. Hierarchy knowledge is usually given by domain experts. Data mining often need to work on different levels. For example, customers should not only know the relationship between Beijing PC sales in 2007 and promotion but also be interested in the connection between Beijing electronics sale and promotion. At this time, hierarchy knowledge is used for all electronic low granular data to generalize into high granularity data, and then start the mining. Figure 4.4 shows that when the conceptual hierarchy tree is enhancing, the rules are:

Math, physics chemistry → science, if it does not meet the requirement, then enhance again:

Science social science → textbook

Until it does meet the requirement

All the rule knowledge can be represented in the form "if…then…" Rule knowledge in data preprocessing can be divided into three categories.

First category is attributes association rule knowledge used to handle with outliers or missing value. It can infer reasonable values of other attributes from some attributes' values. It can reduce the amount of data, but differs in function from range knowledge. Range knowledge can only check values of one attribute at one time and can only judge the attribute itself. While rule knowledge can read data of more than one attributes and predict other attributes' value. It can compare the predicted value with the real one, and judge whether it is an outlier. Attributes association rule knowledge can be expressed as:

$$\begin{aligned} &if(AtrName_1 \text{ opt Value}_1)\Lambda\cdots\Lambda(AtrName_m \text{ opt Value}_m) \\ &then\ (AtrName_k \text{ opt Value}_k)\Lambda\cdots\Lambda(AtrName_l \text{ opt Value}_l) \end{aligned}$$

$AtrName$ stands for attribute name, opt stands for a logic, $\text{opt} \in \{<,=,>,\leq,\geq\}$, and Value means the value of attribute. Knowing the values of $\{AtrName_i, i = 1,\cdots,m\}$, we can predict values of $\{AtrName_j, j = k,\cdots,l\}$.

The second category is classification rule knowledge applied to data discretization. For example, if score of a subject is above 85, we consider it "excellent". This kind of rule knowledge can be expressed as:

$$if\ AtrName \text{ opt Value} then\, AtrName \in \text{Class}$$

$AtrName$ stands for attribute name, opt stands for a logic, $\text{opt} \in \{<,=,>,\leq,\geq\}$, and Value means the value of attribute Class represents a certain class.

The third category is attribute selection rule. Attribute selection rule is used to remove those attributes irrelevant to data mining ontology and reserve those who are relevant. The form is a set of attributes applied to data mining.

$$DMAtr := \{Atr_i, i = 1,\cdots,n\}$$

The fourth category is heuristic rule. It is mainly used to describe expert experience. For example, a customer applied for many credit cards in a short period of time and each card has a large overdraft. For this kind of information, range knowledge may delete the data directly, but 这 heuristic rule can judge this information may mean the person is admitting credit card fraud. Heuristic rule can be expressed as:

$$\begin{aligned} &if(AtrName_1 \text{ opt Value}_1)\Lambda\cdots\Lambda(AtrName_m \text{ opt Value}_m) \\ &then\text{conclusion} \end{aligned}$$

The domain knowledge must be built before data mining by experts or users according to practical problems and data set. If two differ in data set or algorithm, they differ in domain knowledge. So we should use the combination of data set and algorithm as a unique identifier and we name the domain knowledge storing files in the form of "data set + algorithm name". Since XML files have good scalability, we can use them to store domain knowledge. We modify XML file as form of domain knowledge XML storing files.

```
<?xml version--"1.0" standalone--"yes" encoding"UTF-8"?>
<!ELEMENT DomainKnowlege (Datasets, DMMethod, Expression, Category)>
<!ELEMENT Datasets (#PCDATA)>
<!ELEMENT DMMethod (#PCDATA)>
<! ELEMENT Expression (#PCDATA)>
<!ELEMENT Category (Rang*,Type* Hierarchy*,Rule*)>
<!ELEMENT Rang (Name, min, max)>
<!ELEMENT name (#PCDATA)>
<!ELEMENT min (#PCDATA)>
<!ELEMENT max (#PCDATA)>
<!ELEMENT Hierarchy (Name, Tree)>
<!ELEMENT Tree (Name, Tree*)>
<!ELEMENT Rule (If, Then)>
<!ELEMENT If (#PCDATA)>
<!ELEMENT Then (#PCDATA)>
<!ATTLIST Tree TreeType (Normal|Leaf)#REQUIRED>
<!ATTLIST Rule RuleType (Rulel|Rule2|Rule3|Rule4) #REQUIRED>
```

XML file has a very clear hierarchy, so computer can extract information from it easily. Steps of extraction are as follows:

step1: search for the XML files which store domain knowledge according to data set and data mining algorithm.

step 2:read the <Datasets> and <DMMethod> marks of the files, and judge whether they are consistent with data set and data mining algorithm. If not, return to step1.

step 3:get the<Category>mark, and set i=0

step 4:get (i+1)th element in<Category>, and denote it as k. if mark K=</Category>,then end. If mark K is not equal </Category>, there are some possibilities as follows:

If k=<Rang>, then domain knowledge is range knowledge. Get marks <min> and <max> as upper and lower limits of <<Name>>.

If k=<Hierarchy>, then domain knowledge is hierarchy knowledge. Get mark<tree>to build a hierarchy tree. When TreeType=Normal, node is an ordinary node while TreeType=leaf, node is a leaf node.

If k=<Rule>, then domain knowledge is hierarchy knowledge. Get mark<If>as the condition part of rule knowledge and mark<Then>as the conclusion part. And among them, RuleType demonstrates the class rule knowledge belongs to.

Repeat Step4 until the end.

We can express the method of domain driven data cleaning as two steps on the basis of discussion above. The first step is to find out the suitable domain knowledge files according to data set and algorithm, and the second step is to extract domain knowledge from the files and apply it to data set operations. More detailed algorithm can be expressed as:

Step1. Input name of data set and data mining algorithm you are going to deal with, and then computer will search for domain knowledge storing file named "data set name+algorithm name" in domain knowledge file base.

Step2. If computer cannot find such file, we will start data preprocessing out of domain knowledge, else go to step3.

Step 3. Get domain knowledge storing file in the way mentioned above. The methods of handling can be classified into three categories according to the way we get the file.

1. Range knowledge: Delete the records in data set whose attributes are not in the range and replace the missing value with median of the range.
2. Hierarchy knowledge: Upgrade the conceptual hierarchy of attributes in data set according to the structure of conceptual hierarchy tree.
3. Rule knowledge:Judge whether the records satisfy the condition of "if"sentence. If so, do data operation as conclusion instructs.

Step4. Return to step1

After those steps, we finally accomplish domain knowledge driven data preprocessing of certain data set and algorithm. Certainly, there is a disadvantage that we must build specific domain knowledge according to certain data set and algorithm. That means domain knowledge can only apply to increasing data set and constant data mining task, but cannot achieve the goal of knowledge reuse across data sets and algorithms.

(3) Domain Knowledge Driven Data Mining Techniques

Here we will introduce a ontology-based mining method. This method overcomes the shortcoming that traditional data mining algorithm can only produce rules on data content. In this way we can do data mining on high levels and find out top-level or multi-level rules.

Compared with low-level data mining, high-level data mining has some advantages as follows:

First of all, high-level rule can offer a clearer general description of data. Data mining system produce summary of database from low-level information while high-level rule can be considered as a summary of low-level rules. When the system produces many low-level rules of similar forms and contents, high-level rule extraction is particularly useful.

Secondly, the number of high-level rule is far smaller than low-level. Suppose similar search method is used, generally, low-level concepts is converted to high-level concepts, thus we can get fewer rules. In a corresponding way, low-level rule of similar form and content can be replaced with a single high-level rule.

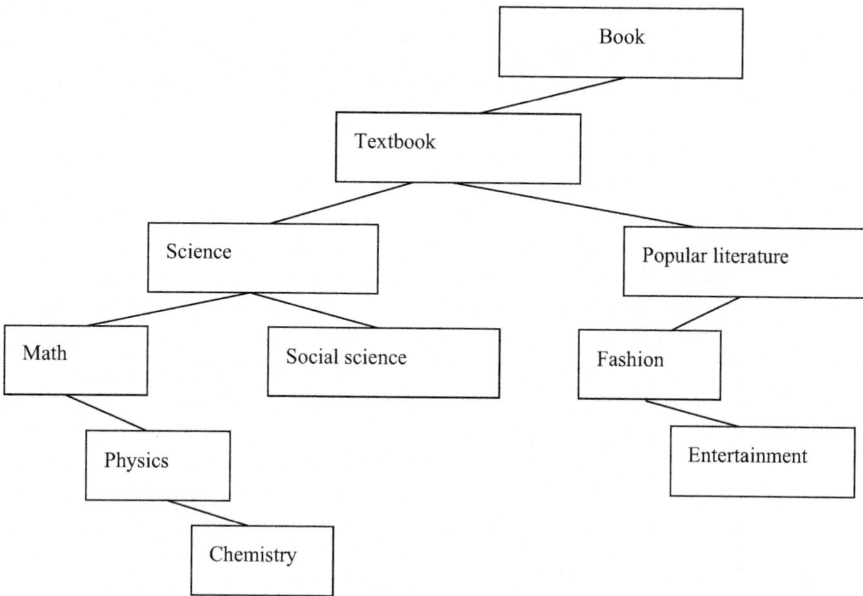

Fig. 4.5 Conceptual hierarchy tree expressed by binary tree

At last, these discoveries can generalize some attributes in different levels. Data mining of multi-level generalization would lead to more significant result and show more ordinary concepts.

We design an algorithm on the basis of conceptual hierarchy tree as follows:

Function of the algorithm: deal with the data in data set automatically according to assigned conceptual hierarchy and merge the data in a certain conceptual level

The first problem to solve is to store the conceptual hierarchy tree. We adopt the method of "child and brother" to store the tree. We can convert the tree to binary tree in this way. We define the node in binary tree as: $Node(value, leftchild, nextsibling)$.

Figure 4.4 can be expressed by binary tree, shown as Fig. 4.5.

Each node of binary tree should include following information: concept name, concept level, leftchild, rightchild. So we can adopt the following algorithm to upgrade the concepts.

```
typedef   struct{                          /*define type of the node in binary tree*/
      String   conceptName;                /*variable name in the data set*/
      Int         conceptlevel;            /*concept level in conceptual hierarchy tree
   (Fig 5-8) */
      *BitreeNode   leftchild;             /*leftchild of the node*/
      * BitreeNode   rightchild;           /*rightchild of the node*/
      Boolean calculable;                  /*whether to calculate at the second time of
   mining*/
} BitreeNode;
Void Rollup(int   Aimlevel, * BitreeNode Root ){
     *BitreeNode p;
     P=Root;
     If p.leftchild<>Null
        p= p.leftchild;
     else if p. conceptlevel =Aimlevel
     {
         Create a new variable (δ) named "p. conceptName"+"new" in the data set,
         and set it equal with variable "p. conceptName";
         if p.rightchild<>Null
             p. calculable=false;
         else
             p. calculable=true;
      }
      else if p. conceptlevel >Aimlevel
         {
             δ=δ+value(p. conceptName);/* value(x) represents the value of x*/
         }
  Void main ()
 { /*suppose k is the conceptual level to be upgraded,  and TreeRoot is the root of
binary tree*/
     Rollup(k, TreeRoot);
     Find out all the nodes that both conceptlevel =k and calculable=true in the data set.
     We use variables these nodes represent and new ones to do data mining; and then
     reset all the nodes' variable "calculable" status
}
```

The main idea of the algorithm is that users can operate on the data set in different hierarchy levels according to their needs. They can upgrade hierarchy levels and construct a new data set on the basis of rules of conceptual hierarchy tree. Later they can adopt various data mining algorithms to operate on the new data set.

(4) Domain Knowledge Driven Evaluation

Data mining is to find out effective, new and potentially useful and finally understandable patterns in large amounts of data. "Effective" means that the pattern we discover can be used to predict; "new" means the pattern is new knowledge rather than common sense; "potentially useful" means the pattern can be used in real applications; "finally understandable" require that the pattern be easily understood. The integrated measurement of patterns' four aspects is called interestingness. Only those patterns which satisfy certain interestingness are useful to users. Since the patterns we get from data mining are really a mass, it is impossible for users to judge whether knowledge we get is useful. Hence it has become an important study focus to evaluate the interestingness of patterns in order to screen knowledge users are interested in [51].

Many documents take study on the interestingness of knowledge. Interestingness divides into objective interestingness and subjective interestingness. Objective interestingness only relates to frame of the pattern and the dependent data of finding the pattern. For example, the interestingness of Rule A→B can be defined as function of p (A)、 p (B) and (A ∧B), in which p (a) indicates a is a true probability. But objective interestingness cannot meet the complexity requirements in the process of finding the pattern. That is because it only concerns about the data itself and ignores the information of the effectiveness of the user's preferences (Piatetsky 1991). For instance, pattern "IF M is a female, THEN M cannot be suffering from prostate disease" possesses a high statistical characteristics, that is, a high interestingness, but obviously users have no interest in the pattern. So subjective interestingness is also the factor considered in defining the interestingness of patterns.

Subjective interestingness includes both accidental possibility and availability (Silberschatz and Tuzhilin 1995, 1996). According to the accidental possibility and availability which patterns possess, we can divide the patterns into 4 categories: (1) Accidental available type; this kind of patterns are both unexpected and practical to users, which therefore users are most interested in. (2) Available unaccidental type; the interestingness of these patterns is general. However, they possess a good availability and can be accepted. (3) Accidental unavailable type; although users are surprised, the rules are unavailable. They are bad patterns. (4) Unaccidental-Unavailable type; obviously, users have no interest in this kind of patterns (Fig. 4.6).

We can know from the previous figure, the subjective measure of the rules should consider both availability and accidental possibility at the same time. This chapter only discusses the measure of accidental possibility. Further reflection is needed about the measure of availability.

Existing researches on the accident rules include: Liu and Hsu (1996) used fuzzy matching techniques to find 2 forms of accident rules, pre-accident and after-accident. It sorts the rules of unexpected form specified only on the basis of the matching score of discovery rule to area rule, failing to measure rule's accidental possibility and to consider uncertainty of the domain knowledge. Liu et al. (1999) used deviation analysis to find accident rules. However, users' domain knowledge

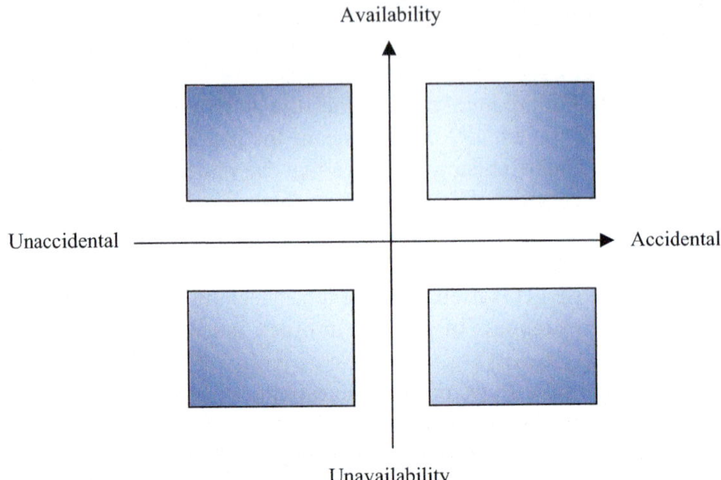

Fig. 4.6 Classification of knowledge subjective interestingness

isn't taken into consideration in the discovery process. And it can not value the rule's accidental possibility. Hussain et al. (2000) used common-sense rule A→X and reference rules to find accident rules, whose frame is $A, B \to \neg X$ and uses relative entropy to value candidate accident rules. In the process of valuing accident rules, it considers rules' credibility and support's degree, but leaves out users' domain knowledge. Padmanabhan and Tuzhilin (1999) discover a sort of rules whose frame is $A, X_1 \to \neg Y$ (X1 is the generalized form of X) for domain knowledge X→Y. But it doesn't propose to measure the rules' accidental possibility. The requirement of domain knowledge is to determine rules' forms and means of discovering accident rules are designed for association rule mining algorithm.

Rule could always be expressed into: $r: X_1 \Lambda X_2 \Lambda \cdots \Lambda X_m \to Y$, CF. Suppose our former rule is: $r_1: U_1 \Lambda U_2 \Lambda \cdots \Lambda U_m \to U^*, \mathrm{CF}_1$, the new one is: $r_2 = V_1 \Lambda V_2 \Lambda \cdots \Lambda V_3 \to V^*, \mathrm{CF}_2$,

We could see that differences come from the following three situations:

1) Preconditions are similar, while the results differ.
2) Preconditions are different, while the results are similar.
3) Preconditions and results are both similar, while confidence levels are different.

We use $SC(U_1, V_1)$ to express the similarity of X in the preconditions in r1 and r2, $SR(U^*, V^*) SC(U_1, V_1)$ to express the similarity of X in the results in r1 and r2.According to its nature- successive or discrete, $SC(U_1, V_1)$ and $SR(U^*, V^*)$ could be computed in two ways.

The first one, precondition is decided, the client set an acceptable warp: $\varepsilon(\varepsilon > 0)$,

If $V_1 \in [U_1 - \varepsilon, U_1 + \varepsilon]$, $SC(U_1, V_1) = 1$;

If $V_1 \notin [U_1 - \varepsilon, U_1 + \varepsilon]$, $SC(U_1, V_1) = 0$

The second one, precondition is among a successive range. Suppose x to be a value with X-nature., and $N_{X_1}(x)$ as all the results that could make it happen. Then, $SC(U_1,V_1)=\frac{N_X(U_1 \cap V_1)}{N_X(U_1)}$.

Suppose $U_1: 10 '' x'' 50$, $V_1: 20 '' x'' 60$, there 80 records satisfy $20 '' x'' 50$ in the data-base, while 100 records satisfy $10 '' x'' 50$, then, $SC(U_1,V_1)=80/100=0.8$

In the same way, we could get the way to compute $SR(U^*,V^*)$:

First, the result is given. The client set an acceptable warp $\varepsilon(\varepsilon>0)$,

If $V^* \in [U^*-\varepsilon, U^*+\varepsilon]$, $SR(U^*,V^*)=1$;

If $V^* \notin [U^*-\varepsilon, U^*+\varepsilon]$, $SR(U^*,V^*)=0$;

Second, result is among a successive range. Suppose y to be a value with Y-nature, and $N_{X_1}(x)$ as all the results that could make it happen. Then, $SR(U^*,V^*)=\frac{N_Y(U^* \cap V^*)}{N_Y(U^*)}$.

Suppose $U^*: 5 '' x'' 30$, $V^*: 20 '' x'' 40$, there 90 records satisfy $20 '' x'' 30$ in the data-base, while 100 records satisfy $5 '' x'' 30$, then $SR(U^*,V^*)=90/100=0.9$

By the above way we find: $SC(U_1,V_1)\in[0,1]$, $SR(U^*,V^*)\in[0,1]$. According to Cask Principle, the semblance is determined by the lower one. So, $TSC(r_1,r_2)=\min SC(U_i,V_i), i=1,\cdots,m$

With the above preparation, we could get the function of two regular accidental degrees. What is more, the differences lie in two aspects: 1 the length of the pre-condition, 2 value of the precondition. We use $TSC(r_1,r_2)$ to measure value, while we use $|N_1-N_2|/(N_1+N_2)$ to express the differences in length.N_1 and N_2 are the length of r_1 and r_2, so there three ways of computing:

1) High similarity in precondition. Two reasons cause the differences, one is the results are different, the other is degree of confidence of precondition is different. At this time the function is:

$$Out\min d(r_1,r_2)=TSC(r_1,r_2)\cdot\left(1-\frac{|N_1-N_2|}{N_1+N_2}\right)\cdot(1-SR(r_1,r_2))\cdot|CF_1-CF_2|$$

2) High similarity in result. Two reasons cause the differences, one is the preconditions are different, the other is degree of confidence of result is different. At this time the function is:

$$Out\min d(r_1,r_2)=(1-TSC(r_1,r_2))\cdot\frac{|N_1-N_2|}{N_1+N_2}\cdot SR(r_1,r_2)\cdot|CF_1-CF_2|$$

3) High similarity in precondition and result, except for degree of confidence. At this tine, difference in degree of similarity is the only reason. So that the function is:

$$Out\min d(r_1,r_2)=TSC(r_1,r_2)\cdot\frac{|N_1-N_2|}{N_1+N_2}\cdot SR(r_1,r_2)\cdot|CF_1-CF_2|$$

The above expressions are maybe not the best ones to compute accidental degree, but they collect all kinds of possibilities, and could find the unexpected rules. However, it leaves us to search the accidental point in which we could accept.

4.3 Research on Unexpected Association Rule Mining of Designed Conceptual Hierarchy Based on Domain Knowledge Driven

With the development of economic globalization, the opening of the national markets continuous improvement, sales industry will face more serious competition. Due to consumers' preferences differ in thousands ways and seriously more and more focus on personality, the original sales mode is no way out. So we must differentiate markets according to consumers' preferences, and how to grasp the consumers' preferences will be a significant practical problem.

Association rules mining in data mining offers a solution to solve the above problem. Actually, association rules among commodities shows part of the customers' preference which are important commercial preference value. But the real situation is there is great distance between data mining of association rules and real application, for example: the number of rules too much to how to select, or the rule is not new (rules are also known). Therefore, we need to design new association rules algorithm to dig the actual action rules which really close to the needs of the user.

This part will use the knowledge discovery theory of domain driving knowledge mentioned above to design an unexpected association rule algorithm of designed conceptual hierarchy based on domain knowledge driven.

4.3.1 Related Technical Problems and Solutions

The core of the unexpected association rule algorithm of designed conceptual hierarchy based on domain knowledge driven is adding domain knowledge to the different stages of mining process. Figure 4.7 shows concept map of the unexpected association rule algorithm of designed conceptual hierarchy based on domain knowledge driven. From the figure, we can realize that three key problems should be solved for the proposed algorithm: first, domain knowledge should be expressed understandable to compute; second, according to users' designed conceptual hierarchy to generate data in real time; third, design more efficient index to evaluate novelty of rules, which will exceed traditional data mining method that is only considering objective interestingness.

The solution of the first problem: this paper through classifying domain knowledge to design XML language to solve the problem of the knowledge representation, which has been stated detailed in the previous section. During the data mining process, computer only needs to read the XML file, and can be processed according to the contents of the file. Because of the different data set and algorithm is suitable for different areas of knowledge, when using a particular data mining method in a particular data set, we need to search matched domain knowledge documents in the knowledge base. So, it is necessary to set special naming rule for files of the domain knowledge, and in this article we will "data set name _ algorithm name" as domain knowledge filename. For example, there is a data set which is carried on

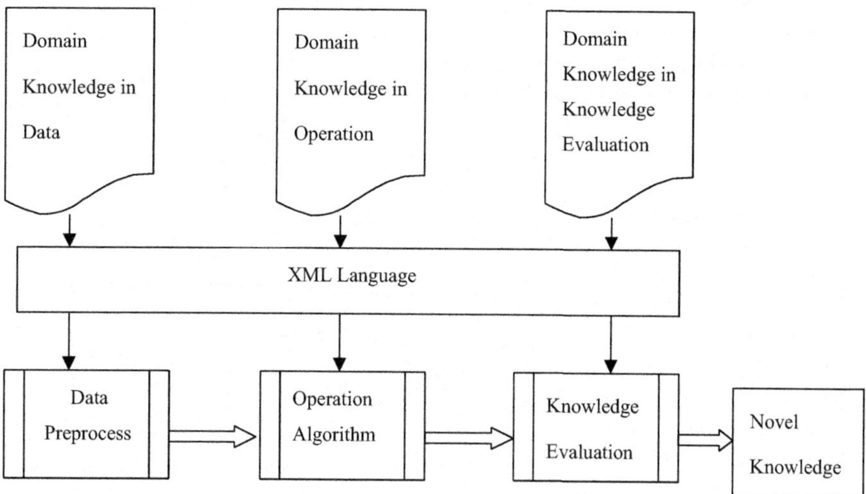

Fig. 4.7 Concept Map of the Unexpected Association Rule Mining

the algorithm of mining is called associationrule, and we should establish a named "dataset_associationrule.xml" files to store its domain knowledge.

The solution of the second problem: users appoint conceptual hierarchy L, if L = 1, then mining original data in dataset directly; if L > 1, finding marked <L_level> in XML files, then reading the level of Nodei node and the corresponding node of the leaf node. After then, integrate the value of the leaf nodes as a node Nodei value, and form a new data set by deleting the value of the leaf nodes from the data, in the end, make association rules mining in new data set. Depending on the type of leaf node values, if the value of leaf nodes are continuous, then integrated approach is addition operations, if the value of leaf nodes are Boolean values, then integrated approach is the logical operations.

Next, solving the third problem: we transform expertise experience and known rules as domain rules, and design a subjective unexpectedness indicator when a new rule relative to these domain rules. The indicator overcomes defect of traditional mining method that always only focus on objective indicators. The proposed indicator can reflect in a certain degree of the users' unexpectedness to rules. Furthermore, the next test is able to show that the proposed indicator can effectively filter the redundancy rules. The following part is introduction of how to calculate the indicator.

4.3.2 The Algorithm of Improving the Novelty of Unexpectedness to Rules

Rules can always be expressed the form $r\ : X_1 \Lambda X_2 \Lambda \cdots \Lambda X_m \rightarrow Y,\ \mathrm{CF}$, that is to say a rule always consists of 3 parts: condition, conclusion and confidence. Thus rule unexpectedness consists of condition unexpectedness OC, conclusion unexpectedness

OR and confidence unexpectedness OF. So the rules of unexpectedness depend on the maximum degree of condition unexpectedness OC, conclusion unexpectedness OR and confidence unexpectedness OF. Suppose original domain rule is $r_1: U_1 \Lambda U_2 \Lambda \cdots \Lambda U_m \to U^*, \mathrm{CF}_1$, and new rule is $r_2 = V_1 \Lambda V_2 \Lambda \cdots \Lambda V_n \to V^*, \mathrm{CF}_2$, then unexpectedness of r_2 to r_1 is: o. $OM(r_1, r_2) = \max[OC(r_1, r_2), OR(r_1, r_2), OF(r_1, r_2)]$.

The following part introduces how to compute conclusion unexpectedness OR, condition unexpectedness OC and confidence unexpectedness OF and then presents the method to compute rule unexpectedness.

(1) Method to Compute Conclusion Unexpectedness OR

Conclusion of association rule only contains one attribute. We use $AR(r)$ to represent the number of attributes that are included in rule r's conclusion. If $AR(r_1) \uparrow AR(r_2)$, then we can conclude that new rules are unexpected to domain rules and we set unexpectedness $OM(r_1, r_2) = 1$. If $AR(r_1) = AR(r_2)$, we have two methods to compute the value. The value of this attribute can be certain or interval type.

We can get a certain value from the first method. $V(AR(r))$ is value of attributes contained in rule r' conclusion. We set an acceptable deviation $\varepsilon(\varepsilon > 0)$ and then represent conclusion unexpectedness as the following equation:

$$OR(r_1, r_2) = \begin{cases} \dfrac{|V(AR(r_2)) - V(AR(r_1))|}{\varepsilon}, V(AR(r_2)) \in [V(AR(r_1)) - \varepsilon, V(AR(r_1)) + \varepsilon] \\ 1, V(AR(r_2)) \notin [V(AR(r_1)) - \varepsilon, V(AR(r_1)) + \varepsilon] \end{cases} \tag{4.1}$$

We assume $U^*: x = 5$, $V^*: x = 6$, $\varepsilon = 0.5$, since $6 \notin [4.5, 5.5]$, $OR(r_1, r_2) = 1$. If $\varepsilon = 2$, since $6 \in [3, 7]$, $COC(r_1, r_2) = \max[OC_i(r_1, r_2)]$

From the second method, we can get an interval. $Range(x)$ is written as length of x, then conclusion unexpectedness is represented as following:

$$OR(r_1, r_2) = 1 - \frac{Range(AR(r_1)) \cap Range(AR(r_2))}{Range(AR(r_1)) \cup Range(AR(r_2))} \tag{4.2}$$

For example, we assume $U^*: 10'' \ x'' \ 50$, $V^*: 20'' \ x'' \ 60$, then $OR(r_1, r_2) = 1 - \dfrac{50 - 20}{60 - 10} = 0.4$.

(2) Method to Compute Condition Unexpectedness OC

Condition usually includes more than attributes. $AC(r)$ represents the number of attributes that are included in rule r's condition and $AC_i(r)$ is the ith attribute. There are three kinds of relations between conditions of two rules, shown as follows:

First, attributes of conditions are exactly the same, it can be expressed as $AC(r_1) = AC(r_2)$. Condition has more than one attributes, so we compute unexpectedness of each attribute ($OC_i(r_1, r_2)$) first and determine comprehensive condition unexpectedness $COC(r_1, r_2) = \max[OC_i(r_1, r_2)]$, $1 \le i \le m$,

m is the number of attributes contained in conditions of r_1 and r_2. $OC_i(r_1, r_2)$ can be computed using the same method as conclusion unexpectedness. Suppose the condition of r_1 is $(0 \le X \le 2)\Lambda(3 \le Y \le 4)$, while r_2's condition is $(0.5 \le X \le 3)\Lambda(3.5 \le Y \le 4.5)$, we can compute conclusion unexpectedness of X is $1-\frac{2-0.5}{3-0}=\frac{1}{2}$ and Y's conclusion unexpectedness is $1-\frac{4-3.5}{4.5-3}=\frac{2}{3}$, so the comprehensive condition unexpectedness can be determined as $COC(r_1, r_2) = \max\left(\frac{1}{2}, \frac{2}{3}\right) = \frac{2}{3}$.

Second, condition attributes of one rule are part of the other. Under this circumstance, we only calculate the unexpectedness of the same attributes in $AC(r_1)$ and $AC(r_2)$ and choose the maximum as comprehensive condition unexpectedness: $COC(r_1, r_2) = \max[OC_i(r_1, r_2)]$, $1 \le i \le k$, k is the number of r_2's attributes. We suppose r_1's condition is $(0 \le X \le 2)\Lambda(3 \le Y \le 4)\Lambda(6 \le Z \le 10)$, r_2's condition is $(3 \le Y \le 5)\Lambda(5 \le Z \le 9)$. They have the same attributes Y and Z, then after computation, unexpectedness of Y is $\frac{1}{2}$ and unexpectedness of Z is $\frac{2}{5}$. Therefore, condition unexpectedness is $COC(r_1, r_2) = \max\left(\frac{1}{2}, \frac{2}{5}\right) = \frac{1}{2}$.

Third, conditions of r_1 and r_2 do not include attributes of each other. Since new attributes in the new rule emerge providing new contents not covered by domain rules, unexpectedness of rule: $COC(r_1, r_2) = 1$.

(3) Method to Compute Confidence Unexpectedness OF

Confidence is a certain value, the method to compute confidence unexpectedness is the same as conclusion unexpectedness of certain type. Suppose confidence of r_1 is 80 % and confidence of r_2 83 %, ε is 5 %, then confidence unexpectedness is: $\frac{83-80}{5}=\frac{3}{5}$.

Basedontheanalysisabove,amethodisproposedtojudgewhether r_2 isredundantto r_1. Supposedomainrules r_1 andanewrule r_2 : $r_1 : (1 \le X \le 5)\Lambda(4 \le Y \le 8) \to (Z = 2), 0.8$, $r_1 : (6 \le X \le 7)\Lambda(2 \le Y \le 10) \to (Z = 2.2), 0.85$. As the same time, we set the acceptable deviation of unexpectedness ε_r and acceptable deviation of confidence ε_f both are 0.5, the threshold of rules' unexpectedness λ_t is 0.7. The steps for computing unexpectedness $OM(r_1, r_2)$ of r_2 to r_1 as follows:

Step 1: determine whether attributes in conclusions of r_1 and r_2 are the same. If they are different, we can conclude that r_2 is unexpected, and $OR(r_1, r_2) = 1$. If they are the same, go to Step 2. The conclusion of r_1 and r_2 has the same discrete attributes in this example.

Step 2: compute conclusion unexpectedness $OR(r_1, r_2)$. If $OR(r_1, r_2) > 1$, set $OR(r_1, r_2) = 1$. Then, go to step 3. We can easily find $OR(r_1, r_2) = \frac{2.2-2}{0.5} = \frac{2}{5}$ in this example.

Step 3: check out characteristics of r_1's and r_2's conditions. If conditions of r_1 and r_2 do not include attributes of each other, then $COC(r_1, r_2) = 1$. Then go to Step 4.

Step 4: choose appropriate algorithm to calculate condition unexpectedness $COC(r_1, r_2)$ based on r_1's and r_2's condition features. If $COC(r_1, r_2) > 1$, then $COC(r_1, r_2) = 1$ and go to Step 5.

In this example, since conditions of r_1 and r_2 include same attributes, we calculate unexpectedness of each attribute separately, and choose the maximum. Because the unexpectedness of X is $1 - \frac{0}{7-1} = 1$, the unexpectedness of Y is $1 - \frac{8-4}{10-2} = \frac{1}{2}$, the comprehensive condition unexpectedness is $COC(r_1, r_2) = \max\left(1, \frac{1}{2}\right) = 1$.

Step 5: compute confidence unexpectedness OF. If $OF(r_1, r_2)$ surpasses threshold, then $OM(r_1, r_2) = 1$ and r_2 is unexpected. Or, go to Step 6.

In this example, confidence of r_1 and r_2 each is 0.8 and 0.85, the acceptable deviation of confidence is 0.5, so confidence unexpectedness is $OF(r_1, r_2) = \frac{0.85 - 0.8}{0.5} = \frac{1}{10}$.

Step 6: set $OM(r_1, r_2) = \max(OR, COC, OF)$. If $OM(r_1, r_2)$ surpasses threshold, then r_2 is unexpected. Otherwise, r_2 is redundant.

In this example, $OR(r_1, r_2) = \frac{2}{5}$, $COC(r_1, r_2) = 1$, $OF(r_1, r_2) = \frac{1}{10}$, so $OM(r_1, r_2) = 1$ which surpasses threshold 0.7, so we can draw the conclusion that is r_2 is unexpected to r_1.

The above steps can be shows to Fig. 4.8.

4.3.3 *Implement of The Unexpected Association Rule Algorithm of Designed Conceptual Hierarchy Based on Domain Knowledge Driven*

The unexpected association rule algorithm of designed conceptual hierarchy based on domain knowledge driven facing three technical problems have been settled in front. The next part is to represent the various stages of domain knowledge by XML language, and then add them to the specific association rules algorithm, then gain final rules of actions after evaluating new rules. Next, we firstly use an example to show XML representation of domain knowledge in every stage of association rule mining process, and then state the unexpected association rule algorithm of designed conceptual hierarchy based on domain knowledge driven while giving the pseudo code.

4.3.3.1 Representation of Domain Knowledge with the XML Language

As an example of the commodities in Fig. 4.5, suppose the user only pay attention to goods of A and B, C, D and don't care about the commodity E, and existing domain knowledge as below: $A \in [5,10]$, $A \Lambda B \rightarrow C, 0.8$. So we gain knowledge of scope, knowledge of attribute selecting, hierarchy knowledge and known rules. The number of knowledge with XML language can be expressed as:

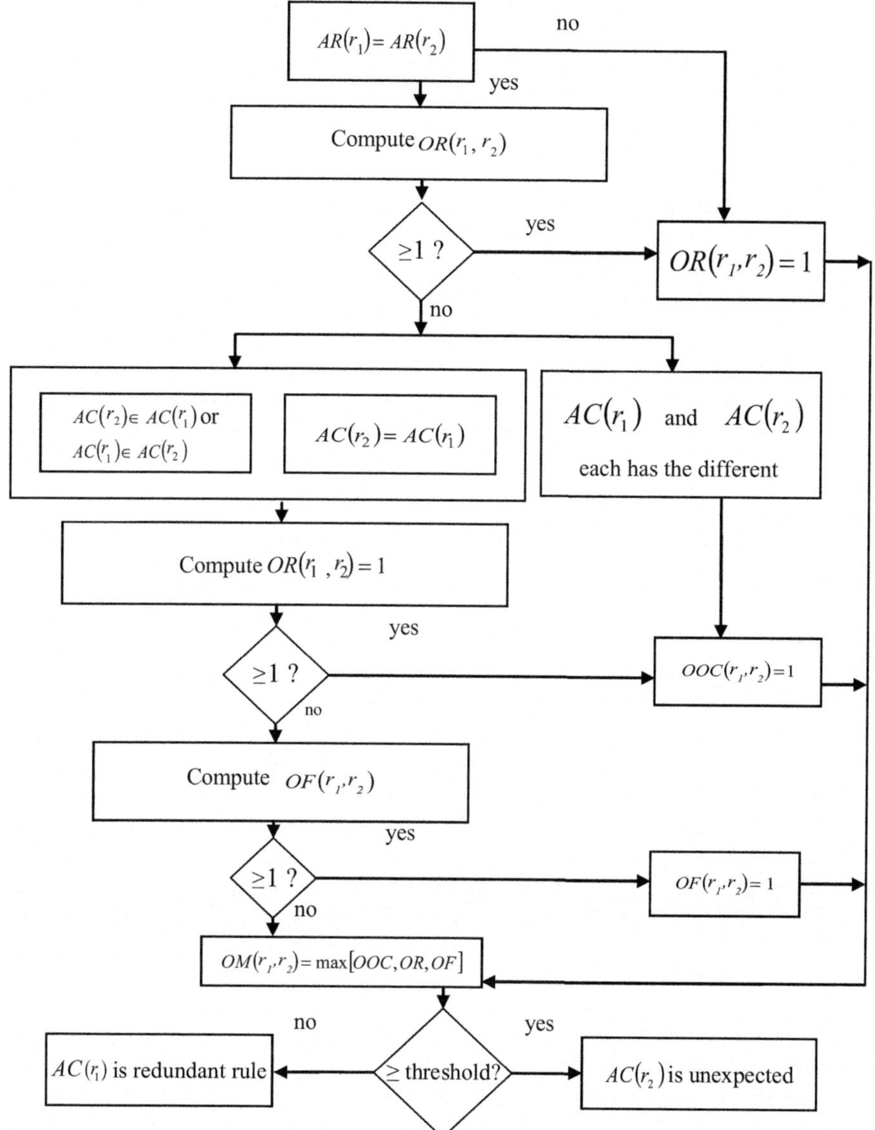

Fig. 4.8 Calculation of Rule Unexpectedness and Judgment of Redundancy

$A \in [5,10]$, $A \wedge B \rightarrow C$,0.8. So we gain knowledge of scope, knowledge of attribute selecting, hierarchy knowledge and known rules. The number of knowledge with XML language can be expressed as:

```
<domain_knowledge>
    <preceeding_knowledge>
        <attribute_select_ knowledge >
          <selection>A|B|C|D</selection>
        </attribute_select_ knowledge >
      <range_knowledge >
          <name>A</name>
          <max>10</max>
          <min>5</min>
      </range_knowledge >
    </preceeding_knowledge>
    <proceeding_knowledge>
        <tree_knowledge>
            <2_level>
        <node>
            <node_name>G</node_name>
            <leaf_node>A|B</leaf_node>
        </node>
        <node>
            <node_name>H</node_name>
            <leaf_node>C|D|E</leaf_node>
        </node>
            </2_level>
        < /tree_knowledge>
    <assessment_knowledge>
        <pre_attribute>A|B</pre_attribute>
        <suf_attribute>C</suf_attribute>
        <confidence>0.8</confidence>
    </assessment_knowledge>
</domain_knowledge>
```

4.3.3.2 Implement of the Unexpected Association Rule Algorithm of Designed Conceptual Hierarchy Based on Domain Knowledge Driven

We use the method mentioned in 4.3.1 to express domain knowledge from each phase of association rules, and put them in a special XML document. Then, the computers not only guide the mining process from reading domain knowledge, but also bring the continued growth of domain knowledge by adding new knowledge to files. Specific algorithm is shown in Fig. 4.9.

Figure 4.9 shows that the steps of the unexpected association rule algorithm of designed conceptual hierarchy based on domain knowledge driven, and the algorithm pseudo code as follows:

Input: data set, XML file, user designed conceptual hierarchy

Output: novel association rules

Suppose: data set is named ”dataset”, mining algorithm is “association rule”, and there are K files in domain knowledge set. The highest of conceptual hierarchy

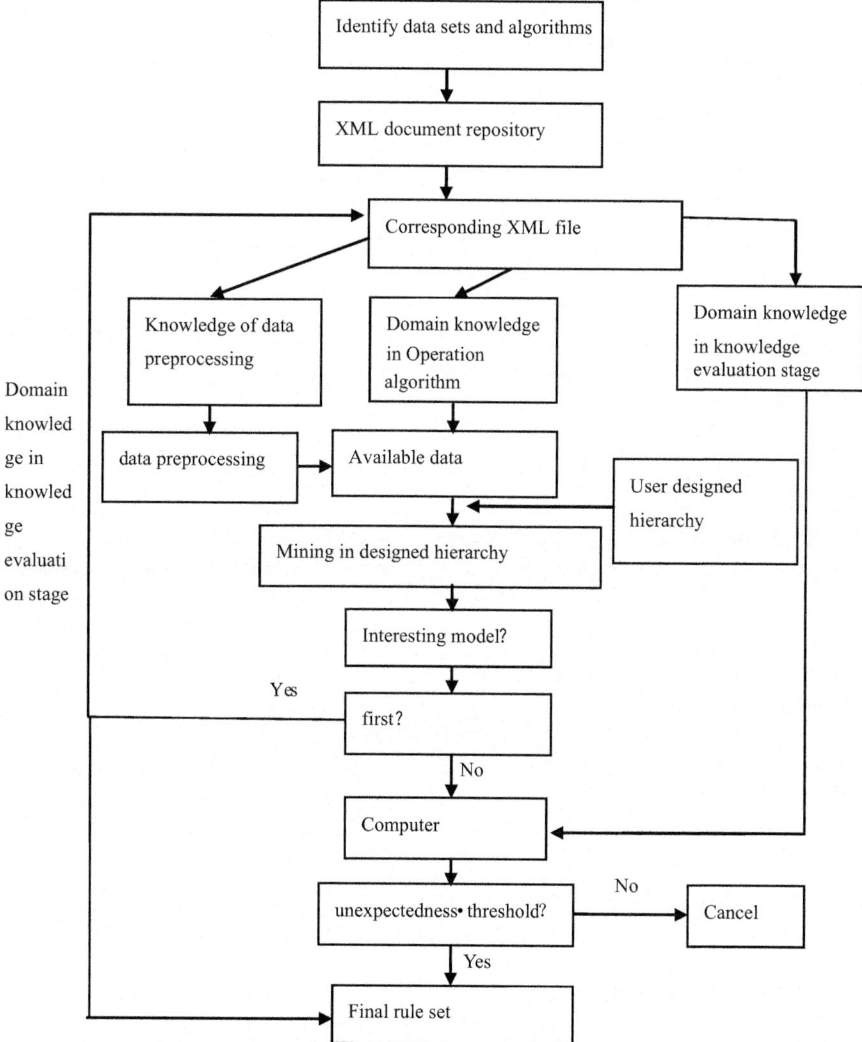

Fig. 4.9 Flow Chart of the Unexpected Association Rule Algorithm of Designed Conceptual Hierarchy Based on Domain Knowledge Driven

tree is Top. The order of the storing knowledge: knowledge of attribute selecting, knowledge of scope, knowledge of rule, hierarchy knowledge and domain knowledge of knowledge evaluation phase.

```
/*search the corresponding file of domain knowledge in knowledge set in according to data set
   name and mining algorithm name */
   For (i=1,i≤k& “dataset_associationrule”!=getname( the ith file in knowledge set),i++);
   If i>K then operate FP tree algorithm to dataset directly; /* show that no domain knowledge
available */
   Else{/*domain knowledge available*/
      Do{/*read content of domain knowledge file */
         label=read dataset_associationrule marks;
         If label==” <attribute_select_ knowledge >”{/*domain knowledge of attribute selecting*/
            read”<selection>”and”</selection>” attribute name;
            form a new data set “dataset_new” by using data of copying variables from original data
set;
         }
         If label== ”<range_knowledge>” {/*domain knowledge of scope */
            Do {attribut=mark the variable name between”<name>”and ”</name>”;
      max=mark value between”<max>”and”</max>”;
      min=mark value between ”<min>”and”</min>”;
               scan the value of attribute in data set “dataset_new”, cancel the record of
Attri_value > max or
               Attri_value <min;
            }Until label==”</ range_knowledge>” /*end the knowledge of scope */
         }
         If label==”< attribute_association_rule>” { /* attribute association rules knowledge */
            Do {expressionA=mark the expression between”<precondition>”and”
</precondition>”;
      expressionB=mark the expression between”< conlusion >”and” </conlusion >”;
               in according to expressionB to revise the record of matching expressionA in
dataset_new;
            }Until label==” </attribute_association_rule>” /*end attribute association rules
knowledge */
         }
         If label==”attribute_category_rule”{ /* attribute category rules knowledge */
      Do{expressionA= mark the expression between”<precondition>”and” </precondition>”;
        expressionB= mark the expression between”< conlusion >”and” </conlusion >”;
                according to expressionB classify the record which is matched expressionA in
dataset_new ;
      }Until label==” </ attribute_category_rule >” /*end attribute category rules knowledge */
```

```
      }
      If label=="<heuristic_rule >"{ /* heuristic rules knowledge */
        Do{expressionA= mark the expression between"<precondition>"and"
</precondition>";
    expressionB= mark the expression between"< conlusion >"and" </conlusion >";
          Search dataset_new expressionA compliance with the record, according to the
          expressionB give an alarm as soon as the location of the record and the (line
          number);
    }Until label==" </heuristic_rule >" /* end heuristic rules knowledge */
      }
      If label==" <tree_knowledge>{/* hierarchy knowledge */
  h=the level of user designed conceptual hierarchy;
  If h==1 operate FP tree algorithm to dataset_new directly;
  Else If h<Top & h>1{search mark h&" _level";/*find domain knowledge of user designed
conceptual hierarchy */
    Do{node=mark attribute name between <node_name>and</node_name>;
      after{ leafi= <leaf_node>do ith attribute name; /*read node of leaf */
      }Until label==</leaf_node>
    If the type of node leaf value is continuous {/*integrating node of leaf by addition */
      Build a new variable named node in dataset_new;
      For(j=1;j<i+1;j++){
        If leaf i is not exiting continue in dataset_new; /* skip the node */
        Else Value(node)=Value(node)+Value(leaf i);
        delet the leaf I in dataset_new;
            }
          }
    If the type of node leaf value is Boolean {/* integrating node of leaf by logic or algorithm
*/
            build a new attribute named node in dataset_new;
      For (j=1;j<i+1;j++){
        if leaf i is not exiting continue in dataset_new; /* skip the node */
        Else Value(node)= Value(node)| Value(leaf i);
        delete leaf i from dataset_new;
            }
    }
  }Until label=="/"&h&"_levl" /*end knowledge of hierarchy */
      }
    }Until label=="</ proceeding_knowledge >"/*end domain knowledge of algorithm
operation */
    get N frequent mode by operating FP tree algorithm to dataset_new;
    For(i=1,i<=N,i++){
    According to the method in 4.3, identify whether the ith frequent mode is the redundancy
rules which is compared to all rules in mark < assessment_knowledge > and < /
assessment_knowledge > in a domain knowledge in relative to the file;
      If ith frequent mode is redundancy, then cancel it;
      Else {keep the rule, and add it to mark between <assessment_knowledge>and
</assessment_knowledge>;}
    }
  }
```

This part applies the knowledge discovery method to association rules mining, and proposes the implement method of designated hierarchy of accident association rule mining based on domain knowledge driven.

This novelty of algorithm lies in:

It can be used to dig in the user designed hierarchy. That is to say, it is able to avoid the shortcoming of traditional algorithms which is computing in all hierarchies by ignoring the demand of customers. As a result, the proposed algorithm not only reduces the computational complexity but also be more in line with the users' preferences.

In order to filter the redundant rules, it provides an indicator to evaluate unexpectedness of rules which can ensure the novelty of the rules.

The proposed algorithm is able to keep the last mining result as the new domain knowledge to guide the next mining process, so as to realize the accumulation of knowledge.

4.3.4 Application of Unexpected Association Rule Mining in Goods Promotion

In this subsection, this algorithm will be validated by a instance in three aspects: (1) whether rule's extent of exceptional can filter redundant rules effectively (2) whether by this algorithm we can obtain results from different layers which are decided by users (3) whether the knowledge data base can be used to cumulate and reuse during the algorithm running. Finally, the feedback-style associated rules applied on product good are analyzed.

4.3.4.1 Extraction of Domain Knowledge

(1) Domain Knowledge of Data Preprocessing—Knowledge of Attribute Selection

Supposed users focus on the relationship of only 20 sorts of food in the supermarket, we adopt one clause of domain knowledge of attribute selection including 20 factors in the data preprocessing stage. This knowledge limit the algorithm to only process on the 20 sorts of foods specified above.

(2) Domain Knowledge in the Algorithm Running Stage—Knowledge of Concept Hierarchy

We can obtain the tree of concept through the connection of relative experts and the research of relationship of different sorts of commodities. The tree can be recorded in XML file as knowledge of concept hierarchy, by the methods introduced above, and then can be used to induce the algorithm to do data mining in different concept level.

(3) Knowledge in the Assessment Stage—Rules Mined Before

Initially, there is no rule about this market. After the first rule, every rule will be filtered by the extent rule exception of knowledge database, which consist of the rules mined earlier. The filter results can be accessed by two ways: use extent rule exception or not.

4.3.4.2 The Feature of Data and Constrain in Algorithm Running Process

(1) Feature of Data

This chapter studies 42463 records of 20 kinds of supermarket food. Data in the set are all bool type. The concept hierarchy relationship of commodities is as shown in Fig. 4.10.

A concept tree have 5 levels is shown in Fig. 4.10, for the equivalence the non-equivalent part have been processed. All the data are bool type, so the "OR" operator will be adapted in leverage of concept. For instance, if "soft cake" = 1, and "cookie" = 1, then "Chinese" = 1; if "soft cake" = 0 and "cookie" = 0, then "Chinese" = 0.

(2) The Constrain of Algorithm

The following constrains should be satisfied in the mining process:

First, the threshold of support, confident and lift are 8 %, 80 % and 1.1, respectively.

Second, the number of rule's prior are limited to under 5.

Finally, the accepted error of all the attributes are 0.1. The unexpected extent of condition, results and integrity are all 0.9, while confident is 0.7.

4.3.4.3 Experimental Results

The mining process have been done in levels from first to fourth concept level, the result is as shown in Table 4.1.

From the table we can draw conclusion as follows: the result of the first level and second level are same because the tree structure of them are nearly same; the rules in the third level are the most numerous, while the fourth only have one.

The three aspects discussed above have been validated in this experiment:

First, filter process are effective. In the third concept level, after adapting the measure of unexpectedness, the rules are reduced to 12 in contrast to original 35, which can validate the effectiveness of filter.

Second, the different results can obtain in different concept level.

Finally, domain knowledge can be cumulated and reused. From the third level result, the number of rule increase from 0 to 12, and the rules influence the assessment of later rules.

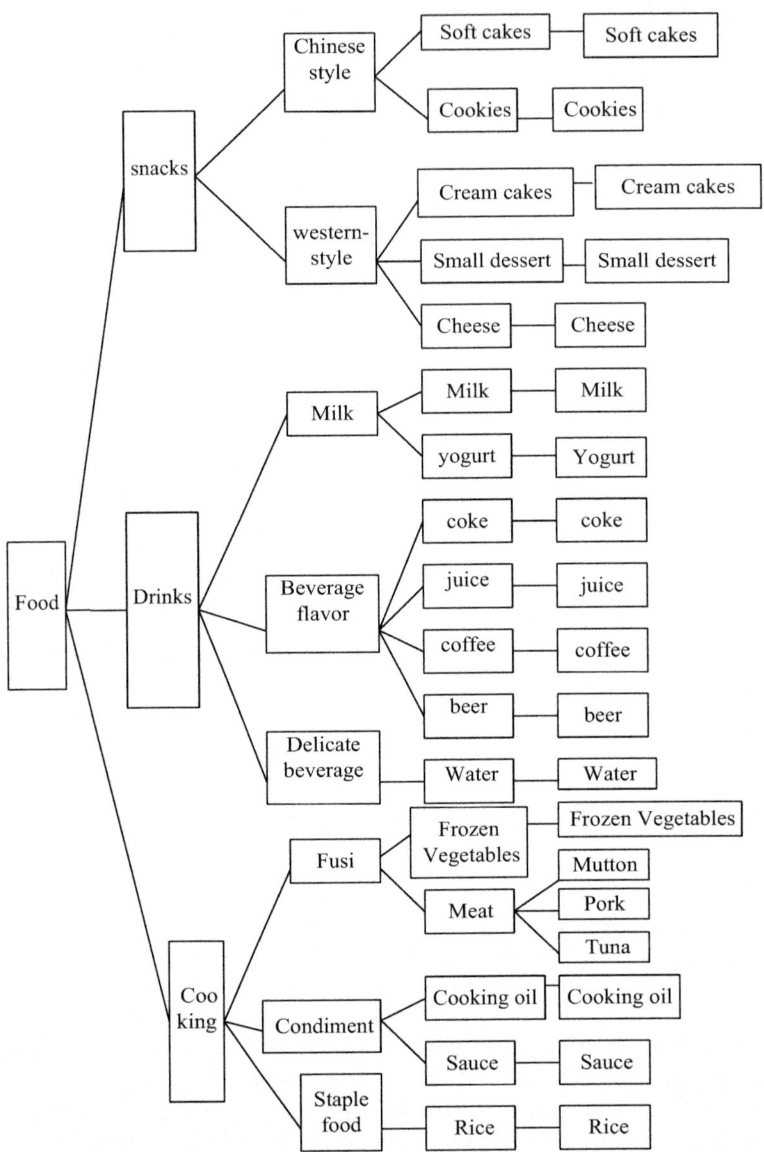

Fig. 4.10 A Concept Hierarchy Tree

4.3.4.4 The Analysis of Experimental Results in Product Promotion

(1) Support, Confidence and Their Applications in Good Promotion

For rules A→B, support represent the probability that both of A and B emerge, e. g. $SP = P(AUB)$. Confidence represent in condition of A emerge, the probability of B emerge, e. g. $CF = P(AUB) / P(A)$. Support means the universality of rules,

Table 4.1 Results of Association Rules

Concept	Support		Confidence		Lift		Rules
	Threshold (%)	Value (%)	Threshold (%)	Value (%)	Threshold	Value	
1	5	6	80	80.2	1.1	1.306	water ^ cookies → Fresh milk
2	5	6	80	80.2	1.1	1.306	water ^ cookies → Fresh milk
3	8	8.1	80	85.9	1.1	1.381	Milk taste drink ^ condiment → Chinese style snacks
		8.7		81.9		1.151	Chinese style snacks ^ condiment → Milk taste drink
		8.4		84.2		1.202	Beverage flavor ^Western cookies → Dairy drink
		10.2		83.5		1.188	Chinese style snacks^ Western cookies → Dairy drink
		10.5		81.5		1.288	Dairy drink^ Western cookies → Chinese style
		8.6		82.9		1.317	snacks Beverage flavor ^ fusi → Chinese style
		8.4		82.0		1.299	snacks Beverage flavor ^ western cookies → Chinese
		12.8		82.0		1.160	style snacks Chinese style snacks ^water → Dairy
		8.6		81.5		1.151	drink Beverage flavor ^ fusi → Dairy drink Chinese
		17.7		81.2		1.146	style snacks ^ Beverage flavor → Dairy drink
		11.1		80.2		1.128	Beverage flavor^ water → Dairy drink
		14.4		80.0		1.257	Condiment → Chinese style snacks
4	10	26.6	80	84.9	1.1	1.154	Drink^Cooking → food snacks

the higher the support degree that this rule apply crowd scale is bigger, so using the rules for promotional influence was even higher. Confidence means the stability of the rules, the higher the confidence that the greater the probability of established rules. The two rules must be combined. If a rule has better support degree, but the probability of this rule is very low, this is clearly not an effective rule. In contrast, while a rule has very good confidence, but only a small percentage of people can be influenced, this rule to promotion had little practical significance. Most of the time, we need to weigh on both.

But it is not enough to only consider the support and confidence, because frequent is not necessarily interesting. For example, there are 85 % of the customers buy milk, but only 80 % of the customer and buy the beer and milk, if will confidence threshold as 80 % will get "beer, milk" this rule, but obviously it is misleading, so also need to calculate lift, which is computed by $lift = (P(AUB)) / [P(A)P(B)]$.

It can be alternatively write as $lift = P(B \mid A) / P(B)$ for $P(AUB) = P(A)P(B \mid A)$. This formula clearly expresses the meaning of lift: relationship between A and B. If lift > 1, A and B are positive related. If lift = 1, A and B are independent; If lift < 1, A and B negative relative. In the example above, lift of "beer, milk" is the negative relative, so the rule is not interesting. So lift can effectively identify some of the boring rules. Based on the above considerations, the test also consider the support degree, confidence and lift, Table 2 lists and at the same time through the three indexes of the rules, but the specific use which rules need to the three indexes balance.

(2) Analysis of Effect of Feedback Rules

This chapter identify the rules which analogy with milk taste drink ^ condiment → Chinese style snacks and Chinese style snacks ^ condiment → Milk taste drink as feedback rules.

This kind of feedback type of the rules of the few scholars discuss application, however an intuitive sense is the second rule compared to the first is the redundancy rules. Because milk taste drink ^ condiment → Chinese style snacks means that the customers bought dairy drinks and condiment will buy Chinese style snacks, so for the businessman only things required to do is putting together these three kinds of goods. Chinese style snacks ^ condiment → milk taste drink means the customers who bought Chinese style snacks and spices at the same time will buy milk drinks, so the choice of the businessman is also put three kinds of goods together. We can see that the second rule cannot provide new knowledge.

But this view need to discuss next, in the one case of no use rules, on another occasion can be useful. Although the two rules for commodities are redundant, they can be further used for goodions promotion field is valuable.

Promotion are making customers buy commodity which they didn't intend to buy by some ways, the condition of its success is to have promotion on an accurately located crowd. If some people would like some kind of goods, to this kind of person to promote only makes mall spend a lot of cost and no reward, even in the short time to obtain the effect also is just the consumption of the borrowed from the future, won't form the absolute sales growth. For instance, the person is like a day spent three times is 10 RMB to drink milk. Even since milk prices fell 10 % more than usual to buy a certain amount of milk, he would not drink milk six times a day, and because the buy milk more, he will end in sales promotion to reduce the number of milk, so just the impact of promotions to offset the. But mall but pay 10 % of the usual price cost but no gain. So the object of sales promotion should be those customers who were not often buy the goods, the consumption of them which increase in the sales promotion stage of consumption is absolutely consumption.

Using the above feedback rules can use to identify promotion applicable object. To the test results, for example, suppose market will promotion dairy drink, the rules Chinese style snacks ^ condiment → Milk taste drink (A kind of customer), Beverage flavor ^Western cookies → Dairy drink (B class customers), Chinese style snacks^ Western cookies → Dairy drink (C customers), Chinese style snacks ^water → Dairy drink (D types of customers), Beverage flavor ^ fusi → Dairy drink (E types of customers), Chinese style snacks ^ Beverage flavor → Dairy drink

(F types of customers), Beverage flavor ^water → Dairy drink (G types of customers) know A, B, C, D, E, F, G the seven types of customers even if not promotions will also buy milk drinks, so the object should be outside the seven type of customers. In extreme cases (assuming no duplication of seven customer) the seven class customers more than 70 % of the total customer, rule out the seven class is not sensitive to promotion of customer, can save a lot of promotion costs so as to improve the efficiency of sales promotion.

But analysis is not over, how to design promotion means is an important question. The most commonly used method is to reduce the price of milk drinks, this is really a can effectively improve the means of sales, but this kind of means can't will be seven class clients from the demarcation customer groups, and will cause a lot of invalidation of the promotion cost. A point of view, if market regulation "and at the same time buy milk drinks and spices can enjoy more favorable price", then the buy driven by price and dairy drinks and condiment customers will increase in a certain degree, the rules Dairy drink^ condiment → Chinese style snacks can infer that clients who Chinese style snacks would increase, again by its inverse rules Chinese style snacks ^ condiment → Milk taste drink, Chinese style snacks^ Western cookies → Dairy drink, Chinese style snacks ^ Beverage flavor → Dairy drink

It can be seen that the milk beverage clients would increase, that is some was not going to buy milk beverage customers in these rules under the function of the dairy drink also buy, but this kind of customer is" and at the same time buy milk drinks and spices can enjoy preferential "article this promotion rule to attract may further purchase was not going to buy the dressing, such rules Chinese style snacks ^ condiment → milk taste drink will enter into a new round of growth, so cycle down. In this way is realized the purpose of sales promotion and at the same time will not sensitive to promotion seven categories of people effectively ruled out, and greatly reduce the cost of sales promotion. The rules of visible feedback not the redundancy rules in business but has an important application value.

This part use the supermarket with a data driven to domain knowledge can be prescribed concept levels of accident association rule mining algorithm on empirical research. The test results show that:

(1) The accident intensity index can effectively filter the redundancy rules, and, to some extent, guarantee the novelty of the rules.
(2) In the field of knowledge driving can be prescribed concept levels of accident association rule mining algorithm to user specifies the specific levels for mining, and get more close to the needs of the user results.
(3) In the field of knowledge driving can be prescribed concept levels of accident association rule mining algorithm can realize the knowledge accumulation and reuse

And then this article from the point of view of real application of association rules do some of the evaluation indexes analytical, and analyses the feedback mode in goods promotion association rules in an important role. Conclusion is feedback mode rules can help sales promotion influencing on more accurate role to target people, and then can increase much more goods promotion effect.

4.4 Conclusions

Traditional data mining algorithms are always data driven, with much existing information ignored, and are usually apart from expert experience. Thus "hidden patterns" from data mining algorithms cannot be directly used for users' decision makings. To overcome the existing shortcomings of data mining, we propose the framework of domain driven intelligent knowledge discovery (DDIKD) process with domain knowledge combined in every step in the process including preprocessing, data mining and post analysis period.

First of all, importance of domain driven intelligent knowledge discovery is emphasized and some relevant definitions are given. Then, we give our framework of domain driven intelligent knowledge discovery (DDIKD). Some relevant literatures are reviewed, and we find out that they combine domain knowledge with data mining only in some steps rather than the whole knowledge discovery process. Our conceptual model of DDIKM is presented with every step described in details.

We propose the method of domain driven association rules mining based on unexpectedness. This method corporate domain knowledge with the whole intelligent knowledge discovery process (including preprocessing, data mining, and post analysis period) and we validated this method in supermarket data analysis. By the above discussion, we present our readers a process of finding knowledge: data mining algorithm recommendation—domain driven data preprocessing—domain driven data mining—knowledge evaluation and post analysis based on unexpectedness.

This chapter does not cover all the proper methods for domain driven intelligent knowledge discovery, but just present the concept of domain driven intelligent knowledge discovery. That is domain knowledge should be combined with every step of knowledge discovery process including the post analysis period.

Chapter 5
Knowledge-incorporated Multiple Criteria Linear Programming Classifiers

Classification is a main data mining task, which aims at predicting the class label of new input data on the basis of a set of pre-classified samples. Multiple Criteria Linear Programming (MCLP) is used as a classification method in data mining area, which can separate two or more classes by finding discriminate hyperplane. Although MCLP shows good performance in dealing with linear separable data, it is no longer applicable when facing with nonlinear separable problem. Kernel-based Multiple Criteria Linear Programming (KMCLP) model is developed to solve nonlinear separable problem. In this method, kernel function is introduced to project the data into a higher-dimensional space in which the data will have more chance to be linear separable. KMCLP performs well in some real applications. However, just as other prevalent data mining classifiers, MCLP and KMCLP learn only from training examples. In traditional machine learning area, there are also classification tasks in which data sets are classified only by prior knowledge, i.e. expert system. Some works combine the above two classification principle to overcome the defaults of each approach. In this section, we combine the prior knowledge and MCLP or KMCLP model to solve the problem when input consists of not only training example, but also prior knowledge.

5.1 Introduction

Multiple Criteria Linear Programming (MCLP) is used as a classification method which is based on a set of classified training examples (Kou et al. 2003). By solving a linear programming problem, MCLP can find a hyperplane to separate two classes. The principle of MCLP classifier is to train on the training set then get some separation model that can be used to predict the label of the new data. However, MCLP model is only applicable for linear separable data. To facilitate its application on nonlinear separable data set, kernel-based multiple criteria linear programming (KMCLP) method was proposed by Zhang et al. (2009), which introduces kernel function into the original MCLP model to make it possible to solve nonlinear separable problem. Likewise, there are also many other prevalent classifiers, such

Y. Shi et al., *Intelligent Knowledge,* SpringerBriefs in Business,
DOI 10.1007/978-3-662-46193-8_5

as Support Vector Machine, Neural Networks, Decision Tree etc., which share the same principle of learning solely from training examples. This inevitably can bring out some disadvantages. One problem is that noisy points may lead to poor result. The other more important one is that when training samples are hard to get or when sampling is costly, these methods will be inapplicable.

Different from the above empirical classification methods, another commonly used method in some area to classify the data is to use prior knowledge as the classification principle. Two well-known traditional methods are Rule-Based reasoning and Expert System. In these methods, prior knowledge can take the form of logical rule which is well recognized by computer. However, these methods also suffer from the fact that pre-existing knowledge cannot contain imperfections (Towell et al. 1990). Whereas, as is known to all, most of the knowledge is tacit in that it exists in people's mind. Thus, it is not an easy task to acquire perfect knowledge.

Recent works combine the above two classification principles to overcome the defaults of each approach. Prior knowledge can be used to aid the training set to improve the classification ability; also training example can be used to refine prior knowledge. In such combination methods, Knowledge-Based Artificial Neural Networks (KBANN) and Knowledge-Based Support Vector Machine (KBSVM) are two representatives. KBANN is a hybrid learning system which firstly inserts a set of hand-constructed, symbolic rules into a neural network. The network is then refined using standard neural learning algorithms and a set of classified training examples. The refined network can function as a highly-accurate classifier (Towell and Shavlik 1994). KBSVM provides a novel approach to incorporate prior knowledge into the original support vector classifier. Prior knowledge in the form of polyhedral knowledge sets in the input space of the given data can be expressed into logical implications. By using a mathematical programming theorem, these logical implications can work as a set of constraints in support vector machine formulation. It is also a hybrid formulation capable of generating a classifier based on training data and prior knowledge (Fung et al. 2002; Mangasarian 2005). Some works are focused on incorporating nonlinear knowledge into nonlinear kernel classification problem (Mangasarian and Wild 2008), because nonlinear prior knowledge is more general in practical application. In addition to the application in classification problem, (Mangasarian et al. 2004) has shown the effectiveness of introduce prior knowledge into function approximation.

In this chapter, we summarize the relevant works which combine the prior knowledge and MCLP or KMCLP model. Such works can extend the application of MCLP or KMCLP model to the cases where prior knowledge is available. Specifically, knowledge-incorporated MCLP model deals with linear knowledge and linear separable classification problem. The prior knowledge in the form of polyhedral knowledge sets can be expressed into logical implications, which can further be converted into a series of equalities and inequalities. Incorporating such kind of constraints to original MCLP model, we then obtain the final knowledge-incorporated MCLP model. It is supposed to be necessary and possible that KMCLP model make better use of knowledge to achieve better outcomes in classifying nonlinear separable data. Linear knowledge can also be introduced into kernel-based MCLP model by transforming the logical implication into the expression with kernel. With this approach, nonlinear separable data with linear knowledge can be easily classified. Concerning the nonlinear prior knowledge, by writing the knowledge into logical expression, the nonlinear knowledge can be added as constraints to the kernel-based MCLP model. It then helps to find the best discriminate hyperplane of the two classes. Numerical tests on the above models indicate that they are effective in classifying data with prior knowledge.

5.2 MCLP and KMCLP Classifiers

5.2.1 MCLP

Multiple criteria linear programming (MCLP) is a classification method (Olson and Shi 2007). Classification is a main data mining task. Its principle is to use the existing data to learn some useful knowledge that can predict the class label of other unclassified data. The purpose of classification problem can be described as follows:

Suppose the training set of the classification problem is $\boldsymbol{X}$, which has n observations in it. Of each observation, there are r attributes (or variables) which can be any real value and a two-value class label G (Good) or B (Bad). Of the training set, the *ith* observation can be described by $\boldsymbol{X}_i=(X_i1,\ldots, X_{ir})$, where i can be any number from 1 to n. The objective of the classification problem is to learn from the training set and get a classification model that can classify these two classes, so that when given an unclassified sample $z=(z_1,\ldots, z_r)$, we can predict its class label with the model.

So far, many classification methods have been developed and widely used in data mining area. Specifically, MCLP is an efficient optimization-based method in solving classification problem. The framework of MCLP is based on the linear discriminate analysis models. In linear discriminate analysis, the purpose is to determine the optimal coefficients (or weights) for the attributes, denoted by $W=(w_1, \ldots, w_r)$ and a boundary value (scalar) b to separate two predetermined classes: G (Good) and B (Bad); that is

$$
\begin{aligned}
&X_{i1}w_1+\cdots+X_{ir}w_r \le b, X_i \in B(Bad)\\
\textit{and}\ &X_{i1}w_1+\cdots+X_{ir}w_r \ge b, X_i \in G(Good)
\end{aligned}
\tag{5.1}
$$

To formulate the criteria and constraints for data separation, some variables need to be introduced. In the classification problem, $X_i w = X_{i1} w_1 + \cdots + X_{ir} w_r$ is the score for the *ith* observation. If all records are linear separable and a sample $\boldsymbol{X}_i$ is correctly classified, then let β_i be the distance from $\boldsymbol{X}_i$ to b, and consider the linear system, $X_i w = b + \beta_i$, $\forall X_i \in G$ and $X_i w = b - \beta_i$, $\forall X_i \in B$. However, if we consider the case where the two groups are not linear separable because of mislabeled

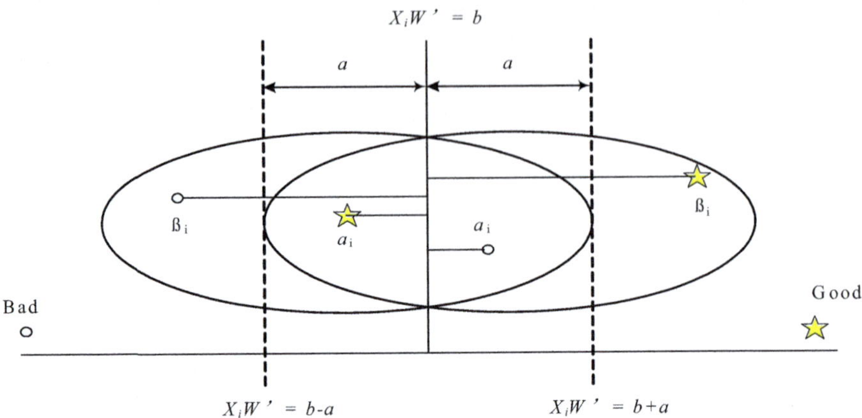

Fig. 5.1 Overlapping of two-class Linear Discriminate Analysis

records, a "soft margin" and slack distance variable α_i need to be introduced. α_i is defined to be the overlapping of the two-class boundary for mislabeled case X_i. Previous equations now can be transformed to $X_i w = b - \alpha_i + \beta_i,\ \forall X_i \in G$ and $X_i w = b + \alpha_i - \beta_i,\ \forall X_i \in B$. To complete the definitions of β_i and α_i, let $\beta_i = 0$ for all misclassified samples and $\alpha_i = 0$ for all correctly classified samples. Figure 5.1 shows all the above denotations in two-class discriminate problem.

A key idea in linear discriminate classification is that the misclassification of data can be reduced by using two objectives in a linear system. One is to maximize the minimum distances (MMD) of data records from a critical value and another is to separate the data records by minimizing the sum of the deviations (MSD) of the data from the critical value. In the following we give the two basic formulations of MMD and MSD (Olson and Shi 2007):

MSD

$$
\begin{aligned}
&\text{Minimize } \alpha_1 + \ldots + \alpha_n \\
&\text{Subject to:} \\
&\quad X_{11}w_1 + \ldots + X_{1r}w_r = b + \alpha_1, \quad for\ \ X_1 \in B, \\
&\quad \ldots \\
&\quad X_{n1}w_1 + \ldots + X_{nr}w_r = b - \alpha_n, \quad for\ \ X_n \in G, \\
&\quad \alpha_i \geq 0, \quad i = 1, \ldots, n, \\
&\quad w \in R^r.
\end{aligned}
\tag{5.2}
$$

MMD

$$\begin{aligned}
&\text{Minimize } \beta_1 + \ldots + \beta_n \\
&\text{Subject to:} \\
&\quad X_{11}w_1 + \ldots + X_{1r}w_r = b - \beta_1, \quad for \ \ X_1 \in B, \\
&\quad \ldots \\
&\quad X_{n1}w_1 + \ldots + X_{nr}w_r = b + \beta_n, \quad for \ \ X_n \in G, \\
&\quad \beta_i \geq 0, \quad i = 1, \ldots, n, \\
&\quad w \in R^r.
\end{aligned} \tag{5.3}$$

Instead of maximizing the minimizing distances of data records from a boundary b or minimizing the sum of the deviations of the data from b in linear discriminate analysis models, MCLP classification considers all of the scenarios of tradeoffs and finds a compromise solution. So, to find the compromise solution of the two linear discriminate analysis models MMD and MSD for data separation, MCLP wants to minimize the sum of α_i and maximize the sum of β_i simultaneously, as follows:

Two-Class MCLP model (Olson and Shi 2007):

$$\begin{aligned}
&\text{Minimize } \alpha_1 + \cdots + \alpha_n \quad and \quad \text{Maximize } \beta_1 + \cdots + \beta_n \\
&\text{Subject to:} \\
&\qquad X_{11}w_1 + \cdots + X_{1r}w_r = b + \alpha_1 - \beta_1, \quad for \ \ X_1 \in B \\
&\qquad \cdots\cdots \\
&\qquad X_{n1}w_1 + \cdots + X_{nr}w_r = b - \alpha_n + \beta_n, \ for \ X_n \in G \\
&\qquad \alpha_1, \cdots, \alpha_n \geq 0, \qquad \beta_1, \cdots, \beta_n \geq 0
\end{aligned} \tag{5.4}$$

To facilitate the computation, a compromise solution approach (Olson and Shi 2007) has been employed to modify the above model so that we can systematically identify the best trade-off between $-\sum\alpha_i$ and $\sum\beta_i$ for an optimal solution. The "ideal value" of $-\sum\alpha_i$ and $\sum\beta_i$ are assumed to be $\alpha^* > 0$ and $\beta^* > 0$ respectively. Then, if $-\sum\alpha_i > \alpha^*$, we define the regret measure as $-d_\alpha^+ = \sum\alpha_i + \alpha^*$; otherwise, it is 0. If $-\sum\alpha_i < \alpha^*$, the regret measure is defined as $d\alpha^- = \alpha^* + \sum\alpha_i$; otherwise, it is 0. Thus, we have (i) $\alpha^* + \sum\alpha_i = d_\alpha^- - d_\alpha^+$, (ii) $|\alpha^* + \sum\alpha_i| = d_\alpha^- + d_\alpha^+$, and (iii) $d_\alpha^-, d_\alpha^+ \geq 0$. Similarly, we derive $\beta^* - \sum\beta_i = d_\beta^- - d_\beta^+$, $|\beta^* - \sum\beta_i| = d_\beta^- + d_\beta^+$, and $d_\beta^-, d_\beta^+ \geq 0$. The two-class MCLP model has been gradually evolved as:

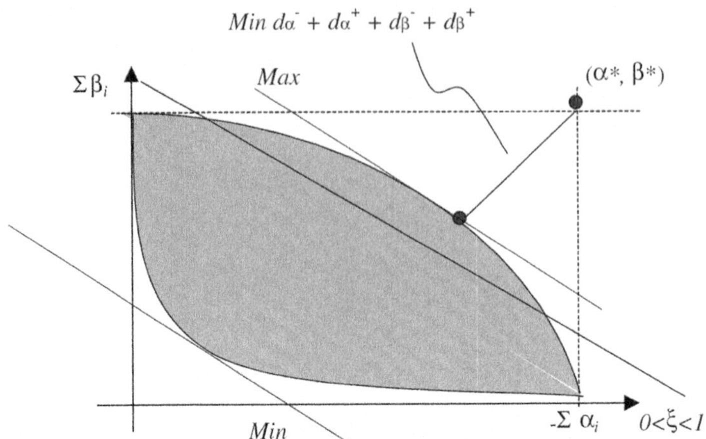

Fig. 5.2 Compromised and Fuzzy Formulations

$$\begin{aligned}
&\text{Minimize} \quad d_\alpha^+ + d_\alpha^- + d_\beta^+ + d_\beta^- \\
&\text{Subject to:} \\
&\qquad \alpha^* + \sum_{i=1}^{n} \alpha_i = d_\alpha^- - d_\alpha^+ \\
&\qquad \beta^* - \sum_{i=1}^{n} \beta_i = d_\beta^- - d_\beta^+ \\
&\qquad X_{11}w_1 + \cdots + X_{1r}w_r = b + \alpha_1 - \beta_1, \quad for \quad X_1 \in B \\
&\qquad \qquad \cdots\cdots \\
&\qquad X_{n1}w_1 + \cdots + X_{nr}w_r = b - \alpha_n + \beta_n, \quad for \quad X_n \in G \\
&\qquad \alpha_1, \cdots, \alpha_n \geq 0, \quad \beta_1, \cdots, \beta_n \geq 0, \quad d_\alpha^+, d_\alpha^-, d_\beta^+, d_\beta^- \geq 0
\end{aligned} \tag{5.5}$$

Here α^* and β^* are given in advance, w and b are unrestricted. With the optimum value of w and b, a discriminate line is constructed to classify the data set.

The geometric meaning of the model is shown as in Fig. 5.2.

To better and clearly understand the methods, we now sum up the notations involved in the models above.

- X the training set of the classification problem with n observations and r attributes,
- W the optimal coefficients (or weights) for the attributes, $W=(w_1, \ldots, w_r)$,
- b a boundary value (scalar) to separate two predetermined classes, the discrimination function is $Wx=b$,
- α_i the overlapping of the two-class boundary for mislabeled case X_i. $\alpha_i = 0$ for all correctly classified samples,

β_i	the distance from X_i to b, $\beta_i = 0$ for all misclassified samples,
α^* and β^*	the "ideal value" of $-\Sigma\alpha_i$ and $\Sigma\beta_i$ for solving the two-criteria model (4),
d_α^-, d_α^+	the regret measure, if $-\Sigma\alpha_i > \alpha^*$, $-d_\alpha + = \Sigma\alpha_i + \alpha^*$; otherwise, it is 0. If $-\Sigma\alpha_i < \alpha^*$, $d_\alpha^- = \alpha^* + \Sigma\alpha_i$; otherwise, it is 0.
d_β^-, d_β^+	the regret measure, if $\Sigma\beta_i > \beta^*$, $d_\beta + = \Sigma\beta_i - \beta^*$; otherwise, it is 0. If $\Sigma\beta_i < \beta^*$, $d_\beta^- = \beta^* - \Sigma\beta_i$; otherwise, it is 0.

5.2.2 KMCLP

MCLP model is only applicable for the linear problem. To extend its application, kernel-based multiple criteria linear programming (KMCLP) method was proposed by (Zhang et al. 2009). It introduces kernel function into the original MCLP model to make it possible to solve nonlinear separable problem. The process is based on the assumption that the solution of MCLP model can be described in the following form:

$$w = \sum_{i=1}^{n} \lambda_i y_i X_i \tag{5.6}$$

here n is the sample size of data set. X_i represents each training sample. y_i is the class label of *ith* sample, which can be $+1$ or -1. Put this w into two-class MCLP model (5.5), the following model is formed:

$$\begin{aligned}
&\text{Minimize} \quad d_\alpha^+ + d_\alpha^- + d_\beta^+ + d_\beta^- \\
&\text{Subject to:} \\
&\alpha^* + \sum_{i=1}^{n} \alpha_i = d_\alpha^- - d_\alpha^+ \\
&\beta^* - \sum_{i=1}^{n} \beta_i = d_\beta^- - d_\beta^+ \\
&\lambda_1 y_1 (X_1 \cdot X_1) + \ldots + \lambda_n y_n (X_n \cdot X_1) = b + \alpha_1 - \beta_1, \quad for \ X_1 \in B \\
&\ldots\ldots \\
&\lambda_1 y_1 (X_1 \cdot X_n) + \ldots + \lambda_n y_n (X_n \cdot X_n) = b - \alpha_n + \beta_n, \quad for \ X_n \in G \\
&\alpha_1, \ldots, \alpha_n \geq 0, \beta_1, \ldots, \beta_n \geq 0, \lambda_1, \ldots, \lambda_n \geq 0, d_\alpha^+, d_\alpha^-, d_\beta^+, d_\beta^- \geq 0
\end{aligned} \tag{5.7}$$

In above model, each X_i is included in the expression $(X_i \cdot X_j)$ which is the inner product of two samples. But with this model, we can only solve linear separable problem. In order to extend it to be nonlinear model, $(X_i \cdot X_j)$ in the model can be replaced with $K(X_i, X_j)$, then with some nonlinear kernel, i.e. RBF kernel, the above model can be used as a nonlinear classifier. The formulation of RBF kernel is $k(x, x') = \exp(-q \| x - x' \|^2)$.

Kernel-based multiple criteria linear programming (KMCLP) nonlinear classifier:

Minimize $d_\alpha^+ + d_\alpha^- + d_\beta^+ + d_\beta^-$

Subject to:

$$\alpha^* + \sum_{i=1}^{n} \alpha_i = d_\alpha^- - d_\alpha^+$$

$$\beta^* - \sum_{i=1}^{n} \beta_i = d_\beta^- - d_\beta^+$$

$$\lambda_1 y_1 K(X_1, X_1) + \ldots + \lambda_n y_n K(X_n, X_1) = b + \alpha_1 - \beta_1, \quad for \ X_1 \in B$$

$$\ldots\ldots$$

$$\lambda_1 y_1 K(X_1, X_n) + \ldots + \lambda_n y_n K(X_n, X_n) = b - \alpha_n + \beta_n, \quad for \ X_n \in G$$

$$\alpha_1, \ldots, \alpha_n \geq 0, \beta_1, \ldots, \beta_n \geq 0, \lambda_1, \ldots, \lambda_n \geq 0, d_\alpha^+, d_\alpha^-, d_\beta^+, d_\beta^- \geq 0 \tag{5.8}$$

With the optimal value of this model (λ, b, α, β), we can obtain the discrimination function to separate the two classes:

$$\begin{aligned} &\lambda_1 y_1 K(X_1, z) + \ldots + \lambda_n y_n K(X_n, z) \leq b, \quad then \ z \in B, \\ &\lambda_1 y_1 K(X_1, z) + \ldots + \lambda_n y_n K(X_n, z) \geq b, \quad then \ z \in G, \end{aligned} \tag{5.9}$$

where z is the new input data which is the evaluated target with r attributes. X_i represents each training sample. y_i is the class label of *ith* sample.

We notice here that a set of optimization variable w is substituted by a set of variables λ in the new model, which is the result of introduction of formulation (6) and thus lead to the employment of kernel function. KMCLP is a classification model which is applicable for nonlinear separable data set. With its optimal solution λ and b, the discrimination hyperplane is then constructed, and the two classes can be separated by it.

5.3 Linear Knowledge-incorporated MCLP Classifiers

5.3.1 Linear Knowledge

Prior knowledge in some classifiers usually consists of a set of rules, such as, if A then $x \in G$ (or $x \in B$), where condition A is relevant to the attributes of the input data. One example of such form of knowledge can be seen in the breast cancer recurrence or nonrecurrence prediction. Usually, doctors can judge if the cancer recur or not in terms of some measured attributes of the patients. The prior knowledge used by doctors in the breast cancer dataset includes two rules which depend on two features of the total 32 attributes: tumor size (T) and lymph node status (L). The rules are (Fung et al. 2005):

If $L\geq 5$ *and* $T\geq 4$ *Then RECUR and If* $L=0$ *and* $T\leq 1.9$ *Then NONRECUR*

The conditions $L\geq 5$ *and* $T\geq 4$ ($L=0$ *and* $T\leq 1.9$) in the above rules can be written into such inequality as $Cx\leq c$, where C is a matrix driven from the condition, x represents each individual sample, c is a vector. For example, if each sample x is expressed by a vector $[x_1,\ldots,x_L,\ldots,x_T,\ldots,x_r]^T$, for the rule: *if* $L\geq 5$ *and* $T\geq 4$ *then RECUR*, it also means: *if* $x_L\geq 5$ *and* $x_T\geq 4$, *then* $x\in RECUR$, where x_L and x_T are the corresponding values of attributes L and T of a certain sample data, r is the number of attributes. Then its corresponding inequality Cx " c can be written as:

$$\begin{bmatrix} 0 & \ldots & -1 & \ldots & 0 & \ldots & 0 \\ 0 & \ldots & 0 & \ldots & -1 & \ldots & 0 \end{bmatrix} x \leq \begin{bmatrix} -5 \\ -4 \end{bmatrix}.$$

where x is the vector with r attributes include two features relevant to prior knowledge.

Similarly, the condition $L=0$ *and* $T\leq 1.9$ can also be reformulated to be inequalities. With regard to the condition $L=0$, in order to express it into the formulation of $Cx\leq c$, we must replace it with the condition $L\geq 0$ *and* $L\leq 0$. Then the condition $L=0$ *and* $T\leq 1.9$ can be represented by two inequalities: $C^1x\leq c^1$ and $C^2x\leq c^2$, as follows:

$$\begin{bmatrix} 0 & \ldots & -1 & \ldots & 0 & \ldots & 0 \\ 0 & \ldots & 0 & \ldots & 1 & \ldots & 0 \end{bmatrix} x \leq \begin{bmatrix} 0 \\ 1.9 \end{bmatrix} \text{ and } \begin{bmatrix} 0 & \ldots & 1 & \ldots & 0 & \ldots & 0 \\ 0 & \ldots & 0 & \ldots & 1 & \ldots & 0 \end{bmatrix} x \leq \begin{bmatrix} 0 \\ 1.9 \end{bmatrix}$$

We notice the fact that the set $\{x\mid Cx\leq c\}$ can be regarded as polyhedral convex set. In Fig. 5.3, the triangle and rectangle are such sets.

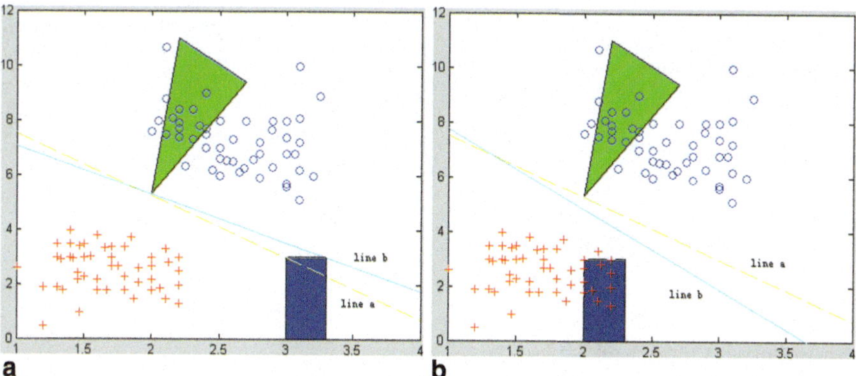

Fig. 5.3 The classification result by MCLP(line a) and Knowledge-Incorporated MCLP(line b)

In two-class classification problem, the result RECUR or NONRECUR is equal to the expression $x \in B$ or $x \in G$. So according to the above rules, we have:

$$Cx \le c \Rightarrow x \in G \;\; (or \;\; x \in B) \tag{5.10}$$

In MCLP classifier, if the classes are linearly separable, then $x \in G$ is equal to $x^T w \ge b$, similarly, $x \in B$ is equal to $x^T w \le b$. That is, the following implication must hold:

$$Cx \le c \Rightarrow x^T w \ge b \;\; (or \;\; x^T w \le b) \tag{5.11}$$

For a given (w,b), the implication $Cx \le c \Rightarrow x^T w \ge b$ holds, this also means that $Cx \le c, x^T w < b$ has no solution x. According to nonhomogeneous Farkas theorem, we can conclude that $C^T u + w = 0, c^T u + b \le 0, u \ge 0,$ has a solution (u, w) (Fung et al. 2002).

The above statement is able to be added to constraints of an optimization problem. In this way, the prior knowledge in the form of some equalities and inequalities in constraints is embedded to the original multiple linear programming (MCLP) model. The knowledge-incorporated MCLP model is described in the following.

5.3.2 Linear Knowledge-incorporated MCLP

Now, we are to explain the knowledge-incorporated MCLP model. This model is to deal with linear knowledge and linear separable data. The combination of the two kinds of input can help to improve the performances of both methods.

Suppose there are a series of knowledge sets as follows:

If $C^i x \le c^i, i = 1,\ldots,k$ Then $x \in G$

If $D^j x \le d^j, j = 1,\ldots,l$ Then $x \in B$

This knowledge also means the convex sets $\{x \mid C^i x \le c^i\}, i = 1,\ldots,k$ lie on the G side of the bounding plane, the convex sets $\{x \mid D^j x \le d^j\}, j = 1,\ldots,l$ on the B side.

Based on the above theory in the last section, we converted the knowledge to the following constraints:

There exist $u^i,\ i = 1,\ldots,k,\ v^j, j = 1,\ldots,l,$ such that:

$$\begin{aligned} &C^{iT} u^i + w = 0, \quad c^{iT} u^i + b \le 0, \quad u^i \ge 0, \quad i = 1,\ldots,k \\ &D^{jT} v^j - w = 0, \quad d^{jT} v^j - b \le 0, \quad v^j \ge 0, \quad j = 1,\ldots,l \end{aligned} \tag{5.12}$$

However, there is no guarantee that such bounding planes precisely separate all the points. Therefore, some error variables need to be added to the above formulas. The constraints are further revised to be:

There exist $u^i,\ r^i,\ \rho^i,\ i = 1,\ldots,k \;\; and \;\; v^j,\ s^j,\ \sigma^j,\ j = 1,\ldots,l,$ such that:

$$
\begin{aligned}
&-r^i \le C^{iT}u^i + w \le r^i, \quad c^{iT}u^i + b \le \rho^i, \quad u^i \ge 0, \quad i = 1,\ldots,k \\
&-s^j \le D^{jT}v^j - w \le s^j, \quad d^{jT}v^j - b \le \sigma^j, \quad v^j \ge 0, \quad j = 1,\ldots,l
\end{aligned}
\tag{5.13}
$$

After that, we embed the above constraints to the MCLP classifier, and obtained the knowledge-incorporated MCLP classifier:

$$
\begin{aligned}
&\text{Minimize} \quad d_\alpha^+ + d_\alpha^- + d_\beta^+ + d_\beta^- + C\left(\sum (r^i + \rho^i) + \sum (s^j + \sigma^j)\right) \\
&\text{Subject to:} \\
&\quad \alpha^* + \sum_{i=1}^{n} \alpha_i = d_\alpha^- - d_\alpha^+ \\
&\quad \beta^* - \sum_{i=1}^{n} \beta_i = d_\beta^- - d_\beta^+ \\
&\quad x_{11}w_1 + \ldots + x_{1r}w_r = b + \alpha_1 - \beta_1, \quad \text{for } A_1 \in B, \\
&\quad \vdots \\
&\quad x_{n1}w_1 + \ldots + x_{nr}w_r = b - \alpha_n + \beta_n, \quad \text{for } A_n \in G, \\
&\quad -r^i \le C^{i'}u^i + w \le r^i, \qquad i=1,\ldots,k \\
&\quad c^{i'}u^i + b \le \rho^i \\
&\quad -s^j \le D^{j'}v^j - w \le s^j, \qquad j=1,\ldots,l \\
&\quad d^{j'}v^j - b \le \sigma^j \\
&\quad \alpha_1,\ldots,\alpha_n \ge 0, \quad \beta_1,\ldots,\beta_n \ge 0, \quad (u^i, v^j, r^i, \rho^i, s^j, \sigma^j) \ge 0
\end{aligned}
\tag{5.14}
$$

In this model, all the inequality constraints are derived from the prior knowledge. The last objective $C(\sum (r^i + \rho^i) + \sum (s^j + \sigma^j))$ is about the slack error variables added to the original knowledge equality constraints. The last objective attempts to drive the error variables to zero. We want to get the best bounding plane (w, b) in formula (1) by solving this model to separate the two classes.

We notice the fact that if we set the value of parameter C to be zero, this means to take no account of knowledge. Then this model will be equal to the original MCLP model. Theoretically, the larger the value of C, the greater impact on the classification result of the knowledge sets.

5.3.3 *Linear Knowledge-Incorporated KMCLP*

If the data set is nonlinear separable, the above model will be inapplicable. We need to figure out how to embed prior knowledge into the KMCLP model, which can solve nonlinear separable problem.

As is shown in the above part, in generating KMCLP model, we suppose:

$$w = \sum_{i=1}^{n} \lambda_i y_i X_i \tag{5.15}$$

If expressed by matrix, the above formulation will be:

$$w = X^T Y \lambda \tag{5.16}$$

where Y is $n*n$ diagonal matrix, the value of each diagonal element depends on the class label of the corresponding sample data, which can be $+1$ or -1. X is the $n*r$ input matrix with n samples, r attributes. λ is a n-dimensional vector $\lambda=(\lambda_1, \lambda_2, \ldots, \lambda_n)^T$.

$$Y = \begin{bmatrix} y_1 & 0 & \cdots & 0 \\ 0 & y_2 & \cdots & 0 \\ \vdots & \vdots & \ddots & \vdots \\ 0 & 0 & \cdots & y_n \end{bmatrix}, \qquad X = \begin{bmatrix} x_{11} & x_{12} & \cdots & x_{1r} \\ x_{21} & x_{22} & \cdots & x_{2r} \\ \vdots & \vdots & \ddots & \vdots \\ x_{n1} & x_{n2} & \cdots & x_{nr} \end{bmatrix}$$

Therefore, w in the original MCLP model is replaced by $X^T Y\lambda$, thus forming the KMCLP model. And in this new model, the value of each λ_i is to be worked out by the optimization model.

In order to incorporate prior knowledge into KMCLP model, the inequalities about the knowledge must be transformed to be the form with λ_i instead of w. Enlightened by the KMCLP model, we also introduce kernel to the expressions of knowledge. Firstly, the equalities in (5.12) are multiplied by input matrix X (Fung et al. 2003). Then replacing w with $X^T Y\lambda$, (5.12) will be:

$$\begin{aligned} &XC^{iT}u^i + XX^T Y\lambda = 0, \quad c^{iT}u^i + b \le 0, \quad u^i \ge 0, \quad i = 1,\ldots,k \\ &XD^{jT}v^j - XX^T Y\lambda = 0, \quad d^{jT}v^j - b \le 0, \quad v^j \ge 0, \quad j = 1,\ldots,l \end{aligned} \tag{5.17}$$

Kernel function is introduced here to replace XC^{iT} and XX^T. Also slack errors are added to the expressions, then such kind of constraints are formulated:

$$\begin{aligned} &-r^i \le K(X, C^{iT})u^i + K(X, X^T)Y\lambda \le r^i, \quad i=1,\ldots,k \\ &c^{iT}u^i + b \le \rho^i \\ &-s^j \le K(X, D^{jT})v^j - K(X, X^T)Y\lambda \le s^j, \quad j=1,\ldots,l \\ &d^{jT}v^j - b \le \sigma^j \end{aligned} \tag{5.18}$$

These constraints can be easily embedded to KMCLP model (5.8) as the constraints acquired from prior knowledge.

Knowledge-incorporated KMCLP classifier:

$$
\begin{aligned}
&\text{Min}(d_\alpha^+ + d_\alpha^- + d_\beta^+ + d_\beta^-) + C\left(\sum_{i=1}^{k}(r^i + \rho^i) + \sum_{j=1}^{l}(s^j + \sigma^j)\right) \\
\text{s.t.}\quad &\lambda_1 y_1 K(X_1, X_1) + \ldots + \lambda_n y_n K(X_n, X_1) = b + \alpha_1 - \beta_1, \quad \text{for } X_1 \in \text{B}, \\
&\vdots \\
&\lambda_1 y_1 K(X_1, X_n) + \ldots + \lambda_n y_n K(X_n, X_n) = b - \alpha_n + \beta_n, \quad \text{for } X_n \in \text{G}, \\
&\alpha^* + \sum_{i=1}^{n} \alpha_i = d_\alpha^- - d_\alpha^+, \\
&\beta^* - \sum_{i=1}^{n} \beta_i = d_\beta^- - d_\beta^+, \\
&-r^i \le K(X, C^{iT})u^i + K(X, X^T)Y\lambda \le r^i, \quad i=1,\ldots,k \\
&c^{iT}u^i + b \le \rho^i \\
&-s^j \le K(X, D^{jT})v^j - K(X, X^T)Y\lambda \le s^j, \quad j=1,\ldots,l \\
&d^{jT}v^j - b \le \sigma^j \\
&\alpha_1, \ldots, \alpha_n \ge 0, \quad \beta_1, \ldots, \beta_n \ge 0, \quad \lambda_1, \ldots, \lambda_n \ge 0, \\
&(u^i, v^j, r^i, \rho^i, s^j, \sigma^j) \ge 0 \\
&d_\alpha^-, d_\alpha^+, d_\beta^-, d_\beta^+ \ge 0
\end{aligned}
\tag{5.19}
$$

In this model, all the inequality constraints are derived from prior knowledge. u^i, $v^i \in R^p$, where p is the number of conditions in one knowledge. For example, in the knowledge *if* $x_L \ge 5$ *and* $x_T \ge 4$, *then* $x \in RECUR$, the value of p is 2. r^i, ρ^i, s^j and σ^j are all real numbers. And the last objective $\text{Min}\sum(r^i + \rho^i) + \sum(s^j + \sigma^j)$ is about the slack error variables added to the original knowledge equality constraints. As we talked in last section, the larger the value of C, the greater impact on the classification result of the knowledge sets.

In this model, several parameters need to be set before optimization process. Apart from C we talked about above, the others are parameter of kernel function q (if we choose RBF kernel) and the ideal compromise solution α^* and β^*. We want to get the best bounding plane (λ, b) by solving this model to separate the two classes. And the discrimination function of the two classes is:

$$
\begin{aligned}
&\lambda_1 y_1 K(X_1, z) + \ldots + \lambda_n y_n K(X_n, z) \le b, \quad \textit{then} \quad z \in B \\
&\lambda_1 y_1 K(X_1, z) + \ldots + \lambda_n y_n K(X_n, z) \ge b, \quad \textit{then} \quad z \in G
\end{aligned}
\tag{5.20}
$$

where z is the input data which is the evaluated target with r attributes. X_i represents each training sample. y_i is the class label of *ith* sample.

5.4 Nonlinear Knowledge-Incorporated KMCLP Classifier

5.4.1 Nonlinear Knowledge

In the above models, the prior knowledge we deal with is linear. That means the conditions in the above rules can be written into such inequality as $Cx \leq c$, where C is a matrix driven from the condition, x represents each individual sample, c is a vector. The set $\{x | Cx \leq c\}$ can be viewed as polyhedral convex set, which is a linear geometry in input space. But, if the shape of the region which consists of knowledge is nonlinear, for example, $\{x | \|x\|^2 \leq c\}$, how to deal with such kind of knowledge?

Suppose the region is nonlinear convex set, we describe the region by $g(x) \leq 0$. If the data is in this region, it must belong to class B. Then, such kind of nonlinear knowledge may take the form of:

$$\begin{aligned} g(x) \leq 0 &\Rightarrow x \in B \\ h(x) \leq 0 &\Rightarrow x \in G \end{aligned} \tag{5.21}$$

Here $g(x)$: $R^r \rightarrow R^p$ $(x \in \Gamma)$ and $h(x)$: $R^r \rightarrow R^q$ $(x \in \Delta)$ are functions defined on a subset Γ and Δ of R^r which determine the regions in the input space. All the data satisfied $g(x) \leq 0$ must belong to the class B and $h(x) \leq 0$ to the class G.

With KMCLP classifier, this knowledge equals to:

$$\begin{aligned} g(x) \leq 0 &\Rightarrow \lambda_1 y_1 K(X_1, x) + \ldots + \lambda_n y_n K(X_n, x) \leq b, (x \in \Gamma) \\ h(x) \leq 0 &\Rightarrow \lambda_1 y_1 K(X_1, x) + \ldots + \lambda_n y_n K(X_n, x) \geq b, (x \in \Delta) \end{aligned} \tag{5.22}$$

This implication can be written in the following equivalent logical form (Mangasarian and Wild 2007):

$$\begin{aligned} &g(x) \leq 0 \quad \lambda_1 y_1 K(X_1, x) + \ldots + \lambda_n y_n K(X_n, x) - b > 0, \text{has no solution } x \in \Gamma. \\ &h(x) \leq 0 \quad \lambda_1 y_1 K(X_1, x) + \ldots + \lambda_n y_n K(X_n, x) - b < 0, \text{ has no solution } x \in \Delta. \end{aligned} \tag{5.23}$$

The above expressions hold, then there exist $v \in R^p$, $r \in R^q$, $v, r \geq 0$ such that:

$$\begin{aligned} &-\lambda_1 y_1 K(X_1, x) - \ldots - \lambda_n y_n K(X_n, x) + b + v^T g(x) \geq 0, (x \in \Gamma) \\ &\lambda_1 y_1 K(X_1, x) + \ldots + \lambda_n y_n K(X_n, x) - b + r^T h(x) \geq 0, (x \in \Delta) \end{aligned} \tag{5.24}$$

Add some slack variables on the above two inequalities, then they are converted to:

$$\begin{aligned} &-\lambda_1 y_1 K(X_1, x) - \ldots - \lambda_n y_n K(X_n, x) + b + v^T g(x) + s \geq 0, (x \in \Gamma) \\ &\lambda_1 y_1 K(X_1, x) + \ldots + \lambda_n y_n K(X_n, x) - b + r^T h(x) + t \geq 0, (x \in \Delta) \end{aligned} \tag{5.25}$$

The above statement is able to be added to constraints of an optimization problem.

5.4.2 Nonlinear Knowledge-incorporated KMCLP

Suppose there are a series of knowledge sets as follows:

If $g_i(x) \leq 0$, Then $x \in B$ ($g_i(x)$: $R^r \to R^{p_i}$ $(x \in \Gamma_i)$, $i = 1,\ldots,k$)

If $h_j(x) \leq 0$, Then $x \in G$ ($h_j(x)$: $R^r \to R^{q_j}$ $(x \in \Delta_j)$, $j = 1,\ldots,l$)

Based on the above theory in last section, we converted the knowledge to the following constraints:

There exist $v_i \in R^{p_i}$, $i = 1,\ldots,k$, $r_j \in R^{q_j}$, $j = 1,\ldots,l$, $v_i, r_j \geq 0$ such that:

$$\begin{aligned} &-\lambda_1 y_1 K(X_1,x) - \ldots - \lambda_n y_n K(X_n,x) + b + v_i^T g_i(x) + s_i \geq 0, \ (x \in \Gamma) \\ &\lambda_1 y_1 K(X_1,x) + \ldots + \lambda_n y_n K(X_n,x) - b + r_j^T h_j(x) + t_j \geq 0, \ (x \in \Delta) \end{aligned} \tag{5.26}$$

These constraints can be easily imposed to KMCLP model (4.8) as the constraints acquired from prior knowledge.

Nonlinear knowledge in KMCLP classifier (Zhang et al. 2002):

$$\begin{aligned} &\text{Min}(d_\alpha^+ + d_\alpha^- + d_\beta^+ + d_\beta^-) + C\Big(\sum_{i=1}^{k} s_i + \sum_{j=1}^{l} t_j\Big) \\ \text{s.t.} \quad &\lambda_1 y_1 K(X_1,X_1) + \ldots + \lambda_n y_n K(X_n,X_1) = b + \alpha_1 - \beta_1, , \quad \text{for } X_1 \in \text{B}, \\ &\vdots \\ &\lambda_1 y_1 K(X_1,X_n) + \ldots + \lambda_n y_n K(X_n,X_n) = b - \alpha_n + \beta_n , \quad \text{for } X_n \in \text{G}, \\ &\alpha^* + \sum_{i=1}^{n} \alpha_i = d_\alpha^- - d_\alpha^+, \\ &\beta^* - \sum_{i=1}^{n} \beta_i = d_\beta^- - d_\beta^+, \\ &-\lambda_1 y_1 K(X_1,x) - \ldots - \lambda_n y_n K(X_n,x) + b + v_i^T g_i(x) + s_i \geq 0, \qquad \text{i}=1,\ldots,\text{k} \\ &s_i \geq 0, \qquad \text{i}=1,\ldots,\text{k} \\ &\lambda_1 y_1 K(X_1,x) + \ldots + \lambda_n y_n K(X_n,x) - b + r_j^T h_j(x) + t_j \geq 0, \qquad \text{j}=1,\ldots,l \\ &t_j \geq 0, \quad \text{j}=1,\ldots,l \\ &\alpha_1,\ldots,\alpha_n \geq 0, \quad \beta_1,\ldots,\beta_n \geq 0, \quad \lambda_1,\ldots,\lambda_n \geq 0, \\ &(v_i, r_j) \geq 0 \\ &d_\alpha^-, d_\alpha^+, d_\beta^-, d_\beta^+ \geq 0 \end{aligned} \tag{5.27}$$

In this model, all the inequality constraints are derived from the prior knowledge. The last objective $C(\sum_{i=1}^{k} s_i + \sum_{j=1}^{l} t_j)$ is about the slack error. Theoretically, the larger the value of C, the greater impact on the classification result of the knowledge sets.

The parameters need to be set before optimization process are C, q (if we choose RBF kernel), α^* and β^*. The best bounding plane of this model decided by (λ, b) of the two classes is the same with formula (5.20).

5.5 Numerical Experiments

All above models are linear programming models which are easily solved by some commercial software such as SAS LP and MATLAB. In this paper, MATLAB6.0 is employed in the solution process. To prove the effectiveness of these models, we apply them to four data sets which consist of knowledge sets and sample data. Among them, three are synthetic examples, one is real application.

5.5.1 *A Synthetic Data Set*

To demonstrate the geometry of the knowledge-incorporated MCLP, we apply the model to a synthetic example with 100 points. These points are marked by "o" and "+" in Fig. 5.3 which represent two different classes. Original MCLP model (5) and knowledge-incorporated MCLP model (14) are applied to get the separation lines of the two classes. Figure 5.3 depicts the results of the separation lines (***line a*** and ***line b***) generated by the two models.

The rectangle and the triangle in Fig. 5.3 are two knowledge sets for the classes. ***Line a*** is the discriminate line of the two classes by the origional MCLP model (C=0), then ***line b*** is generated by the Knowledge-Incorporated MCLP model (C=1). From the above figure, we can see that the separation line changed when we incorporated prior knowledge into MCLP(C is set to be 1), thus results in two different lines ***a*** and ***b***. And when we change the rectangle knowledge set's position, the line b is also changed with it. This means that the knowledge does have effect on the classifier, and our new model seems valid to deal with the prior knowledge.

5.5.2 *Checkerboard Data*

For knowledge-incorporated KMCLP which can handle nonlinear separable data, we construct a checkerboard dataset (Fig. 5.4) to test the model. This data set consists of 16 points, and no neighboring points belong to one class. The two squares in the bottom of the figure are prior knowledge for the classes (Fung et al. 2003). In this case, we can see the impressive influence of the knowledge on the separation curve.

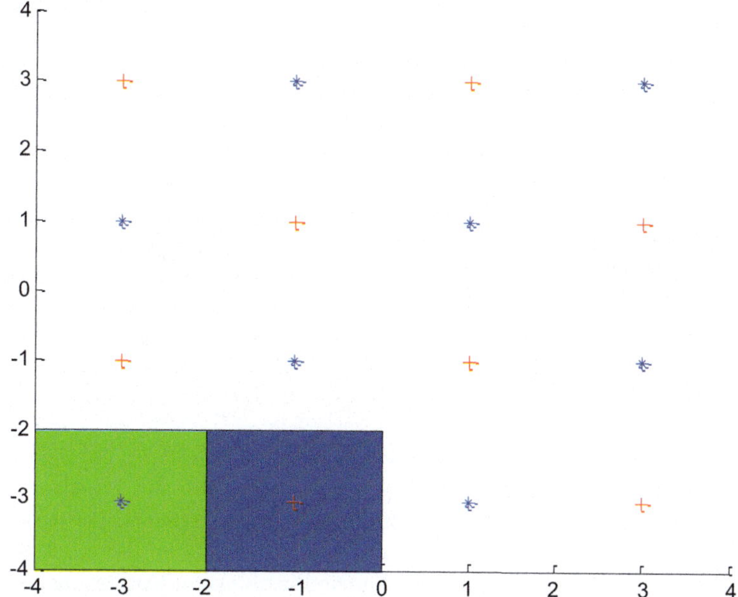

Fig. 5.4 The checkerboard data set

Experiments are conducted with the knowledge-incorporated KMCLP model with $C = 0$, 0.001, 0.01, 0.1 and 1. And, after grid search process, we choose the best suitable value for parameters: $q = 1$, $\alpha^* = 10^{-5}$, $\beta^* = 10^6$. The results of the separation curve generated by knowledge-incorporated KMCLP are showed in Fig. 5.5.

We notice the fact that when $C = 0.01$(Fig. 5.5a) or even smaller value, the separation curve can not be as sharp as that of a bigger value of C like in Fig. 5.5b. And bigger C means more contribution of prior knowledge to the optimization result. Obviously in this checkerboard case, sharper line will be more preferable, because it can lead to more accurate separation result when faced with larger checkerboard data.

However in Fig. 5.5b, we also find when set $C = 0$ the separation curve can also be sharp. It seems to have no difference with $C = 0.1$ and 1. This demonstrates the original KMCLP model can achieve a preferable result by itself even without knowledge.

5.5.3 *Wisconsin Breast Cancer Data with Nonlinear Knowledge*

Concerning real word cases, we apply the nonlinear knowledge model (27) to Wisconsin breast cancer prognosis data set for predicting recurrence or nonrecurrence of the disease. This data set concerns 10 features obtained from a fine needle aspirate (Mangasarian and Wild 2007; Murphy and Aha 1992). Of each feature, the mean, standard error, and worst or largest value were computed for each image, thus resulting in 30 features. Besides, two histological features, tumor size and lymph

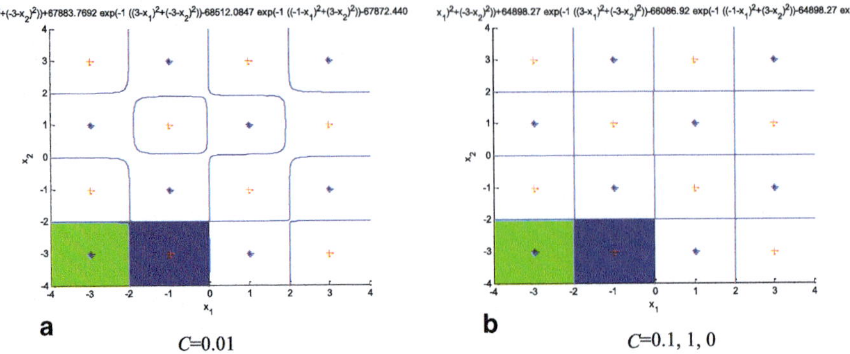

Fig. 5.5 The classification results by Knowledge-Incorporated KMCLP on checkerboard data set. **a** $C=0.01$. **b** $C=0.1, 1, 0$

node status, obtained during surgery for breast cancer patients, are also included in the attributes. According to the characteristic of the data set, we separate the features into four groups F1, F2, F3 and F4, which represent the mean, standard error, worst or largest value of each image and histological features, respectively. We plotted each point and the prior knowledge in the 2-dimensional space in terms of the last two attributes in Fig. 5.6. The three geometric regions in the figure are the corresponding knowledge. And the points marked by "o" and "+" represent two different classes. With the three knowledge regions, we can only discriminate a part of "o" data. So we need to use multiple criteria linear programming classification method plus prior knowledge to solve the problem.

The prior knowledge involved here is nonlinear knowledge. The whole knowledge consists of three regions, which correspond to the following three implications:

$$\left\|\begin{pmatrix} 5.5\times x_{iT} & 5.5\times 7 \\ x_{iL} & 9 \end{pmatrix}\right\| + \left\|\begin{pmatrix} 5.5\times x_{iT} & 5.5\times 4.5 \\ x_{iL} & 27 \end{pmatrix}\right\| - 23.0509 \le 0 \Rightarrow X_i \in RECUR$$

$$\begin{pmatrix} -x_{iL} + 5.7143\times x_{iT} - 5.75 \\ x_{iL} - 2.8571\times x_{iT} - 4.25 \\ -x_{iL} + 6.75 \end{pmatrix} \le 0 \Rightarrow X_i \in RECUR$$

$$\frac{1}{2}(x_{iT} - 3.35)^2 + (x_{iL} - 4)^2 - 1 \le 0 \Rightarrow X_i \in RECUR$$

Here, x_{iT} is the tumor size, and x_{iL} is the number of lymph nodes of training sample X_i. In Fig. 5.6, the ellipse near to the upper-right corner is about the knowledge of the first implication. The triangular region corresponds to the second implication. And the ellipse in the bottom corresponds to the third implication. The red circle points represent the recurrence samples, while the blue cross points represent non-recurrence samples.

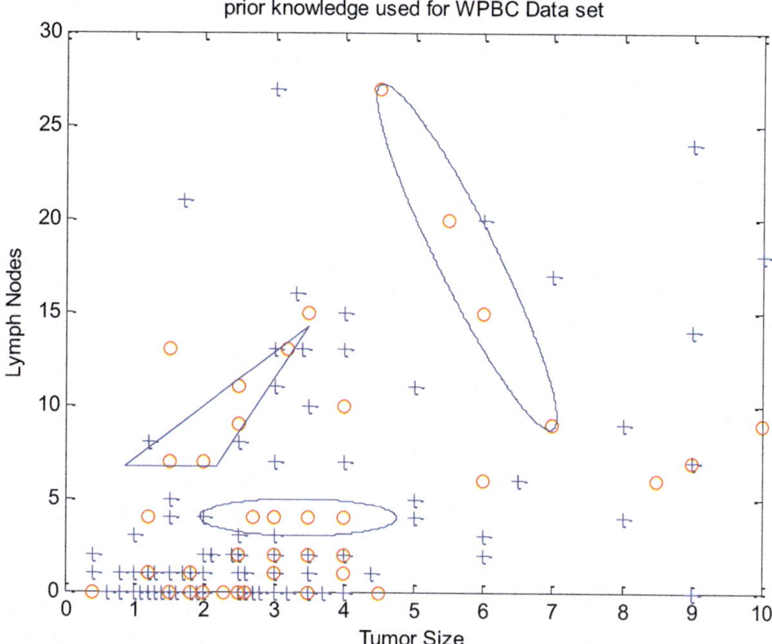

Fig. 5.6 WPBC data set and prior knowledge

Before classification, we scaled the attributes to [0, 1]. And in order to balance the samples in the two classes, we need to randomly choose 46 samples, which is the exact number of the recurrence samples, from the nonrecurrence group. We choose the value of q from the range $[10^{-6}, \ldots, 10^{6}]$, and find the best value of q for RBF kernel is 1. Leave-one-out cross-validation method is used to get the accuracy of the classification of our method.

Experiments are conducted with respect to the combinations of four subgroups of attributes. $C=0$ means the model takes no account of knowledge. The results are shown here.Tab 5.1

The above table shows that classified by our model with knowledge ($C=1$), the accuracies are higher than the results without knowledge ($C=0$). The highest improvement of the four attributes groups is about 6.7%. Although it is not as much as we expected, we can see the knowledge dose make good results on this classification problem. Probably, the knowledge here is not as precise as can pro-

Table 5.1 The accuracies of classification on Wisconsin breast cancer data set.

	F1 and F4 (%)	F1, F3 and F4 (%)	F3 and F4 (%)	F1,F2,F3 and F4 (%)
$C=0$	51.807	59.783	57.609	63.043
$C=1$	56.522	66.304	63.043	64.13

duce noticeable improvement to the precision. But it does have influence on the classification result. If we have much more precise knowledge, the classifier will be more accurate.

5.6 Conclusions

In this section, we summarize the relevant works which combine the prior knowledge and MCLP or KMCLP model to solve the problem when input consists of not only training example, but also prior knowledge. Specifically, how to deal with linear and nonlinear knowledge in MCLP and KMCLP model is the main concerning of this paper. Linear prior knowledge in the form of polyhedral knowledge sets in the input space of the given data can be expressed into logical implications, which can further be converted into a series of equalities and inequalities. These equalities and inequalities can be imposed to the constraints of original MCLP and KMCLP model, then help to generate the separation hyperplane of the two classes. In the same way, nonlinear knowledge can also be incorporated as the constraints into the KMCLP model to make it possible to separate two classes with help of prior knowledge. All these models are linear programming formulations, which can be easily solved by some commercial software. With the optimum solution, the separation hyperplane of the two classes can be formulated. Numerical tests indicate that these models are effective when combining prior knowledge with the training sample as the classification principle.

Chapter 6
Knowledge Extraction from Support Vector Machines

Support Vector Machines have been a promising tool for data mining during these years because of its good performance. However, a main weakness of SVMs is its lack of comprehensibility: people cannot understand what the "optimal hyperplane" means and are unconfident about the prediction especially when they are not the domain experts. In this section we introduce a new method to extract knowledge with a thought inspired by the decision tree algorithm and give a formula to find the optimal attributes for rule extraction. The experimental results will show the efficiency of this method.

6.1 Introduction

Support Vector Machines, which were widely used during these years for data mining tasks, have a main weakness that the generated nonlinear models are typically regarded as incomprehensible black-box models. Lack of comprehensibility makes it difficult to apply in fields such as medical diagnosis and financial data analysis (Martens 2008).

We briefly introduce two fundamental kinds of rules. (Martens 2008): Propositional rule, which is most frequently used, is simple "If … Then … "expressions based on conventional propositional logic; The second is M-of-N rules which usually expressed as "If {at least/exactly/at most} M of the N conditions $(C_1, C_2 \ldots C_N)$ are satisfied Then Class = 1". Most of the existing algorithms extract propositional rules while only little algorithm, such as TREPAN, could extract the second rules. (Martens 2008).

There are several techniques to extract rules from SVMs so far, and one potential method of classifying these rule extraction techniques is in terms of the "translucency", which is of the view taken within the rule extraction method of the underlying classifier. Two main categories of rule extraction methods are known as decompositional and pedagogical (Diederich 2004). Decompositional approach is closely

Y. Shi et al., *Intelligent Knowledge,* SpringerBriefs in Business,
DOI 10.1007/978-3-662-46193-8_6

related to the internal workings of the SVMs and their constructed hyperplane. On the other hand, pedagogical algorithms consider the trained model as a black box and directly extract rules which relate the inputs and outputs of the SVMs.

There are some performance criteria to evaluated the extracted rules, Craven and Shavlik (Craven 1996) listed such five criteria as follows:

1) Comprehensibility: The extent to which extracted representations are humanly comprehensible.
2) Fidelity: The extent to which the extracted representations model the black box from which they were extracted.
3) Accuracy: The ability of extracted representations to make accurate predictions on previously unseen cases.
4) Scalability: The ability of the method to scale to other models with large input spaces and large number of data.
5) Generality: The extent to which the method requires special training regimes or restrictions on the model architecture.

However, the last two are hard to quantize, so we consider the first three criteria only.

First we should introduce coverage to explain accuracy and fidelity better. If the condition (that is, all the attribute tests) in a rule antecedent holds true for a given instance, we say that the rule antecedent is satisfied and the rule covers the instance. Let n_{covers} be the number of instances covered by the rule R and D be the number of instances in the data. Then we can define coverage as:

$$coverage(R) = \frac{n_{covers}}{|D|} \tag{6.1}$$

Then we can define accuracy and fidelity easily. Let $n_{correct}$ be the number of instances correctly classified by R and $n_{coincide}$ be the number of instances which prediction by R coincides with prediction by the SVM decision function. We define them as:

$$accuracy(R) = \frac{n_{corrent}}{n_{covers}} \tag{6.2}$$

$$fidelity(R) = \frac{n_{coincide}}{n_{covers}} \tag{6.3}$$

There is not a definition about comprehensibility acknowledged by all. In this paper we define it as the number of attribute tests in rule antecedent in the simplest form, which means if there are two antecedents such as **If** $a_1 > \alpha$ and **If** $a_1 < \beta$ they can be simplified to the form **If** $\alpha < a_1 < \beta$.

However, the major algorithms for rule extraction from SVM have some disadvantages and limitations. There are two main decomposition methods: SVM+Prototypes and Fung. The main drawback of SVM+Prototypes is that the extracted rules are neither exclusive nor exhaustive which results in conflicting or missing rules for the classification of new data instances. The main disadvantage of Fung is that each of the extracted rules contain all possible input variables in its conditions, making the approach undesirable for larger input spaces as it will extract complex rules lack of interpretability, which is same to SVM+Prototypes. How to solve this problem? Rules extracted from decision tree are of good comprehensibility with remarkably less antecedents as the decision tree is constructed recursively rather than construct all the branches and leaf nodes at the same time. So our basic thought is to integrate the advantage of decision tree with rule extraction methods.

6.2 Decision Tree and Support Vector Machines

6.2.1 *Decision Tree*

Decision Tree is widely used in predictive model. A decision tree is a recursive structure that contains a combination of internal and leaf nodes. Each internal node specifies a test to be carried out on a single attribute and its branches indicate the possible outcomes of the test. So given an instance for which the associated class label is unknown, the attribute values are tested again the decision tree. A path is traced from the root to a leaf node which holds the class prediction.

A crucial step in decision tree is **splitting criterion**. The splitting criterion indicates the splitting attribute and may also indicate either a split-point or a splitting subset. The splitting attribute is determined so that the resulting partitions at each branch are as pure as possible. According to different algorithms of splitting attribute selection people have developed lots of decision tree algorithms such as ID3, C4.5 and CART.

6.2.2 *Support Vector Machines*

For a classification problem in which the training set is given by

$$T = \{(x_1, y_1), \ldots, (x_l, y_l)\} \in (R^n \times \{-1, 1\})^l, \tag{6.4}$$

where $x_i = (|x_i|_1, \ldots, |x_i|_n)^T \in R^n$ and $y_i \in \{-1, 1\}, i = 1, \ldots, l$, standard C-SVM constructs a convex quadratic programming

$$\min_{w,b,\xi} \quad \frac{1}{2}\|w\|^2 + C\sum_{i=1}^{l} \xi_i, \tag{6.5}$$

$$s.t. \;\; y_i\,((w \cdot x_i) + b) \geq 1 - \xi_i, i = 1, \ldots, l, \tag{6.6}$$

$$\xi_i \geq 0, i = 1, \ldots, l, \tag{6.7}$$

where C is the penalty parameter to compromise this conflict of two terms in the objective function.

6.3 Knowledge Extraction from SVMs

6.3.1 *Split Index*

We need to sort and find the attribute of optimal performance for splitting. There are two methods for this purpose: F-value and RFE (Deng and Tian 2009).

F-value aims at displaying the difference of each attribute. For a certain attribute k, it defines:

$$[x]_k^+ = \frac{1}{l_+} \sum_{y_i=1} [x_i]_k, k = 1, \ldots, n, \tag{6.8}$$

$$[x]_k^- = \frac{1}{l_-} \sum_{y_i=-1} [x_i]_k, k = 1, \ldots, n, \tag{6.9}$$

$$[x]_k = \frac{1}{l} \sum_{i=1}^{l} [x_i]_k, k = 1, \ldots, n, \tag{6.10}$$

and then defines the F-value of attribute k as:

$$F(k) = \frac{([x]_k^+ - [x]_k)^2 + ([x]_k^- - [x]_k)^2}{\frac{1}{l_+ - 1} \sum_{y_{i=1}} ([x_i]_k - [x]_k^+)^2 + \frac{1}{l_- - 1} \sum_{y_{i=-1}} ([x_i]_k - [x]_k^-)^2} \tag{6.11}$$

The numerator reflects the extent of difference between positive and negative points on attribute k while the denominator reflects the extent of variance of positive points and negative points respectively on attribute k. So the larger $F(k)$ is, the better the attribute k could distinguish these two categories.

RFE, which is short for **recursive feature elimination**, delete the attribute with minimal absolute value component of the vector w during each iteration. On the other hand it reveals that the attribute k, which correspond to the maximal absolute value component of $w: w_k$, is the most important attribute as it changes slightly it could result in the maximal change in the result of decision function.

But two figures as follows show a dilemma that we may not get a desired result while taking each one separately into consideration. Figure 6.1 shows that the attribute x_1 has a maximal w_1 as the gradient of the decision line, but $F(1)$ is too low,

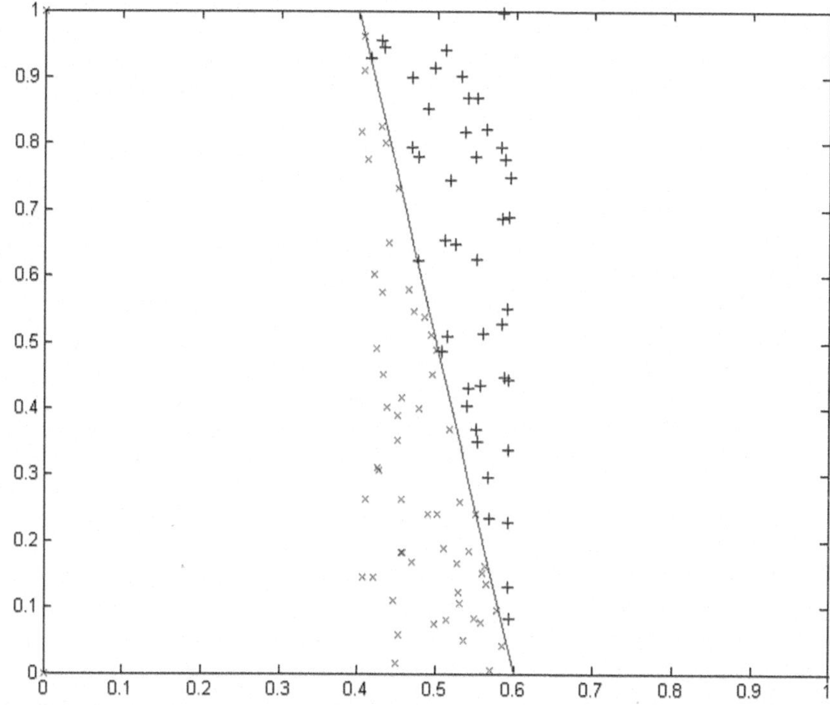

Fig. 6.1 Example of attribute with large w_1 but low $F(1)$

so the attribute x_1 is not a good attribute for splitting. Figure 6.2 shows that x_1 has a large $F(1)$ but a small w_1 and similarly we won't select x_1 as the splitting attribute.

So we could say both F-value and RFE are not always effective and stable and so they are not an excellent criterion to evaluate the splitting capacity.

Here we introduce a new criterion called **Split Index** to balance the effect of these two factors. The Split Index of attribute k could be computed as the formula:

$$SI(k) = F(k) * |w_k| \tag{6.12}$$

It is easy to compute and obviously we should normalize the training data to make sure that all the attributes are under the same condition. We assume that the training data we mentioned later has been normalized.

In order to test the rationality of (6.12) we use it in the two data showed in the figures above. The attribute x_2 has maximal SI value rather than x_1 which has large component w_1 on the first data. When applying to the second data the attribute x_2 has maximal SI value rather than x_1 which has larger $F(1)$. The results are better using SI value for splitting after computation.

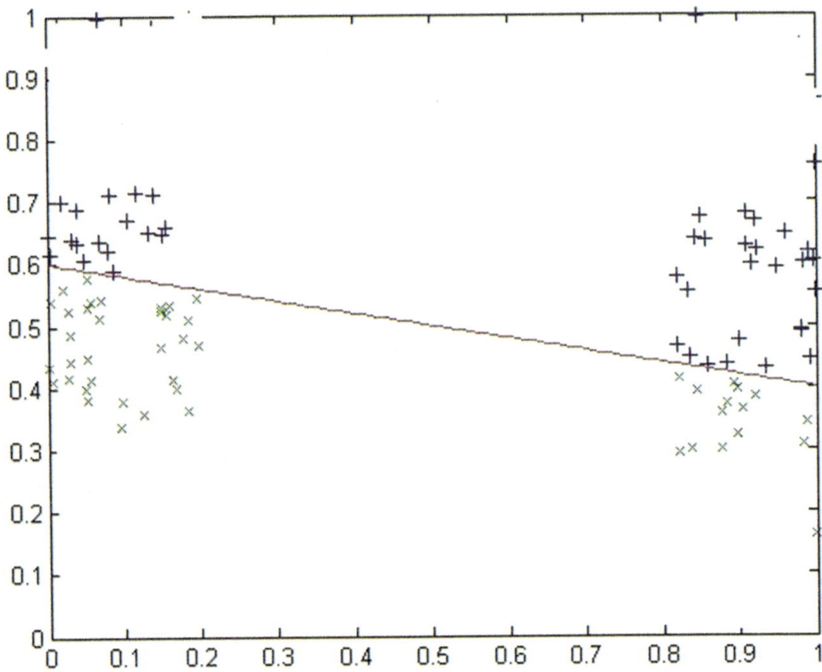

Fig. 6.2 Example of attribute with large $F(1)$ but low w_1

6.3.2 *Splitting and Rule Induction*

We choose the attribute k_i with maximal SI value as the splitting attribute during the *i*th iteration. In order to get rules with good comprehensibility we want to get subsets of k_i as pure as possible, which means we want to extract rules like **if** $a_{k_1} \le \alpha$ **then label** -1 and **if** $a_{k_1} \ge \beta$ **then label 1** with a perfect accuracy. α and β are named split points, which should make sure that the instances are covered as much as possible with coincide label. In addition a constraint inequality must be satisfied: $\alpha \le \beta$.

If $\alpha = \beta$ the algorithm ends with two rules mentioned above because all the attributes are covered. While $\alpha < \beta$ the rules cannot give the label of instances with $\alpha < a_{k_1} < \beta$, and a_{k_1} is of no use to these instances. We define the rest instances which satisfy $\alpha < a_{k_1} < \beta$ as the training data for the second iteration with a_{k_1} deleted and select a new attribute a_{k_2} with maximal SI value. The procedure could hold on until some stopping criteria are matched.

The method to compute α and β is crucial because the split points are closely related to the quality and performance of the extracted rules. The first method is to compute the cross point that the optimal decision hyperplane learned by SVM intersect the normalized border as showed in Fig. 6.3. The advantage is stability as they

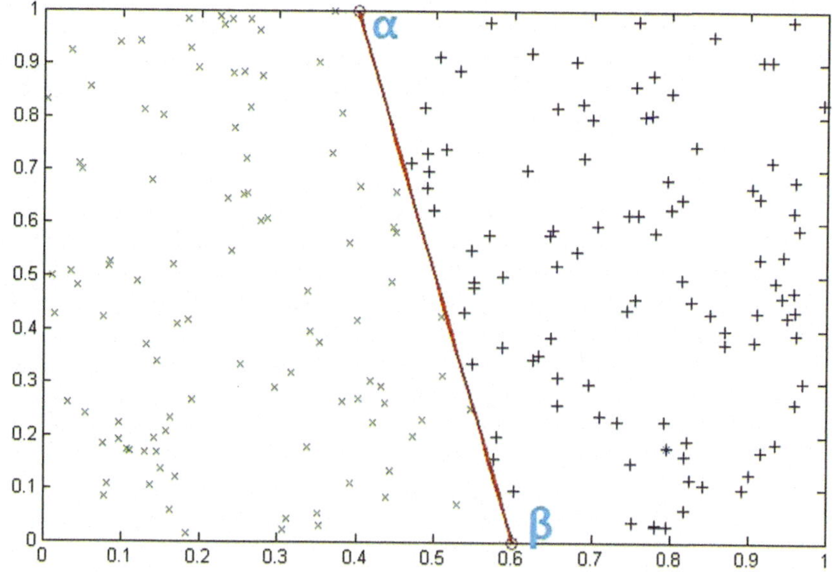

Fig. 6.3 and β are cross points the decision hyperplane intersect the border

are inducted directly from the SVM decision hyperplane. But the intuitive solutions may be hard to compute especially dealing with high dimensional data.

The main idea is to construct a statistic which is a good estimation of the split points and easy to compute. First we assume that the negative and positive points satisfied $0 \le a_{k_1} \le \alpha_i$ and $\beta_i \le a_{k_1} \le 1$ respectively on attribute k_i during ith iteration. So if $\alpha_i \le \beta_i$ we can induct these two rules:

$$\textit{if} \quad a_{k_i} \le a_i, \quad \textit{then} -1 \tag{6.13}$$

$$\textit{if} \quad a_{k_i} \ge a_i, \quad \textit{then}\ 1 \tag{6.14}$$

The accuracy of these two rules is 100% on the training data.

If $\alpha_i > \beta_i$ the accuracy of these two rules descends and we should find a better estimation. Set $S_{i_{pos}}$ to be the set that contains the value of attribute k_i on positive instances and $a_{i_{pos}}$ that satisfies:

$$a_{i_{pos}} \ge \alpha_i \tag{6.15}$$

$$\forall a_s \in S_{i_{pos}} \quad \textit{we have } a_{i_{pos}} \le a_s \tag{6.16}$$

Then we can yield this rule based on the fact that $a_{i_{pos}}$ is no less than α_i and β_i:

$$if\ a_{k_i} \geq a_{i_{pos}},\quad then\ 1 \tag{6.17}$$

According to (6.13) we yield another rule:

$$if\ a_{k_i} > \alpha_i,\quad then\ 1 \tag{6.18}$$

Its accuracy is also 100% and we consider (6.17) and (6.18) at the same time. We set the statistics $\overline{\beta}_i$ to be the median of $a_{i_{pos}}$ and α_i:

$$\overline{\beta}_i = (a_{i_{pos}} + \alpha_i)/2 \tag{6.19}$$

Now (6.17) and (6.18) could be replaced by:

$$if\ a_{k_i} \geq \overline{\beta}_i,\quad then\ 1 \tag{6.20}$$

Similarly we have corresponding rule on the negative instances:

$$if\ a_{k_i} \leq \overline{\alpha}_i,\quad then\ -1 \tag{6.21}$$

While:

$$\overline{\alpha}_i = (a_{i_{neg}} + \beta_i)/2 \tag{6.22}$$

$\overline{\alpha}_i$ and $\overline{\beta}_i$ are convergent with little error compared to α_i, β_i, $a_{i_{pos}}$ and $a_{i_{neg}}$. We can get formula as follows:

$$\overline{\alpha}_i = \begin{cases} \alpha_i & if\ \alpha_i \leq \beta_i; \\ (a_{i_{neg}} + \beta_i)/2 & else. \end{cases}$$

$$\overline{\beta}_i = \begin{cases} \beta_i & if\ \alpha_i \leq \beta_i; \\ (a_{i_{pos}} + \alpha_i)/2 & else. \end{cases}$$

And two yielded rules could have unique form:

$$if\ a_i \leq \overline{\alpha}_i,\quad then\ -1 \tag{6.23}$$

$$if\ a_i \geq \overline{\beta}_i,\quad then\ 1 \tag{6.24}$$

But one problem should be taken into consideration: the estimated statistics $\bar{\alpha}$ and $\bar{\beta}$ are strongly relied on α_i and β_i because they can also change the value of $a_{i_{pos}}$ and $a_{i_{neg}}$ according to (6.15). If there is an outlier the statistics biases too much. We mark α_{abnor} for this "abnormal" training data and α_{nor} while deleting the outlier. $|\alpha_{abnor} - \alpha_{nor}|$ may be great as the outlier plays an important role.

To eliminate the influence of outliers we need to make the data set linear separable in order that the label is coincided with what the SVM predict. According to the thought of pedagogical rule extraction algorithm known as **learn what SVM has learned** we could make the training set linear separable through 3 steps: (1) perform linear SVM on the normalized training data and get the decision function; (2) change the label into what the decision function predicts; (3) do the **second learning** on the linear separable data and get new decision function. After these steps we erase the outliers and $\bar{\alpha}$ and $\bar{\beta}$ are good approximation of split points.

In order to stop the iteration we construct two stopping criterion: (1) no attribute left; (2) $\alpha_i = \beta_i$ such that all the instances are covered by the rules extracted. Nevertheless, sometimes these criteria are too idealized. We should do some changes to make the criteria practical. If we take **comprehensibility** into consideration we should limit the number of antecedent because rules with too many antecedents are hard to comprehend and interpret especially when the training data is of high dimension. So the first criterion could be changed as follows: (1) The number of antecedents reaches the maximal threshold (5 usually).

On the other hand some rules may be redundant because their coverage is too low. We can prune them to keep the rules in rule set efficient and easy to understand. We can also integrate a rule into a "father" rule which developed during the last iteration with one antecedent less. This process could repeat, but it may reduce the accuracy of the "pruned" rules. Now the stopping criteria could be changed into:

1) The number of antecedents reaches the maximal threshold (5 usually) or no attribute left.
2) $\alpha_i = \beta_i$ Such that all the instances are covered by the rules extracted.
3) Too little instances remain in the training data.

For these rules are on the normalized data we should convert them into rules on original training data. The final step is to refer to the meaning of each attribute and change the norm such as "attribute k" into its real meaning.

Now we can summarize the algorithm as follows:

Algorithm 6.1 (Rule extraction from SVM using Split Index)

1) Divide the data into two parts: training data and test data;
2) Normalize the training set and do linear SVM on it, change the label into what the SVM predict;
3) Do linear SVM and get the decision function;
4) Compute Split Index value and choose the attribute a_{k_i} with maximal value as splitting attribute;
5) Compute α_i and β_i, then extract two rules respectively;

6) Delete the points covered by these two rules and make the instances rest to consist of the new training data with a_{k_i} deleted;
7) Repeat step 3–6 with $i \leftarrow i+1$ until any of the stopping criterion is matched;
8) Get the rule set and prune redundant rules;
9) Yield corresponding rules on original training data;
10) Do tests on test data and evaluate the criterion of the rules in rule set;

6.4 Numerical Experiments

We choose the wine data as our experimental data from UCI repository.

The data is the result of a chemical analysis of wines grown in the same region in Italy but derived from three different cultivars. The analysis determined the quantities of 13 constituents found in each of the three types of wines, and we select two types among the three for our two-class classification task and the first 130 instances are reserved. For the comprehensibility of our results we need to illustrate the meaning of each attribute for detail:

1) Alcohol;
2) Malic acid;
3) Ash;
4) Alcalinity of ash;
5) Magnesium;
6) Total phenols;
7) Flavanoids;
8) Nonflavanoid phenols;
9) Proanthocyanins;
10) Color intensity;
11) Hue;
12) OD280/OD315 of diluted wines;
13) Proline

We randomly select 65 instances as training data while the rest consist of the test data. During the first iteration the a_{13} has the maximal SI value and we have $\alpha_1 = 0.5043$, $\beta_1 = 0.326$, $a_{1_{pos}} = 0.5257, a_{1_{neg}} = 0.3138, \bar{\alpha}_1 = 0.32, \bar{\beta}_1 = 0.515$ after computation. According to (6.23) and (6.24) we yield two rules:

$$\textit{if } a_{13} \le 0.32, \quad \textit{then } 1 \tag{6.25}$$

$$\textit{if } a_{13} \ge 0.515, \quad \textit{then} \text{-}1 \tag{6.26}$$

On the second iteration the splitting attribute is a_2, and we have $\alpha_2 = 0.2617$, $\beta_2 = 0.2483$,

$a_{2_{pos}} = 0.3087, a_{2_{neg}} = 0.2416, \breve{\alpha}_2 = 0.245, \overline{\beta}_2 = 0.2852$, so we get two rules:

$$if\ a_2 \le 0.245, \quad then\ 1 \tag{6.27}$$

$$if\ a_2 \ge 0.2852, \quad then\text{-}1 \tag{6.28}$$

On the second iteration the splitting attribute is a_3 and there are only two instances in the training data, so we end the algorithm according to the stopping criterion (3). Then we yield rule set on the original training data:

$$R1: if\ \text{Pr}oline \le 726.64, \quad then\ 1 \tag{6.29}$$

$$R2: if\ \text{Pr}oline \ge 1000, \quad then - 1 \tag{6.30}$$

$$R3: if\ 726 < \text{Pr}oline < 1000\ and\ Malic\ Acid \le 1.62, \quad then\ 1 \tag{6.31}$$

$$R4: if\ 726 < \text{Pr}oline < 1000\ and\ Malic\ Acid \ge 1.74, \quad then - 1 \tag{6.32}$$

The following table shows the performance of rules on the test data (Table 6.1):

Table 6.1 EXPERIMENTAL RESULTS ON WINE TEST DATA

Rule	Fidelity	Accuracy	Coverage	Number of antecendent
R1	0.94	0.97	36/65	1
R2	0.95	1	20/65	1
R3	1	1	1/65	2
R4	1	1	4/65	2

Chapter 7
Intelligent Knowledge Acquisition and Application in Customer Churn

7.1 Introduction

Almost all of the entrepreneurs desire to have brain trust generated decision to support strategy which is regarded as the most critical factor since ancient times. With the coming of economic globalization era, followed by increasing competition, rapid technological change as well as gradually accrued scope of the strategy. The complexity of the explosive increase made only by the human brain generates policy decision-making appeared to be inadequate.

Extension theory is a new discipline engaged in studying the extension properties of things as well as its law and methods (Cai et al. 2003; Cai 1994). Bibliography (Han and Micheline 2006) combined the Extension theory with artificial intelligence, database technology, and software engineering to come up a software system called Extension Strategy Generating System (ESGS) which enable computer to mock human strategy generation. The idea of ESGS is an inevitable trend towards scientific and intelligent decision-making. However, There would have strategic explosion which would definitely lead to an increase in optimal evaluation of artificial workload, If it was not controlled appropriated during the procedure of strategy generation on computer.

In recent years, Data mining as an important instrument for knowledge discovery has been widespread concerned by scholars from all over the world (Han and Micheline 2006; Olson and Shi 2007). It has already been employed in Finance and insurance (Olson and Shi 2007), Marketing (Chen and Hu 2005), bio-medical treatment (Larry et al. 2004), Internet customer analysis (Nie et al. 2006) etc. However, the pattern knowledge obtained from data mining is only the description of characteristic of things, which requires a further combination of expert experience, and finally come out the strategy for solution relying on analysis of business experts.

A website is one of China's major portal sites, "one of the four major portals in China". the company is always maintain the leading position of the industry in china in the development of Internet applications, services and other technology. Since its inception in June 1997, by virtue of advanced technology and high quality service, it is welcomed by the majority of Internet users, and named as China's top

Y. Shi et al., *Intelligent Knowledge,* SpringerBriefs in Business,
DOI 10.1007/978-3-662-46193-8_7

ten sites two times by the China Internet Network Information Center (CNNIC). in 2010 its turnover is 5.7 billion Yuan. Now it provides the online game, e-mail, news, blog, forum, search engine and virtual community services.

Although the website company own a large number of charge-mail registered users. However, some customers are lost due to the intense competition and other objective reasons. The acquirement of the 245 rule is through applying decision tree data mining algorithm to divide user into “the existing user, the freezing user and the lost user” and predict the user type. However, It cannot acquire strategy which promote user transformation from those rules, Actually, the freeze user and the normal user can transform into each other in certain condition. Finding transformation knowledge among different users will provide subordinate strategy for strategy.

7.2 The Data Mining Process and Result Analysis

To get intelligent knowledge for prevention of the customers churn through data mining, project group launched the four phases of work according to the following six steps.

The Four phases are:

1. Data Exploration Phase
2. Experimental Mining Phase
3. Data mining Phase
4. Validation and Follow-ups

The six steps are:

1. Understand the process flow, and the distribution of the data, build up the data map.
2. Discuss the selected dataset, compile data dictionary
3. Pre selection of the data fields
4. Determine the process method for the data mining field
5. Determine the data mining plan.
6. Using MCLP software, input integrated and cleaned data in the table of TXT file, then make dataset partition, modeling, get the scoring model step by step, and visualize the results collated. The following figure is data map for customer churn prevention (Fig. 7.1):

Data collection and consolidation

1. A list is selected by the data field of the data dictionary, and data retrieval based on the data retrieval method
2. Compile the log processing program, transform the data into structured data
3. Label the structured data based on the labels from the service department, authenticated by the technical department
4. Data consolidation
5. Cleaning transformation and discretization.

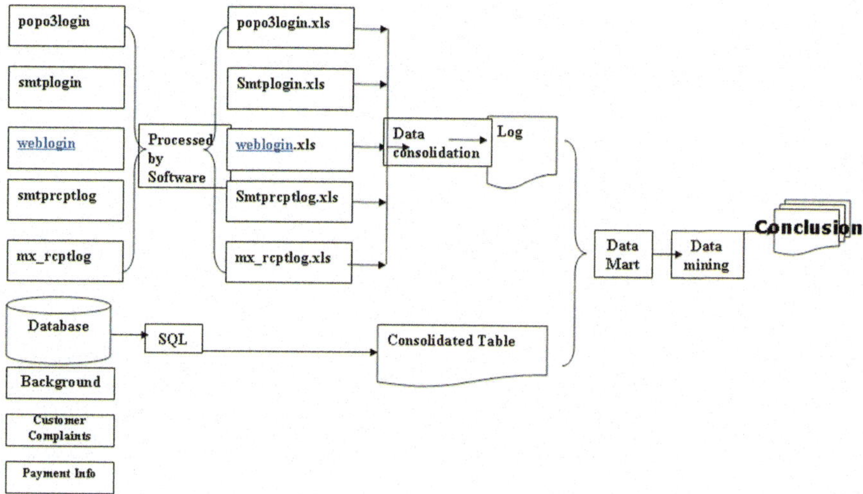

Fig. 7.1 Data map for customer churn prevention

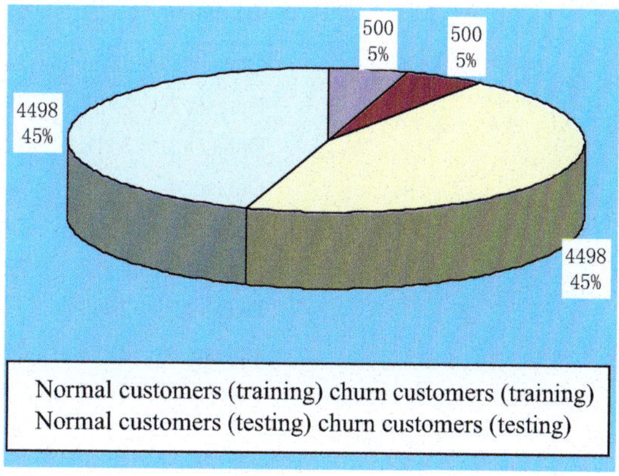

Fig. 7.2 Selections for training samples and test samples

By above five steps, we get 4998 records of churn customers and 4998 records of normal customers. Then we used cross-validation method for ten times, each time we selected 500 records randomly to constitute the training sample from the two data sets respectively, and the remaining data as test sample. Finally we got 10 groups of training samples and test samples. As shown in Fig. 7.2:

Data mining Modeling.

We selected 10 groups on the basis of sample data to set up the evaluation model, the training and testing results show as follows, smooth lines shows our scoring models with high stability. The results are as shown in Fig. 7.3:

In this project, we use cross validation algorithm to generate the 9 groups of score voting machines, their predictive accuracy as shown in Table 7.1:

The combination of the 9 votes consisted 10 MCLP score models, if score[i]> 5 it will be judged as normal, score[i]<=5 will be judged for the churn of customers.

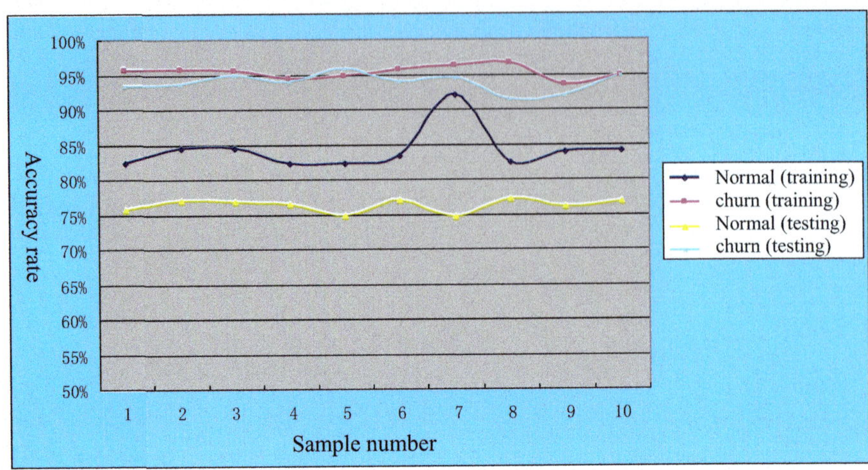

Fig. 7.3 Training and testing results

Table 7.1 Cross validation table

Cross validation	Testing data sets(3382churn+65493 normal)			
	Churn	Accuracy (%)	Normal	Accuracy (%)
Dataset 1	2506	74.0982	46,777	71.4229
Dataset 2	2451	72.4719	47,336	72.2764
Dataset 3	2518	74.4530	46,940	71.6718
Dataset 4	2505	74.0686	46,728	71.3481
Dataset 5	2509	74.1869	46,844	71.5252
Dataset 6	2467	72.945	46,951	71.6886
Dataset 7	2565	75.8427	46,534	71.0510
Dataset 8	2535	74.9556	46,518	71.0274
Dataset 9	2475	73.1815	46,496	70.9938

The score precision measurement has a lot of kinds of methods, including the cumulative distribution structure of the KS value method. It was confirmed to be able to identify more efficient data sets, which are widely applied in the field of credit risk management. We explain the MCLP score model performance from the view of distribution density and cumulative distribution as following.

Table 7.2 below is a distribution density table based on MCLP scoring systems with two types of customers, the first column score is in the range of [1, 10], the second column LOST is the scores of all the number and percentage of the churn customers, the third bar CURRENT shows scores of all the number and the percentage of the normal customers. As can be seen from the charts, the 5382 churn of customers mainly in the low field; for the 69,473 regular customers, the score paragraph mainly in high field. Among them, the churn of customers' score gathered in the scores of 1, of the total churn number 55.797 %, and the normal customer vscore gathered in the scores of 10, accounting for all the normal customer number of 46.196 %.

Table 7.2 The predictive accuracy of Churn prediction

Score	Churn (5382 records)	Normal (69,473 records)
	Percentage	Percentage
1	55.797101	13.196924
2	7.785210	4.115982
3	4.923820	2.961789
4	3.994797	3.118842
5	3.493125	3.269969
6	3.010033	3.923370
7	3.530286	4.588624
8	3.660349	6.107300
9	4.998142	12.521299
10	8.807135	46.195902

A more intuitive density distributions figure is shown in Fig. 7.4, the yellow line represents the distribution of churn customers, blue lines represent the distribution of normal customers, as we can see, the yellow line represents the churn customers and the blue line for normal customers are basically linear separable, thus the MCLP method has good applicability to solve churn problems. (Table 7.3)

Sum up the above distribution density data, we get the distribution function (cumulative distribution):

From the table, we can see the maximum separation of the churn customers and normal customers appears in the arrow pointing to the score=5 position. that is to say, if our model on the customer's score is $score[i] > 5$, then it can be assumed that the customer loyalty is high, do not churn; if our model's score is $score[i] <= 5$, then it can be assumed that the customer is in the state to be loss, we need to take measures to let them stay.

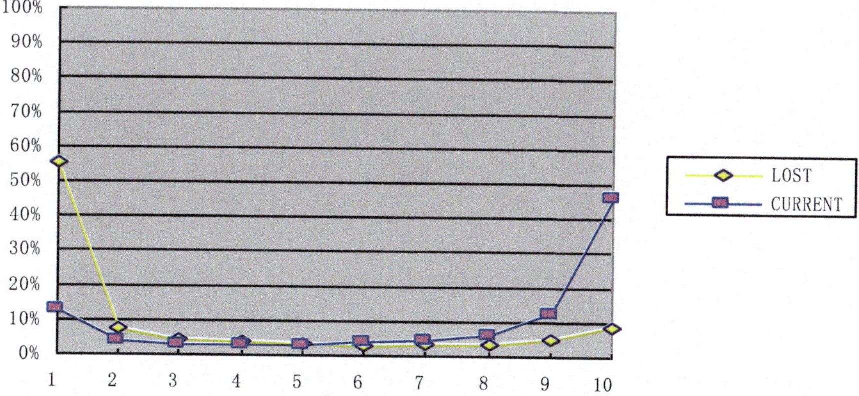

Fig. 7.4 Density distributions figure

Table 7.3 distribution function lists

SCORE	Churn	Normal	Absolute degree of separation
	ACCUMULATE	ACCUMULATE	PERCENTAGE
0	0.000000%	0.000000%	0.000000%
1	55.797101%	13.196924%	42.600177%
2	63.582311%	17.312907%	46.269405%
3	68.506132%	20.274695%	48.231436%
4	72.500929%	23.393537%	49.107392%
5	*75.994054%*	*26.663506%*	*49.330548%*
6	79.004088%	30.586876%	48.417212%
7	82.534374%	35.175500%	47.358874%
8	86.194723%	41.282800%	44.911923%
9	91.192865%	53.804098%	37.388767%
10	100.000000%	100.000000%	0.000000%

The following Fig. 7.5 is for the KS graphical display:

Set the origin of coordinates (0, 0), we see that, for the yellow line marked churn customers, there's a big jumps for cumulative distribution in scores 1, growing from 0 to 55.797 %, shows that a large number of customers are accumulated in the scores 1, from 1 to 10 the growth is with relative ease; and for the blue line marking the normal customers, cumulative distribution from scores of 1–9 with relative ease, when increased from 9 to 10, the cumulative distribution grows from 53.804098 to 100 %, a large number of customers is statistically in the numerical. While the two

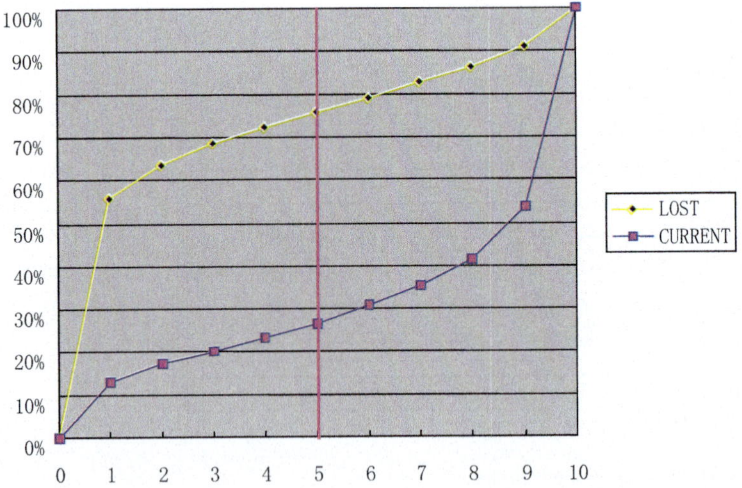

Fig. 7.5 KS score chart

customer maximum separation values appeared in scores of 5 (pink line), the churn customers in scores of 5 have accumulation of 75.994054 %, normal customers for 26.663506 %, KS = |75.994054 % − 26.663506 %| = 49.330548 %, MCLP based vote scoring models of two types of customers is distinguished more clearly.

Conclusion and Management Recommendations for the first stage:

1. Determine whether a customer is churn based on the score of the customer.
2. Analyzing the MCLP model document, find out the characteristics of churn customers by See5 and SPSS.
3. Actions are taken based on the predicted churn customer list and the churn characteristics.

The application of the project result is a complicated, systematic task. The log files are retrieved from the functional department, and processed into structured documents. The functional department designs the application measures, and forwards the feedback to the technical department, mining the new data and build up a reinforcing cycle.

The following is the second stages of the intelligent knowledge management.

7.3 Theoretical Analysis of Transformation Rules Mining

7.3.1 From Classification to Transformation Strategy

Generated by classification can provide a reference for strategy. The existing category mining is based on classical set theory and fuzzy set theory. The classical theory requires each object in Data Universe must belong to one set and only one or the other. The classical collection uses the characteristic function of range {0, 1} to qualitatively describe whether one thing has certain property, A corresponding classification is "within class is the same, among class is the different", But it cannot be used to quantitatively describe the degree of possessing certain property things (Cai et al. 2003). The fuzzy set uses the membership function of range {0, 1} to describe the degree of certain things which are undergoing differences during the intermediate transition. But for the membership degree on the domain object to 0 or 1 are also indiscriminate, is still "within the class is the same" expression. Neither classical set nor fuzzy set study the changes among the categories of things, therefore both of them cannot directly describe the conversion between "non" and "is" in certain condition (Cai 1994). Frankly speaking, many things can divided into two parts according to P property. The part which does not have the nature of P can be further divided into two categories, one is "can be convert into holding P property" and the other is "cannot be transformed into possessing the nature of P" under certain condition. In the actual production, For instance, unqualified products can turn to be qualified after some processing. For example, The number of axles of a workshop production require qualified diameter $D = 50 \pm 0.1$ mm,the unqualified diameter $d > 50.1$ cm, Considering the "re-lathe processing" of transformation measures, are then taken to turning the product into qualified ones.

In recent years, Extension theory has been initially applied in the field of data mining, and achieved good result. Bibliography (Li et al. 2004) have had outlook-style description on extension application in Data mining. Bibliography (Chen et al. 2006) proposed the conception of Extension Knowledge, which regards the expanding mode as the basic knowledge of the extension knowledge, The Transform Implication of Transmission theory of Extension is the change of knowledge, Extension introduce correlation function to alter contradiction problem into quantitative knowledge by quantification procedure. Bibliography (Zhang and He 2001) exploit methods of the corresponding potential knowledge by utilizing properties of matter element including divergence, relevance, and implication, arousing our concerns on potential information category. Bibliography (Li et al. 2006) analyzed the existing problem caused within the data mining process based on extension theory, and also proposed a new data mining application based on extension transformation through establishing matter-element set in enterprise data. Bibliography (Huang and Chen 2006) further proposed measures for fundamental improvement of data quality promoted by consulting data mining, which promotes the development of transformation of the extension domain in matter-element set. Bibliography (Gao 2002) use extension transformation to turn false proposition into true proposition, infeasibility to feasibility, and come out the idea transform infeasibility to feasibility from the point of change, It also comes out the conception and theories of change knowledge through the study of extension transformation. Bibliography (Tan et al. 2000) gives out the conception and assumption of extension classification, The above reference laid the foundation for our further research. Decision tree classification which has stronger interpretability of classification principle is one of the most commonly used data mining measures (Han and Micheline 2006; Nie et al. 2006). The paper studied the acquisition methods of transformation strategies among one category of thing from the basic idea and methods of extension set, and also engaged in mining rules and knowledge of transformation strategies among one category of thing, and go further to design the implementation of Algorithm.

7.3.2 Theoretical Analysis of Transformation Rules Mining

The basic extension theories of transformation rules mining contain three parts: First and foremost is the extension theory of matter-element, which indicates that everything has the possibility of development and change, The second is the extension transformation theory, that is the property of things will change through certain transformation; The last comes to the theory of extension set, which reflects the degree of transformation of the nature of things. Its definition can be stated as follows:

Definition1 Set U as universe, u is any element in U, k is a mapping of U to real domain I, the given transformation of $T=(TU, Tk, Tu)$ refers to the following equation.

$$\tilde{E}(T) = \{(u, y, y') \mid u \in T_U U, y = k(u) \in I, y' = T_k k(T_u u) \in I\}$$

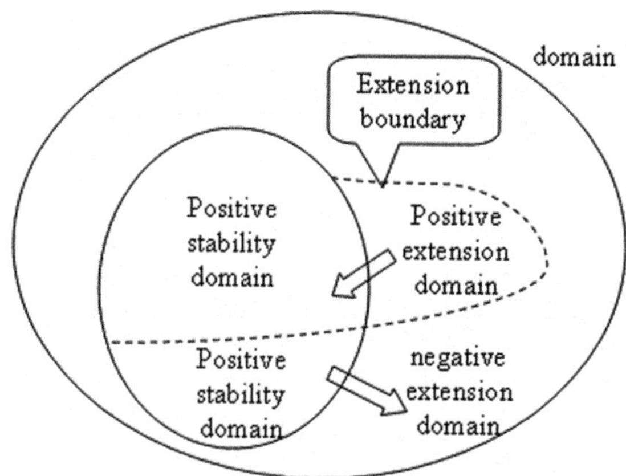

Fig. 7.6 Domain division of element transformation under extension set

The above set is a extension set of U universe, $y = k(u)$ is correlation function of $\tilde{E}(T)$. $y' = T_k k(T_u u)$ is extension function of $\tilde{E}(T)$. T_U T_k T_u is separately the transformation of universe U, correlation quasi-function K, and element u.

On the conditions of $T \neq e$, $\underset{\cdot}{E}_+(T)$ is the positive extension domain of $\tilde{E}(T)$, $\underset{\cdot}{E}_-(T)$ is the negative domain of $\tilde{E}(T)$, $E_+(T)$ is positive stable domain of $\tilde{E}(T)$, $E_-(T)$ is negative stable domain of $\tilde{E}(T)$, $J_0(T)$ is extension bounding of $\tilde{E}(T)$.

Positive extension domain indicates that element which initially does not belong to E turn to a part of E after the implementation of A transformation; while the Negative extension domain reflects element which initially does not belong to E remain the same after A transformation; Positive stability domain refers to element which originally belong to E remain belongs to E after the implementation of A transformation, Similarly, Negative stability domain refers to element which originally does not belong to E is still not part of E after A transformation. Extension boundary refers to element which existed at the border of extension transformation and its extension function is zero. Extension boundary describe the qualitative change point which indicates that elements surpass the point will definitely produce qualitative change. The diagram is shown in Fig. 7.6.

Extension utilize extension set to represent the degree of things holding certain property, and indicates things of certain property can be changed into things that lack of such property, Similarly, things absent of certain property can be altered into things holding such property. In order to make the description more clear and accurate, you should use two definitions together to describe the variability and the process of quantitative and qualitative change of elements.

Bibliography (Nie et al. 2006) transform T from element extend to transformation of correlation function or universe. Element transformation (including affair element and matter element transformation), correlation function transformation and universe transformation, are collectively known as extension transformation. And therefore, make further effort to dig rules of classification transformation on the basic of connecting classification with transformation through extension set

Rule mining which is the extension and expansion of data mining refers to Decision-making strategy come from the process of rule knowledge transformation obtained from data mining, then go through extension transformation and finally enter into category things transformation. According to different business and variable demands, matter element set can alter into another set through special extension transformation. For instance, the churned client might transform to the loyal ones under certain condition. Similarly, the normal customer might turn to be the churned ones under certain condition.

Decision tree as data set classifier has been widely used in data mining. However, it resulted in a static subset of classification of data which only describe the characteristics of different branches of leaves. The branch number is too large, although it produces numerous rules. The proportion of rules truly interested is too small when dealing with the complex data. And therefore effective measures aiming to prevent the loss of customers only relied on classification rules are invalid. Using matter element extension set to represent the results of Decision tree mining so that it can transform the static rule set into changing, dynamic extension rule set, It can transform static descriptive knowledge discovery to dynamic strategy generation. The following describe the acquirement of strategy based on Decision tree extension transformation.

7.3.3 The Algorithm Design and Implementation of Transformation Knowledge

Decision tree is a tree structure similar to flow chart, where each internal node represents a test on attribute, each branch represents output of test, and each leaf node represents a category. Decision tree is mainly based on the summarized data attribute values, from the tree top-level node(root node)to leaf node traversal which store the forecast sample, for example,

Rule 1: Total Types of Mail <=0

Average No. of logon by POP3 on the second week <=0
Total No. of log on by Web <=0
Standby mail service status = not selected
Percentage of Service Period 7 <=0.25
Total Payment in the past 3 months = 0
→Churn [0.736]

Rule 2: Total No. of logon by WEB <=0

Standby mail service status = not selected
Percentage of payment method 11 >0.2941177
Total Payment in the past 3 months = 0
Contact mailbox = No
Contact method = No
ID Number = No
→Freeze [0.757]

Through this procedure can transform the decision tree into a "if-then" form of classification rules. Take rules obtained by see5 measures for example, In the following form:

"Rule 2: (198/14, lift 2.7)

whether use mobile-mail services=0
POINTS <=6
The length of occupied time >92
Type = 6
→ class 0 [0.925]"

In the above form, 198 of rule 2 represents the record number which meet the rule in training set, while 14 represents the record number which does not meet the rule in training set, Predicting Accuracy Rate (PAR)=(198−14+1)/(198+2)=0.925, Enhance degree of lift=PAR/the relative frequency of the occurrence of such class in training set=0.925/0.343=2.7.

7.3.3.1 The Method of Obtaining Transformation Knowledge

In order to obtain strategies of classification transformation rules turn to change through extension transformation mining On the foundation of decision tree classification rule connecting with extension set theory. Take A, B two types of conversion as example.

Set up A as:

$$\{D_{\cdot+}(T)\} = \{D_i | D_i = \begin{bmatrix} I_i, & d_1, & u_{i1} \\ & d_2, & u_{i2} \\ & d_r, & u_{ir} \end{bmatrix}, K_i < 0, K_i \cdot K_i(T) < 0, i \in J_{D_{\cdot+}}\}$$

J_D is index set of information unit D_i which meet the condition of $K_{ip}^{\circ+} < 0, K_{ip} \cdot K_{ip}(p) < 0$, the later sign is similar, so no long explain

$$\left\{I_{\cdot+}(T)\right\} = \left\{I_i | I_i = (O_i, c_j, v_{ij}), D_i \in \left\{D_{\cdot+}(T)\right\}, i \in J_{D_{\cdot+}}\right\}$$

Set all of relevant characteristics of $c_j (j = 1, 2, \cdots, m)$ and $d_p (p = 1, 2, \cdots, r)$ as $\{j_0\}$, change the property value of rules hold the same property in the two types of rule based on A<-B replacement transformation; there must be transformation set called T_{AB} which make A=>B by transforming the rule existed in B but not in A through adding transformation;

The reliability is $\frac{|D_{\cdot+}(T)|}{|D_{-}(T)|}$, support degree is the transformation knowledge of $\frac{|D_{\cdot+}(T)|}{|D|}$, which indicates that about $j \subset \{j_0\}$, if $I = (O, c_j, v_j)$ have $v_j \in V_{\cdot+j}(T)$, then $D_i = \begin{bmatrix} & d_1, & u_{i1} \\ I_i, & d_2, & u_{i2} \\ & d_r, & u_{ir} \end{bmatrix}$ which originally belong to E will turn to not belong to E after the implement of T transformation, among which $V_{\cdot+j}(T) = \begin{bmatrix} Minv_{ij} & Maxv_{ij} \\ i \in J_{D_{\cdot+}} & i \in J_{D_{\cdot+}} \\ j \in \{j_0\} & j \in \{j_0\} \end{bmatrix}$

For example:

Through original knowledge

"Rule 2: (198/14, lift 2.7)

whether using mobile-mail services=0

POINTS <=6

the length of occupied time >92

Type =6

→class B[0.925]

Rule 3: (6, lift 2.7)

whether using mobile-mail services = 1

POINTS <=6

the length of occupied time <=795

→ class A [0.875]"

Obtain transformation rule knowledge

"Rule6: (6/9) support: 4.25 % ID: 240–235

Under:

POINTS <=6(same)

92< occupied time <=795(same)

Trans:

whether using mobile-mail services =1 to =0

Add: none

→class A to B [61.70%]"

ID: 240–235 is the source rule number generating transformation rule.

Below the word "under" will list rules existed in category A but not in category B. (add "same" signal in the rear)

Below the word "Trans:" will list rules had the same attribute but different value, and convert the antecedent value among condition category based on target category value

"Add: "refers to copy rules existed in B but not in A as an additional transformation condition.

Table 7.4 Statics of transformation rule's record

	The record number	The record number which correspond to antecedent	The record number which correspond to consequent
A	$\lvert D(A)\rvert$	Fa	Ra
B	$\lvert D(B)\rvert$	Fb	Rb
Subtotal	$\lvert D\rvert$	F	R

"POINTS<=6", "92< the length of occupied time <=795" and "whether use mobile-mail services=1" are the antecedent of rule knowledge, "whether use mobile-mail services=0" and "none" are the consequent of rule knowledge.

7.3.3.2 Evaluation Index of Transformation Knowledge

Set the record number of $\{A\}\cup\{B\}$ in database table as $|D|$, set the record number which correspond to antecedent in $\{A\}$ as Fa, set the record number which correspond to consequent in $\{A\}$ as Ra, set the record number which correspond to antecedent of transformation rule knowledge T_{iAB} in $\{B\}$ as Fb, set the record number which correspond to consequent of this in $\{B\}$ as Rb, set all the record number which meet antecedent of rule set as F, and all the record number which meet consequent of rule set as R, set the record number which accord with A rule set in $\{D\}$ as $|D(A)|$, set the record number which accord with B rule set in $\{D\}$ as $|D(B)|$, The following table 1 clearly reflect those evaluation index (Table 7.4). the accuracy rate of rules

$$P_{iAB} = (\mathrm{Rb}+1)/(\mathrm{Rb}+\mathrm{Ra}+2) \tag{7.1}$$

anticipative conversion rate

$$Tr = Fa / F \tag{7.2}$$

the support degree of the rule

$$S = \frac{|F|}{|D(B)|} \tag{7.3}$$

the reliability

$$R = \frac{|Rb|}{|R|} \tag{7.4}$$

For instance, In the "Rule6: (6/9) support: 4.25% ID: 240−235", 6 refers to the record number which meet transformation condition. 9 refer to the record number which meet antecedent of A "under" condition. support: 4.25% refers to reliability.

7.3.3.3 Implementation Steps

1. **Read in the original rule set**

Take See5 (http://www.rulequest.com.) decision tree software for example, the initial rule set saved in out text file as the form of text file, Rule format as shown in the above example, in which 198 of rule2 represents the record number which meet the rule in training set, 14 represents the record number which does not meet the rule in training set, Predicting accuracy rate=(198−14+1)/(198+2)=0.925, Enhance degree of lift 2.7=prediction accuracy rate/the relative frequency of occurrence of such class in training set. Classification rules will be read into database in turn, stored into the rule table.

2. **Pretreatment of rule set**

Expurgate the same rules generated by rereading in the process, establish keyword of full-text index and so forth.

3. **Set mining parameters**

Set the following parameters by user:

1) ,"Mining rules transform from class__ into class__", such as class0, and class1,etc, shown in the mentioned example.
2) ,"The number of rules have the same content > = ——", such as "POINTS < = 6"and"92 < the length of occupied time< = 795" in rules 2 and rule 3.
3) ,"The number of rules have the same content< = ——", such as the different value of antecedent in" whether use mobile-mail services" in rule 2 and rule 3 in the example.
4) ,"The predicting transformation rate of extension rule> = ——%", the conversion rate of applying predicting extension rule=the record number consisted with transformation rule in rule set/all the record number consisted with antecedent of rule set.

4. **Tule Mining**

Search for rules have many similarity and less discrepancies, by comparing the output generated by transformation rules

5. **Rule evaluation index calculation**

In order to evaluate the practicality and novelty of extension rule, you should calculate the indicators, such as accuracy rate, predicting transformation rate, support degree and credibility.

6. **Demonstrate results report**

The results of mining provide the list of transformation rules and the summary report of mining condition.

7.3.3.4 Mining Algorithm of Transformation Knowledge

The following shows the brief algorithm of transformation knowledge mining:

Input: The result set based on decision tree data mining (two class are respectively represented by A and B), and the minimum record number n from elements of the two set.

Output: matter element of A might transform into strategy of B under the condition of TkK(TRR).

Method:

(1) The elements in A, B should be respectively represented as multi-dimensional matter element w1 and w2, R1m and R2m analysis indicate the first m matter element in W1 an W2.
(2) The number of matter element for i=0 to A
(3) The number of matter element for j=0 to B
(4) Set integer total equal to 0
(5) Set the dimension of R1i as iN, set the dimension of R2j as jN;
(6) For k=0 to iN
(7) For kk=0 to jN
(8) If R1ir is the K-dimension feature, then value is the same as the value of KK-dimension of R2j
(9) Total=total+1
(10) End k,kk circulation
(11) If total is greater or equal to the system input value N, then output one transformation knowledge of R1i and R2j
(12) End i, j circulation
(13) End.

7.4 Conclusions

We briefly analyzes the measures of the acquisition strategy, combined extension theory with research result to come up with strategy knowledge measures of acquiring customer transformation through data mining and extension transformation, and implement through designing algorithm programming. The practicality of this method is confirmed by preliminary test.

First of all, import all the decision tree rules into rule base, as is shown in Fig. 7.7.

Then set the parameters (such as transform users from freeze user to normal user) to engage in mining strategy to come out dozens of strategies, the rule 6 of the former Sect. 3.2 is the case in point, from which indicates that users among the scope of POINTS<=6 and the length of occupied time between 92 and 795 can reduce their loss, as long as advising them not to use mobile-mail services. This intui-

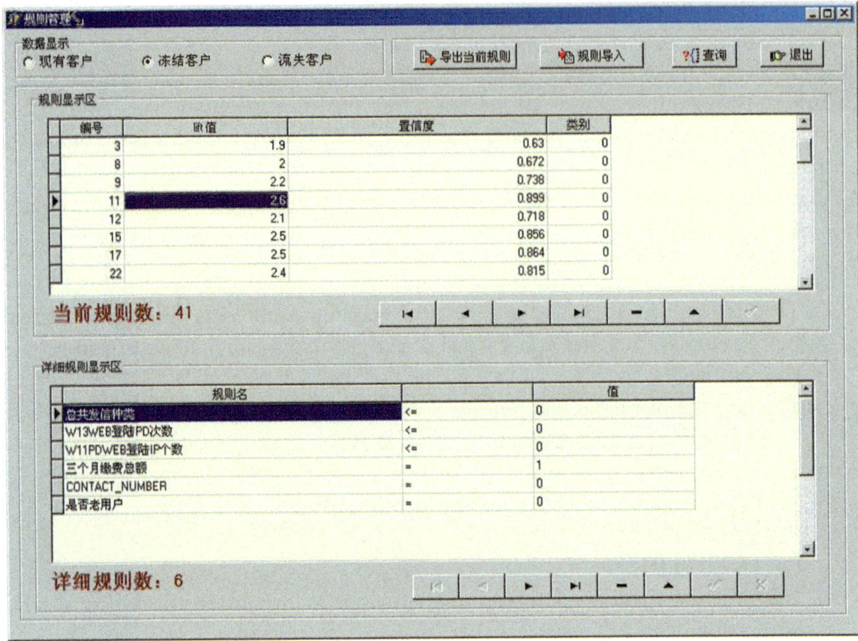

Fig. 7.7 Example software library of transformation knowledge acquisition

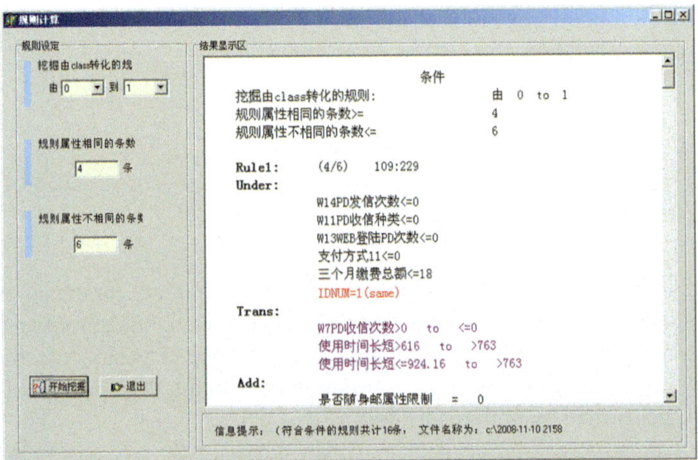

Fig. 7.8 Extension strategy mining interface

tive transformation knowledge plays a pivotal role on taking effective operational measures. The interface is shown as in Fig. 7.8:

We found that there are two paths for transformation knowledge mining by combining decision tree method with extension set theory.

1. The indirect rule mining method refers to further digging on the basis of traditional decision tree rule. After generating a static rule set through data mining of decision tree, coming the second excavation of the rule set.
2. Extension strategy direct mining method refers to directly dig out transformation knowledge on original data base by improving traditional decision tree algorithm.

The chapter mainly based on the first path to achieve the acquisition of transformation knowledge, the second path has more practicality and need further research. In the research process, we also found that transformation of classification of things need certain condition, the definition of transformation condition for qualitative and quantitative analysis is also research direction. there would be great application prospection by taking advantage of the result of extension theory research which connect traditional data mining with extension set, and with extension transformation as well as extension logical theory to dig out "can't to can, not to yes" strategy by using methods of extension data mining.

Chapter 8
Intelligent Knowledge Management in Expert Mining in Traditional Chinese Medicines

In the research of intelligent knowledge acquirement, it is hard to integrate domain knowledge to the algorithms, which involves some key issues as follows. First, how to accomplish the structured representation of domain knowledge, which can help computers understand human languages. Second, results of data mining algorithms refreshing with the change of domain knowledge; finally, needing a friendly interface, which can help the experts represent structured domain knowledge, and make the interaction between the experts and the computers conveniently during setting and adjusting the parameters of algorithms.

This chapter proposes a semantics-based improvement of Apriori algorithm, which can integrate domain knowledge to mining and its application in traditional Chinese Medicines. The algorithm can recognize the changes of domain knowledge and re-mining. That is to say, the engineers need not to take part in the course, which can realize intellective acquirement.

8.1 Definition of Semantic Knowledge

It's necessary to represent domain knowledge in a structured way, which makes dynamic recognizing and domain knowledge be applied conveniently. In the improving algorithm, we represent domain knowledge in semantic way and define three classes of semantic knowledge, that is to say, abstract semantic, classification semantic and composed semantic. Representing ways reflects different categories, different levels of domain concept and the logical relationship among the concepts.

Abstract semantic Definition 8.1 Abstract semantic is a superior abstract of concepts, which achieves more general semantic knowledge, denoted by K^A. We have:

$$K^A = \left\{ k_1^A, k_2^A \ldots k_n^A \right\} \tag{8.1}$$

Y. Shi et al., *Intelligent Knowledge,* SpringerBriefs in Business,
DOI 10.1007/978-3-662-46193-8_8

Here, $k_n^A: \forall Ii, Ij, \cdots, Ik \rightarrow S_n^A, k_n^A$ indicates the nth abstract semantic knowledge.

For instance, in traditional Chinese medicine, dizzy and dazzled are both included by giddiness, which means the eyes are unable to see clearly and is a common symptom of arteriosclerosis, cervical spondylosis and low blood pressure. The relationship can be shown as Fig. 8.1.

Classification semantic Definition 8.2 Classification semantic groups the concepts according to the values of attributes, denoted by K^C

$$K^C = \left\{k_1^C, k_2^C \ldots k_n^C\right\} \tag{8.2}$$

Here, $k_n^C: f^i(xj) \rightarrow S_n^C$ indicates the ith symptom item or the classification of a traditional Chinese medicine when its attribute value is x_j.

$$k_n^C \xrightarrow{isa} S_n^C$$

For example, when type of pulse is slippery pulse, tight pulse, long pulse or taut pulse, it's classified as weak pulse. Moreover, a hypertension patient who has been ill for less than 1 year will be classified as an early period patient; the one who has been sick for 1–3 years will be classified as a medium period patient; the one who has been ill for more than 3 years will be classified as a long-term patient. The relationship can be described by the following figure (Fig. 8.2):

Composed Semantic Definition 8.3 Composed Semantic is that more than one concept are composed as a new concept, denoted by K^P.

$$K^P = \left\{k_1^P, k_2^P \ldots k_n^P\right\} \tag{8.3}$$

Here, $k_n^P: I_i \wedge I_j \wedge \cdots \wedge I_k \rightarrow S_n^p$ means that many symptoms or medicine appearance at the same time would compose a new conception.

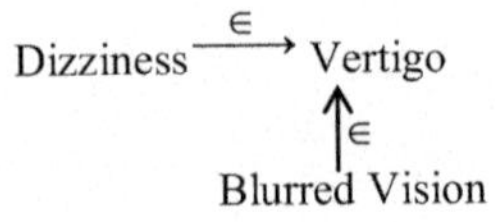

Dizziness $\xrightarrow{\in}$ Vertigo

$\uparrow \in$

Blurred Vision

Fig. 8.1 An example of abstract semantic

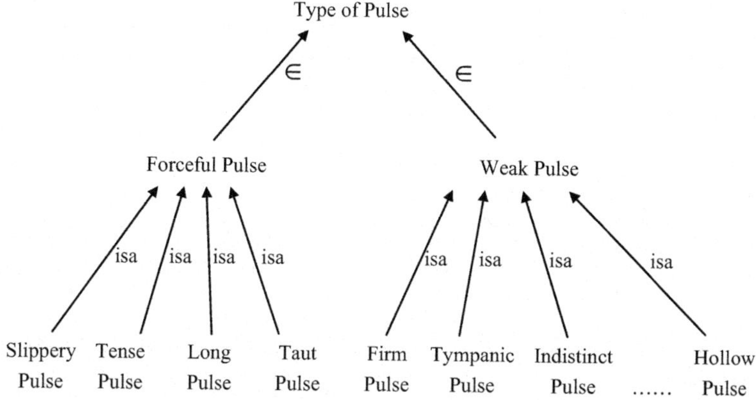

Fig. 8.2 An example of classification semantic

If the patient suffers from thirsty and bitter taste simultaneously, we could describe it as hot-tempered instead of thirsty and bitter taste. The relationship can be shown as Fig. 8.3.

Before data mining, knowledge engineers should communicate and associate with specialists in order to find out the characters and design structuring plan of target domain according to the task. When it comes to the structurized definitions, we must guarantee all-sidedness and integrity of knowledge while avoiding to gender variance and conflict in the process of structuring.

Furthermore, we need provide friendly user interface and help customer administrate domain knowledge flexibly in visible mode in order to define and maintain domain knowledge in dynamic state in the operation of system. Specially, the users could maintain domain knowledge conveniently and flexibly through the interface when the system is operating. The interface is shown as in Fig. 8.4. The system would integrate new domain knowledge into algorithm to mine new knowledge in the process of executing algorithm.

Specialists could make domain knowledge structuring before and in the process of mining through user interface and integrate new finding into domain knowledge as an input of next mining so as to search new knowledge endlessly on a basis of mining results' estimation last time.

8.2 Semantic Apriori Algorithm

In our method, algorithm and domain knowledge is integrated in a loose way. On one hand, the extensibility and flexibility of the algorithm can be improved. Algorithm improvement cannot influence definition and contents of domain knowledge. On the other hand, it is not necessary to modify algorithm when domain knowledge is changed. This helps to enhance the flexibility of mining system, and also to reuse algorithm and domain knowledge.

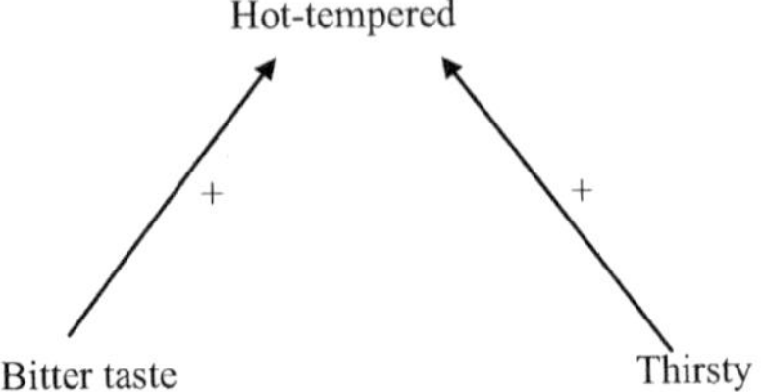

Fig. 8.3 An example of composed semantic

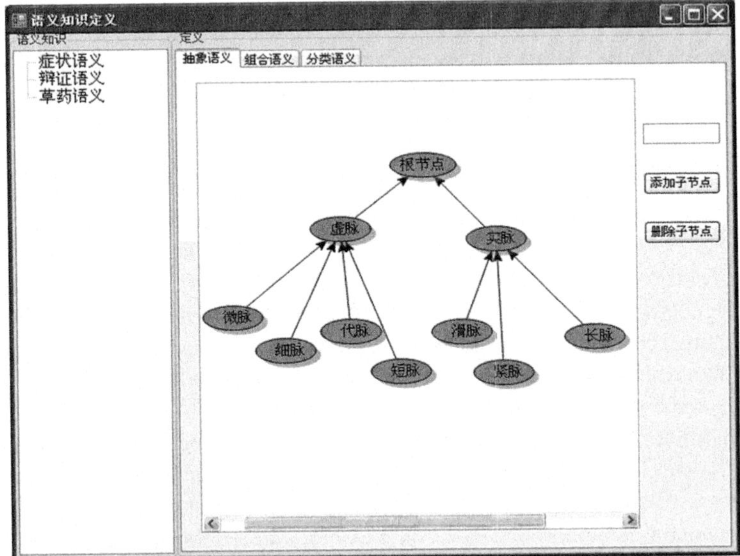

Fig. 8.4 User interface for semantic knowledge definition

Our semantic Apriori algorithm works as follows. Firstly, we read domain knowledge from knowledge base and store it into memory. Secondly, when we read transactions, our algorithm scans all the items, and compares them with three kinds of semantic knowledge. If related semantic knowledge is found, original items are processed with new semantic, and transform into new items.

Semantic Apriori algorithm is as follows:

Procedure: Semantic Apriori Input: dataset D, minimum support (min-sup), minimum confidence (min-conf), abstract semantic K^A ,classification semantic K^C , combination semantic K^P ,and order of semantic execution O .

Among them, find_frequent_1_item(*D*D, minSup) and Apriori_gen(L_{k-1},misSup) is function of generating candidate frequent itemsets and strong association rules respectively.

The major difference between semantic Apriopri and traditional Apriori is that semantic Apriori algorithm mines domain knowledge dynamically without participation of knowledge engineers. The algorithm is the repeated mining process and can feedback the mined results. This algorithm changes traditional "black box" mining into "white box" mining.

8.3 Application Study

8.3.1 Background

Hypertension refers to the artery systolic blood pressure and (or) diastolic blood pressure increased. It is often accompanied by functional or organic change of heart, brain, kidney and retinal.

China is a country with high rate of hypertension. It is estimated that the number of people affected now is 200 million, an increase of 100 million since 1991. There is a significant rising trend of hypertension.

Epidemiological studies showed that more than 115/75 mmHg blood pressure can increase the mortality of cardiovascular events. Hypertension the important risk factors of myocardial infarction, heart failure and chronic kidney disease (CKD) in stroke. 50–60% occurrence of stroke and 40–50% occurrence of myocardial infarction is related to blood pressure increase. More than 7 million cases of death are due to hypertension worldwide, and has become the leading death risk factor. In China, medical cost is estimated to reach 130 billion Yuan due to cardiovascular disease and medical treatment for hypertension is as high as 36.6 billion Yuan every year. As one of the highest incidence of cardiovascular disease, hypertension has become the burden of our society.

In our country, the current treatment for hypertension has two ways: western medicine therapy and TCM treatment. Western medicine treatment for hypertension, often drops blood pressure, and even to normal level. But as for improvement of dizziness and headache, western medicine therapy performs worse. However, TCM treatment emphasizes integral treatment, thus has more ideal performance.

When hypertension patients have symptoms such as headaches, dizziness, head expansion and insomnia, traditional Chinese medicine doctors think it is due to liver-kidney Yin deficiency, hand Yin deficiency. Through traditional Chinese medicine treatment, these symptoms can be improved with blood pressure dropped at the same time.

Although traditional Chinese medicine treatment of hypertension disease is advantageous, there isn't unified treatment method. Therefore it is significant for both improvement of curing hypertension and thought inheritance of old and famous traditional Chinese medicine doctors to sum up clinical experiences of hypertension, especially those of old and famous traditional Chinese medicine doctors.

We selected 313 cases of hypertension treatment from national wide database of old and famous Chinese medicine doctors. We preprocessed the data by merging synonyms and standardizing data, and also deleted attributes with little contribution and those that experts are not interested in (such as occupations, place of birth, height, etc.). After the preprocessing process, 23 symptoms characteristics and 44 commonly-used herbal medicines are used as data source. We use our semantic Apriori method to find association rules between symptoms characteristics and herbal medicines that are used in order to discover knowledge about characteristics of TCM treatment of hypertension.

8.3.2 Mining Process Based on Semantic Apriori Algorithm

Due to the domain knowledge of different experts is not completely same, it is necessary to add personal mining process in accordance with their own field of knowledge to meet the need of experts from different fields of mining.

In addition, to assess the knowledge from mining, then put new found knowledge as a new field of knowledge into the next step in order to achieve the cycle of the mining process.

In the following example, according to different areas knowledge, make use of Semantic precession Apriori algorithm by three mining. Each mining maintains data and algorithms unchanged while domain knowledge changed, in order to achieve different purposes and different levels of knowledge discovery. At last, we can get knowledge which is actionable as well as users interested in.

At first, we get 47 strong association rules by using classical Apriori algorithm, mining results shown in Table 2 “the first mining column” and mining user interface shown in Fig. 8.5.

In second mining, according to the first mining results to analyze, evaluate, refine rules while to combine the experience and interests of experts form a new field of knowledge. After then, make new knowledge into abstract semantics, classification semantics and in the form of a combination of semantic, Table 8.1 lists some of the semantic knowledge. Using algorithm Semantic Apriori to mine again, the results obtained has been greatly improved in quality, and will also filter some experts are not interested in knowledge to reduce the knowledge redundancy, results shown in Table 8.2 "second mining column” and mine user interface shown in Fig. 8.6.

Based on the second mining results, the third mining will further convert abstracted, combined and grouping knowledge into new areas of knowledge, third precession mining results shown in Table 8.2 “the third excavation”.

Through spiral mining constantly, the quality of the knowledge gained has been significantly improved, for example, we can get the following two rules after first mining:

dry mouth ⇒ Chrysanthemum (sup=0.11, conf=0.52)
bitter taste in mouth ⇒ Chrysanthemum (sup=0.16, conf=0.42)

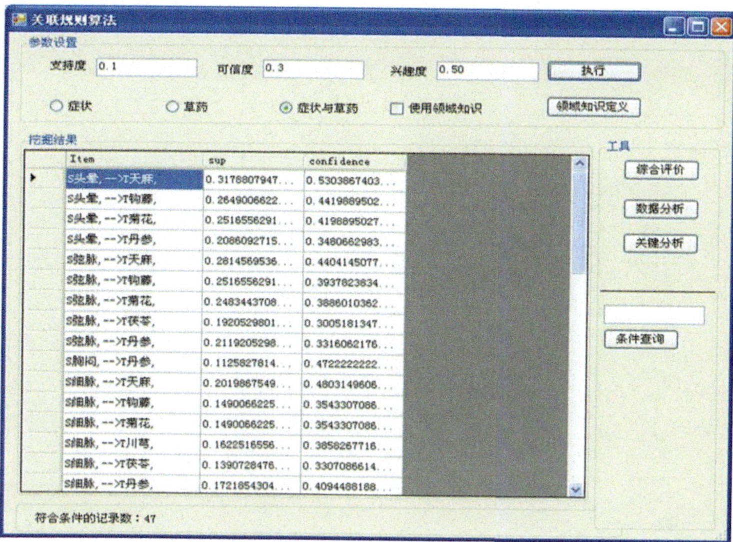

Fig. 8.5 Results of the first dData mining process

Table 8.1 Semantic knowledge fragment during the second mining process

Abstract Semantics	
Brash	Fretful or palpitations or insomnia
Numbness	Numb or cramp or tenderness
……	
Classification Semantics	
Blood pressure classification	If 140<=systolic blood pressure<=159 and 90<=diastolic blood pressure<= 99 then Level 1 If 160<=systolic blood pressure<=179 and 100<=diastolic blood pressure<=109 then Level 2 If systolic blood pressure>=180 and diastolic blood pressure>=110 then Level 3
Pulse classification	If pulse=excess pulse or pulse=slippery pulse or pulse=tight pulse or pulse=long pulse or pulse=stringy pulse then excess pulse
	If pulse=faint pulse or pulse=thready pulse or pulse=regularly intermittent puls or pulse=short pulse then feeble pulse
……	
Combination semantic	
Irascibility flourishing	Dry mouth and bitter taste in mouth
……	

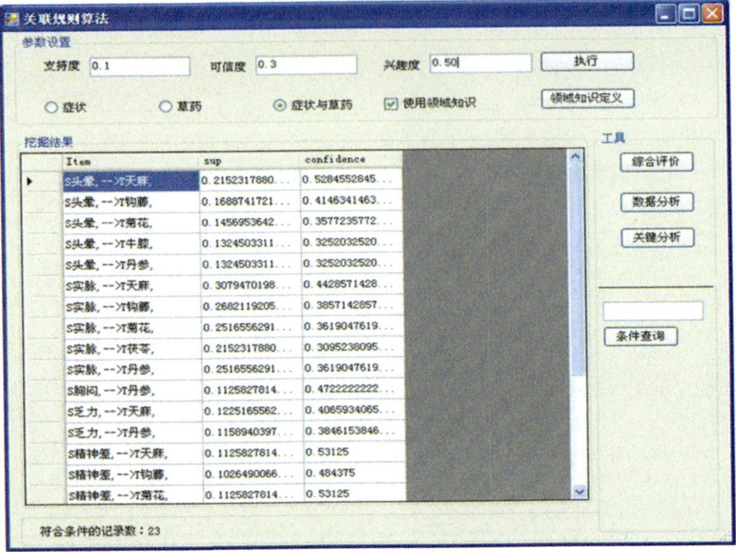

Fig. 8.6 Results of the third data mining process

Table 8.2 Comparison of three mining conditions and results

		First mining	Second mining	Third mining
Semantic domain knowledge		–	Table 1	Omit
Data		315 records	315 records	315 records
Technique	Algorithm	Classical apriori	Semantic apriori	Semantic apriori
	Support degree	0.1	0.1	0.1
	Confidence degree	0.3	0.3	0.3
Results comparison	The total number of rules	47	30	23
	Newly discovered number of rules	–	22	8
	The number of rules to filter out	–	8	4
	The number of rules when support degree increases	–	11	10
	The number of rules when support degree decreases	–	3	3
	The number of rules when confidence degree increases	–	6	4
	The number of rules when confidence degree decreases	–	2	2

When domain experts analysis the mining results, they point out that if hypertensive patients suffering the symptoms of dry mouth and bitter taste in mouth, then patients belonging to irascibility flourishing, and upper hyperactivity of liver yang. According to this field of knowledge, in the second mining, dry mouth and bitter taste in mouth will be combined into the new semantics: irascibility flourishing, and use Semantic Apriori re-mining, we gain a new knowledge:

Irascibility flourishing ⇒ Chrysanthemum, Spica Prunellae (sup=0.07, conf=0.61)

We can see that it is significantly different from the knowledge of the first mining. First, although the support degree decreases in new knowledge, the confidence is significantly improved. Besides chrysanthemum, we also find that spica prunellae is commonly used drugs to clear irascibility flourishing. But in the first mining, no matter what dry mouth or bitter taste in mouth has lower confidence degree for spica prunellae which failed to get the knowledge about the spica prunellae.

Based on method mentioned above, after three spiral mining, we can gain the number of rules from the first 47 has been reduced to 23. By comparing, it is easy to find that every time the knowledge gained by the spiral mining process has been greatly improved in quality. At the same time, due to the combine the domain knowledge into the mining process, in particular the expert preferences, experience, knowledge and wisdom, results more easily are accepted and used in the real world.

Reference

Aggarwal CC, Yu PS (1998) A new framework for itemset generation. ACM, New York

Agrawal R, Imielinski T, Swami A (1993) Data mining: a performance perspective. IEEE Trans Knowl Data Eng 5:914–925

Alavi M (2000) Managing organizational knowledge. In: Zmud RW (Eds) Framing the domains of it management research: glimpsing the future through the past. Pinnaflex Educational Resources, Cincinnati

Alavi M, Leidner D (2001) Review: knowledge management and knowledge management systems: conceptual foundations and research issue. MIS Quarterly 25(1):107–135

Ambrosino R, Buchanan BG (1999) The use of physician domain knowledge to improve the learning of rule-based models for decision-support. In: Proceedings of the AMIA Symposium

Anand SS, Bell DA, Hughs JG (1996) EDM: a general framework for data mining based on evidence theory. Data Knowl Eng 18:189–223

Apte C, Liu B, Pednault EPD, Smyth P (2002) Business applications of data mining. Commun ACM 45(8):49–53

Arias JA, Pinquier J, André OR (2005) Evaluation of classification techniques for audio indexing. In: Proceedings of 13th European Signal Processing Conference, Antalya, Turkey

Awad EM, Ghaziri HM (2004) Knowledge management. Prentice Hall, Upper Saddle River

Baker J, Burkman J, Jones DR (2009) Using visual representations of data to enhance sense making in data exploration tasks. J Assoc Inf Syst 10(7):533–559

Barquin R, Edelstein H (1997) Building, using, and managing the data warehouse. Prentice Hall, Upper Saddle River

Bayes T, Price R (1763) An essay towards solving a problem in the doctrine of chances. PhilosTrans R Soc Lond 53(0):370–418

Beckman TJ (1999) The current state of knowledge management. In: Liebowitz J (Eds) Knowledge management handbook. CRC, Boca Raton, pp 1-1–1-22

Bendoly E (2003) Theory and support for process frameworks of knowledge discovery and data mining from ERP systems. Inf Manage 40(7):630–647

Berger P, Luckman T (1966) The social construction of reality. Doubleday, Garden City

Bose I, Mahapatra RK (2001) Business data mining: a machine learning perspective. Inf Manage 39(3):211–225

Bower G, Hilgard E (1981) Theories of learning. Prentice hall, Englewood Cliffs

Breiman L, Friedman J, Olshen R, Stone C (1984) Classification and regression trees. Wadswroth, Belmont

Brezillion P, Pomerol J (1999) Contextual knowledge sharing and cooperation in intelligent assistant systems. Le Travail Humain 62(3):223–246

Brydon M, Gemino A (2008) You've data mined. Now what? Commun Assoc Inf Sys 22:603–616

Y. Shi et al., *Intelligent Knowledge*, SpringerBriefs in Business,
DOI 10.1007/978-3-662-46193-8

Cabena P, Hadjinian P, Stadler R, Verhees J, Zanasi A (1997) Discovering data mining from concepts to implementation. Prentice Hall, Upper Saddle River

Cai W (1994) The matter-element model and Its application. Science and Technology Document Publishing House, Beijing

Cai LB, Zhang CQ (2007) The evolution of KDD: towards domain-driven data mining. Int J Pattern Recogn Artif Intell 21(4):677–692

Cai W, Yang CY, He B (2003) Principium of extension logic. Science, Beijing

Cao L et al (2006) Domain-driven data mining: a practical methodology. Int J Data Warehous Min 2(4):49–65

Cao L, Zhang C (2007) Domain-driven, actionable knowledge discovery. IEEE Intell Syst 22(4):78–88

Cao L, Yu P, Zhang C, Zhao Y (2010) Domain driven data mining. Springer, New York

Cauvin S, Braunschweig B (1993) Graphical knowledge representation in the ALEXIP system for petrochemical process supervision. Appl Artif Intell Eng 2:219–233

Chen YQ, Hu LF (2005) Study on data mining application in CRM system based on insurance trade. In: Proceedings of the 7th international conference on Electronic commerce ICEC '05, ACM Press, pp 839–841

Chen M, Han J, Yu P (1996) Data mining: an overview from a database perspective. IEEE Trans Knowl Data Eng 8:866–883

Chen WW, Yang CY, Huang JC (2006) Extension knowledge and extension knowledge reasoning. J Harbin Inst Technol 38(7):1094–1096

Cohen WW (1995) Fast effective rule induction, machine learning. In: Proceedings of the Twelfth International Conference

Collins HM (2001) Tacit knowledge, trust and the Q of sapphire. Soc Stud Sci 31(1):71–85

Craven MW, Shavlik JW (1996) Extracting tree-structured representations of trained networks. In: Touretzky DS, Mozer MC, Hasselmo ME (Eds) Advances in neural information processing systems Vol 8. The MIT Press, Cambridge, pp 24–30

Deng NY, Tian YJ (2004) New method in data mining: support vector machines. Science press, Beijing

Deng NY, Tian YJ (2009) Support vecotr machines: theory, algorithms and extensions. Science press, Beijing

Despres C, Chauval D (2000) A thematic analysis of the thinking in knowledge management. In: Despres C, Chauvel D (eds) The present and the promise of knowledge management. Butterworth Heinemann, Boston, pp 55–86

Dictionary of Military and Associated Terms, US Department of Defense (2005)

Diederich J, Barakat N (2004) Hybrid rule-extraction from support vector machines[C]//Cybernetics and Intelligent Systems, IEEE Conference on IEEE 2:1271–1276

Dieng R, Corby O, Giboin A, Ribière M (1999) Methods and tools for corporate knowledge management. Int J Hum Comput Stud 51(3):567–598

Dunn JC (1974) Well separated clusters and optimal fuzzy partitions. J Cybern 4(3):95–104

Fayyad UM, Piatetsky SG, Smyth P (1996a) From data mining to knowledge discovery in database. AI Magazine 17(3):37–54

Fayyad UM, Piatetsky SG, Smyth P (1996b) The KDD process for extracting useful knowledge from volumes of data. Commun ACM 39(11):27–34

Fayyad UM, Piatetsky SG, Smyth P (1996c) From data mining to knowledge discovery: an overview. In Fayyad UM, Piatetsky SG, Smyth P, Uthurusamy R (Eds) Advances in knowledge discovery and data mining. AAAI/The MIT Press, Menlo Park, pp 1–34

Fayyad UM, Piatetsky SG et al (1996d) From data mining to knowledge discovery in databases. AI magazine 17(3):37–54

Feigenbaum EA (1977) The art of artificial of intelligence: themes and case studies of knowledge engineering, The fifth international joint conference on artificial intelligence, Cambridge, pp 1014–1029

Frawley WJ, Piatetsky-Shapiro G, Matheus CJ (1991) Knowledge discovery in databases: an overview. In: Piatetsky-Shapiro G, Frawley WJ (Eds) Knowledge discovery in databases. AAAI/MIT Press, Menlo Park, pp 1–27

Frawley WJ, Piatetsky-Shapiro G et al (1992) Knowledge discovery in databases: an overview. AI magazine 13(3):57–70

Freed N, Glover F (1981) Simple but powerful goal programming models for discriminant problems. Eur J Oper Res 7:44–60

Freitas AA (1999) On rule interestingness measures. Knowl Based Sys 12:309–315

Fung GM, Mangasarian OL, Shavlik JW (2002) Knowledge-based support vector machine classifiers. In: NIPS 2002 Proceedings, Vancouver, pp 9–14

Fung GM, Mangasarian OL, Shavlik JW (2003) Knowledge-based nonlinear kernel classifier. COLT, pp 102–113

Gao H (2002) Applied research of extension approach in data mining algorithm, Master's dissertation, Dalian Maritime University

Geary RC (1954) The contiguity ratio and statistical mapping. Incorporated Stat 5(3):115–127+129–146

Geng LQ, Hamilton HJ (2007) Choosing the right lens: finding what is interesting in data mining. Stud Comput Intell 43:3–24

Gibert K, Rodríguez SG, Annicchiarico R (2013) Post-processing: bridging the gap between modelling and effective decision-support. Math Comput Model 57:1633–1639

Goldkuhl G, Braf E (2001) Contextual knowledge analysis—understanding knowledge and its relations to action and communication. In: Proceedings of 2nd European Conference on Knowledge Management, IEDC-Bled School of Management, Slovenia, p 197

Graco W, Semenova T et al (2007) Toward knowledge-driven data mining, International workshop on Domain driven data mining. ACM, California, pp 49–54

Gray B, Orlowska ME (1998) Clustering categorical attributes into interesting association rules. In: Proceedings ofSecond Pacific Asia Conference on Knowledge Discovery in Databases, Melbourne, pp 132–143

Gu S, Tang X (2004) How to synthesize experts opinions building consensus form different perspectives, The Fifth International Symposium on Knowledge Management and Systems Sciences, Japan, pp 291–295

Guillet FJ, Hamilton HJ (2007) Quality measures in data mining. Springer, New York

Han J, Kamber M (2006) Data mining: concepts and techniques. Morgan Kaufmann, San Fransisco

Han J, Kamber M, Pei J (2011) Data mining: concepts and techniques. Morgan Kaufmann, Waltham

Harrison AW, Rainer RK JR (1992) The influence of individual differences on skill in end-user computing. J Manage Inf Sys 9(1):93–111

Hou JL, Sun MT, Chuo HC (2005) An intelligent knowledge management model for construction and reuse of automobile manufacturing intellectual properties. Int J Adv Manuf Technol 26(1):169–182

http://searchdatamanagement.techtarget.com/sDefinition/0,sid91_gci211894,00.html, 2005. Accessed 17 Sept 2013

Huang YL, Chen JH, Shen WC (2006) Diagnosis of hepatic tumors with texture analysis in non-enhanced computed tomography images[J]. Acad Radiol 13(6):713–720

Huang X, Zhang L (2009) A comparative study of spatial approaches for urban mapping using hyperspectral ROSIS images over Pavia City, northern Italy[J]. Int J Remote Sens 30(12): 3205–3221

Hussain F, Liu H et al (2000) Exception rule mining with a relative interestingness measure. In: Terano T, Liu H, Chen A (eds) Knowledge discovery and data mining. current issues and new applications, vol 1805, Springer, Berlin, pp 86–97

Igbaria M, Parsuraman S (1989) A path analytic study of individual characteristics, computer anxiety, and attitudes toward microcomputers. J Manage 15(3):373–388

Jackson J (2002) Data mining: a conceptual overview. Commun Assoc Inf Syst 8:267–296

Jang JSR, Sun CT, Mizutani E (1997) Neuro-fuzzy and soft computing: a computational approach to learning and machine learning. Prentice Hall, Upper Saddle River

Jourdan Z, Rainer RK, Marshall TE (2008) Business intelligence: an analysis of the literature. Inf Syst Manage 25(2):121–131

Kamber M, Shinghal R (1996) Evaluating the interestingness of characteristic rules. In: Proceedings of 2nd international conference on knowledge discovery and data mining, Portland, USA

Klemettinen M, Mannila H, Ronkainen P, Toivonen H, Verkamo AI (1994) Finding interesting rules from large sets of discovered association rules. In: Proceedings of the 3rd international conference on information and knowledge management, Gaithersburg, ACM Press

Klosgen W (1996) A multipattern and multistrategy discovery assistant. In: Fayyad U et al (eds) Advances in knowledge discovery and data mining. AAAI Press/MIT Press, Menlo Park, pp 249–271

Knowledge W The free encyclopedia, http://en.wikipedia.org/wiki/Knowledge

Kotagiri R (2008) Contrast pattern mining and application. IEEE Data Mining Forum, Hong Kong

Kou G, Liu X, Peng Y, Shi Y, Wise M, Xu W (2003) Multiple criteria linear programming to data mining: models, algorithm designs and software developments. Optim Methods Softw 18:453–473

Kuo YT, Lonie A et al (2007) Domain ontology driven data mining: a medical case study. International workshop on Domain driven data mining. ACM, California, pp 11–17

Lavrac N, Flach P, Zupan B (1999) Rule evaluation measures: a unifying view. In: Slovenia B, Dzeroski S, Flach PA (eds) In: Proceedings of the ninth international workshop on inductive logic programming, Springer-Verlag, pp 174–185

Lee W, Stolfo SJ (2000) A framework for constructing features and models for intrusion detection systems. ACM Trans Inf Syst Secur 3(4):227–261

Li LX, Li HW, Yang CY (2004) Study on the application of extenics in data mining. Eng Sci 6(7):53–79

Li XS, Shi Y, Li AH (2006) Study on enterprise data mining solution based on extension set. J Harbin Inst Technol 38(7):1124–1128

Li XS, Shi Y, Zhang LL (2010) From the information explosion to intelligent knowledge management. Science Press, Beijing

Li XS, Xiang ZB, Zhang HL, Zhu ZX (2012) A novel method for extension transformation knowledge discovering. In Wang H et al (eds) APWeb 2012 workshops. LNCS 7234, pp 43–50

Li XS, Li LP, Chen ZX (2014) Toward extenics-based innovation model on intelligent knowledge management. Ann Data Sci. doi:10.1007/s40745-014-0009-5

Liu B, Hsu W (1996) Post-analysis of learned rules, the 13th national conference on artificial intelligence, Portland, Citeseer

Liu B, Hsu W, Chen S (1997) Using general impressions to analyze discovered classification rules. In: Proceedings of the 3rd international conference on knowledge discovery and data mining, Vancouver, Canada, pp 31–36

Liu H, Lu H, Feng L et al (1999) Efficient search of reliable exceptions [M]//Methodologies for knowledge discovery and data mining. Springer, Berlin, pp 194-204

Ludwig J, Livingstone G (2000) What's new using prior models as a measure of novelty in knowledge discovery. In: Proceedings of the 12th IEEE conference on tools with artificial intelligence

Mangasarian OL (2005) Knowledge-based linear programming. SIAM J Optim 15:375–382

Mangasarian OL, Wild EW, (2006) Nonlinear knowledge in kernel approximation, IEEE Transactions on Neural Networks

Mangasarian OL, Wild EW (2007) Nonlinear knowledge in kernel machines, Computational and Applied Mathematics Seminar, Mathematics Department University of California at San Diego

Mangasarian OL, Shavlik JW, Wild EW (2004) Knowledge-based kernel approximation. J Mach Learn Res 5:1127–1141

Margaret R (2005) What is data? - Definition from WhatIs.com. http://searchdatamanagement.techtarget.com/sDefinition/0,sid91_gci211894,00.html. Accessed 17 Sept 2013

Martens D et al (2008) Rule extraction from support vector machines: an overview of issues and application in credit scoring. Stud Comput Intell 80:33–63

Martin X, Salomon R (2003) Tacitness, learning, and international expansion: a study of foreign direct investment in a knowledge-intensive industry. Organ Scie 14(3):297–311

Mcgarry K (2005) A survey of interestingness measures for knowledge discovery. Knowl Eng Rev 20(1):39–61

Mertins PH, Vorbeck J (2003) Knowledge management concepts and best practices. Springer, London

Murphy PM, Aha DW (1992) UCI machine learning repository, www.ics.uci.edu/~mlearn/ML Repository.html. Accessed 17 Sept 2013

Negash S (2004) Business intelligence. Commun Assoc Inf Sys 13:177–195

Nemati HR, Steiger DM et al (2002a) Knowledge warehouse: an architectural integration of knowledge management, decision support, artificial intelligence and data warehousing. Decis Support Syst 33(2):143–161

Nemati HR, Steiger DM, Iyer LS, Herschel RT (2002b) Knowledge warehouse: an architectural integration of knowledge management, decision support, artificial intelligence and data warehousing. Decis Support Syst 33:143–161

Nie GL, Zhang LL, Li XS, Shi Y (2006) The analysis on the customers churn of charge email based on data mining, Sixth IEEE International Conference on Data Mining—Workshops, Hong Kong, China, pp 843–847

Nonaka IR (1991) The knowledge creating company. Harvard Bus Rev 69(6):96–104

Nonaka IR (2009) Speech at the Chinese academy of sciences

Nonaka IR, Reinmoeller P, Senoo D (1998) The 'ART' of knowledge: systems to capitalize on market knowledge. Eur Manage J 16(6):673–684

Nonaka IR, Toyama R, Konno N (2000a) SECI, Ba, and leadership: a unifying model of dynamic knowledge creation. In Teece DJ, Nonaka I (eds) New perspectives on knowledge-based firm and organization. Oxford University, New York

Nonaka IR, Toyama R et al (2000b) Ba and leadership: a unified model of dynamic knowledge creation. Long Range Plan 33(1):5–34

Olson D, Shi Y (2007) Introduction to business data mining. McGraw-Hill/Irwin, Englewood Cliffs

Othman ZA, Baker AA, Othman Z, Rosli S (2009) Development of the data preprocessing agent's knowledge for data mining using rough set theory. In: Wen P, Li Y, Polkowski L, Yao Y, Tsumoto S, Wang G (eds) Rough sets and knowledge technology, the 4th international conference. RSKT, Australia

Overby E, Bharadwaj A, Sambamurthy V (2006) Enterprise agility and the enabling role of information technology. Eur J Inf Syst 15(2):120–131

Padmanabhan B, Tuzhilin A (1999) Unexpectedness as a measure of interestingness in knowledge discovery. Decis Support Syst 27(3):303–318

Pan XW (2005) Research on some key knowledge of knowledge management integrating context. Graduate University of Zhejiang University, pp 23–28

Pass S (1997) Discovering in a value mountain of data, ORMS Today, pp 24–28

Peng Y, Kou G, Shi Y, Chen Z (2008) A descriptive framework for the field of data mining and knowledge discovery. Int J Inf Technol Decis Mak 7(4):639–682

Piatetsky SG (1991) Discovery, analysis, and presentation of strong rules, knowledge discovery in databases, vol 229. AAAI/MIT Press, Menlo Park, pp 229–248

Piatetsky SG, Matheus CJ (1992) Knowledge discovery workbench for exploring business databases. Int J Intell Syst 7(7):675–686

Piatetsky SG, Matheus CJ (1999) Knowledge discovery databases: an overview. In: Piatetsky SG, Frawley WJ (eds) Knowledge discovery in databases. AAAI Press/MIT Press, Menlo Park, pp 1–27

Piatetsky SG, Frawley WJ, Brin S et al (1997) Discovery, analysis and presentation of strong rules. Comput Stat 16:387–398

Polanyi M (1996) The tacit dimension. Doubleday and Co, Garden City

Polese G, Troiano M, Tortora G (2002) A data mining based system supporting tactical decisions. SEKE, Ischia, pp 681–684

Price R (1771) Observations on reversionary payments, by Printed for T. Cadell, in the Strand in London

Quinlan J (1986) Induction of decision trees. Mach Learn 1:81–106
Rachkovskij D (2001) Representation and processing of structures with binary sparse distributed codes. IEEE Trans Knowl Data Eng 13(2):261–276
Scholtz J, Wiedenbeck S (1990) Learning second and subsequent programing languages: a problem of transfer. Int J Hum-Comput Interact 2(1):51–72
Shearer C (2000) The CRISP-DM model: the new blueprint for data mining. J Data Warehous 5(4):13–19
Shekar B, Natarajan R (2004) A framework for evaluating knowledge-based interestingness of association rules. Fuzzy Optim Decis Mak 3:157–185
Shi Y (2000) Humancasting: a fundamental method to overcome user information overload. Information 3(1):127–143
Shi Y (2001) Multiple criteria multiple constraint-level (MC2) linear programming: concepts, techniques and applications, World Scientific Publishing
Shi Y (2009) Multiple criteria optimization based data mining methods and applications: a systematic survey. Knowl Inf Syst 24(3):369–391
Shi Y, Li XS (2007) Knowledge management platforms and intelligence knowledge beyond data mining. In: Shi Y, Olson D, Stam A (eds) Advance in multiple criteria decision making and human systems management. IOS, Amsterdam, pp 272–288
Shi Y, Yu PL (1989) Goal setting and compromise solutions. In: Karpak B, Zionts S (eds) Multiple criteria decision making and risk analysis using microcomputers. Springer, Berlin, pp 165–204
Shi Y, Wise M, Luo M, Lin Y (2001) Data mining in credit card portfolio management: a multiple criteria decision making approach. In: Koksalan M, Zionts S (eds) Advance in multiple criteria decision making in the new millennium. Springer, Berlin, pp 427–436
Shi Y, Tian YJ, Kou G, Peng Y, Li JP (2011) Optimization based data mining: theory and applications. Springer, New York
Silberschatz A, Tuzhilin A (1995) On subjective measures of interestingness in knowledge discovery, First International Conference on Knowledge Discovery and Data Mining, Montreal, Canada, pp 275–281
Silberschatz A, Tuzhilin A (1996) What makes patterns interesting in knowledge discovery systems. IEEE Trans Knowl Data Eng 8(6):970–974
Sinha AP, Zhao H (2008) Incorporating domain knowledge into data mining classifiers: An application in indirect lending. Decis Support Syst 46(1):287–299
Smyth P, Goodman RM (1992) An information theoretic approach to rule induction from databases. IEEE Trans Knowl Data Eng 4(4):301–316
Surdeanu M, Turmo J (2005) Semantic role labeling using complete syntactic analysis, the Ninth conference on computational natural language learning ann arbor, Michigan, Association for Computational Linguistics
Tan X, Wang L, Zhuo M (2000) Research on discovery of classification rules based on decision tree. J YunNan Univ (Natural Sciences Edition) 22(6):415–419
Tan PN, Kumar V, Srivastava J (2002) Selecting the right IM for association patterns. In: Proceedings of the eighth international conference on knowledge discovery and data mining, Edmonton, Canada, pp 32–41
Tan PN, Steinbach M, Kumar V (2005) Introduction to data mining. Addison Wesley, Upper Saddle River
The American Heritage Dictionary of the English Language (2003) Houghton Mifflin Company
Toivonen H, Klemettinen M, Ronkainen P et al (1995) Pruning and grouping discovered association rules, in ECML-95 workshop on statistics, machine learning, and knowledge discovery in databases, New York, USA
Towell GG, Shavlik JW (1994) Knowledge-based artificial neural networks. Artif Intell 70:119–165
Towell GG, Shavlik JW, Noordewier MO (1990) Refinement domain theories by knowledge-based artificial neural network. In: the proceedings of the eighth national conference on artificial intelligence, pp 861–866
Vapnik VN (1995) The nature of statistical learning theory. Springer New York, New York
Wang ZT (2004) Knowledge system engineering. Science Publication, Beijing

Wasserman S, Faust K, Iacobucci D (1995) Social network analysis: theory and methods[J]

Webb G (2008) Finding the real pattern. IEEE Data Mining Forum, Hong Kong

Weizenbaum J (1966) A computer program for the study of natural language communication between man and machine. Commun ACM 9(1):36–45

What is data?—A definition from Whatis.com

What is data?—A word definition from the Webopedia (2003) http://www.webopedia.com/TERM/D/data.html. Accessed 17 Sept 2013

Wiig KM (1995) Knowledge management: the central management focus for intelligent-acting organization. Schenma Press, Arlington, p 157

Wiig KM (1997) Knowledge management: where did it come from and where it go? Expert Syst Appl 13(1):1–14

Wikipedia (2008) Knowledge

Wong AKC (2008) Association pattern analysis for pattern pruning, pattern clustering and summarization. IEEE Data Mining Forum, Hong Kong

Yang CY, Zhang YJ, Cai W (2002) Extension set and its application. Math Pract Theory 32(2): 301–308

Yang Q, Yin J, Ling C, Chen T (2007) Postprocessing decision trees to extract actionable knowledge. IEEE Trans Knowl Data Eng 19(1):43–56

Yao YY, Zhong N (1999) An analysis of quantitative measures associated with rules In: Proceedings of the third Pacific-Asia conference on knowledge discovery and data mining, Beijing, China, pp 479–488

Yao H, Hamilton HJ, Butz CJ (2004) A foundational approach to mining item set utilities from databases In: Proceedings of the 4th SIAM international conference on data mining

Yoon JP, Kerschberg L (1993) A framework for knowledge discovery and evolution in database. IEEE Trans Knowl Data Eng 5:973–979

Yu PL (1980) Behavior bases and habitual domains of human decision/behavior-concepts and applications. In: Fandel G, Gal T (eds) Multiple criteria decision-making, theory and applications. Springer Verlag, New York, pp 511–539

Yu PL, Chen YC (2010) Dynamic MCDM, habitual domains and competence set analysis for effective decision making in changeable spaces

Yu LTH, Chung FL, Chan SCF, Yuen SMC (2004) Using emerging pattern based projected clustering and gene expression data for cancer detection, Proceedings of the second conference on Asia-Pacific bioinformatics. Aust Comput Soc 29(4):75–84

Yu XD, Shi Y, Zhang LL, Nie GL, Huang A (2014) Intelligent knowledge beyond data mining: Influence of habitual domains. Commun Assoc Inf Syst 34:985–1000

Zeleny M (2002) Knowledge of enterprise: knowledge management technology? Int J Inf Technol Decis Mak 1(2):181–207

Zeleny M (2006) From knowledge to wisdom: on being informed and knowledgeable, becoming wise and ethical. Int J Inf Technol Decis Mak 4(5):751–762

Zeleny M (2007) Human systems management: integrating knowledge, management and systems. World Scientific, Hackensack

Zhang YL, He B (2001) Potential information mining based on matter-element extensibility. Math Pract Theory 31(5):569–575

Zhang S, Zhang C, Yan X (2003) Post-mining: maintenance of association rules by weighting. Inf Syst 28:691–707

Zhang LL, Li J, Shi Y (2005) Study on improving efficiency of knowledge sharing in knowledge-intensive organization, WINE, pp 816–825

Zhang LL, Li J, Zheng X, Li X, Shi Y (2008) Study on a process-oriented knowledge management model. Int J Knowl Syst Sci 5(1):37–44

Zhang D, Shi Y, Tian Y, Zhu M (2009a) A class of classification and regression methods by multiobjective programming. Front Comput Sci China 3:192–204

Zhang D, Tian Y, Shi Y (2009b) Nonlinear knowledge in kernel-based multiple criteria linear programming classifier In: Proceedings of MCDM 2009, LNCCIS, pp 622–629

Zhang LL, Li J et al (2009c) Foundations of intelligent knowledge management. Hum Syst Manage 28(4):145–161

Zhang LL, Li J, Shi Y, Liu X (2009d) Foundations of intelligent knowledge management. Hum Syst Manage 28:145–161

Zhong YX (2004) An introduction to cognetics—unified theory of information, knowledge and intelligence. China Engineering Science 6(6)

Zhong W (2004) Duality system in applied mechanics and optimal control[M]. Springer Science & Business Media

Zhong YX (2007) On the laws of information-knowledge-intelligence transforms. J Beijing Univ Post Telecommun 30(1):1–8

Zhu Z (2002) Knowledge management: learning from diverse styles. In: Proceedings of KSS'2002 & MCS'2002, Shanghai, China

Zhu Z, Gu J et al (2008) Toward domain-driven data mining. International symposium on intelligent information technology application workshops, IEEE

Index

Y. Shi et al., *Intelligent Knowledge*, SpringerBriefs in Business,
DOI 10.1007/978-3-662-46193-8

The manufacturer's authorised representative in the EU is Springer Nature Customer Service Centre GmbH, Europaplatz 3, 69115 Heidelberg, Germany. If you have any concerns regarding our products, please contact ProductSafety@springernature.com

Printed and bound by CPI Group (UK) Ltd, Croydon, CR0 4YY

25/03/2026

02078177-0016